Newco

A Southern Couple Finds Their Perfect Retirement Home In Santa Barbara

TO Richard

with Many Thanks
For all you do !
Best wishes

Bob

Robert M. Fulmer

Published by ECI
Santa Barbara, CA 93103

Chapter Opening Illustrations by Pat Fulmer

IL quote from internationalliving.com

"Walk on the Ocean" quote from Glen Phillips,
Toad the Wet Sprocket, Sony 1991

Cover Design and Photo by Robert M. Fulmer
Title Page Photo by Fal Oliver, Design by Brad Wallace

Library of Congress Cataloging in Publication Data
Fulmer, Robert M.
Newcomers in Paradise / Robert M. Fulmer

LCCN 2009912903

Book webpage:
http:///newcomersinparadise.com

Newcomers in Paradise
is dedicated to

Santa Barbara Newcomers,

the folks who helped us discover paradise
in Santa Barbara,

and

Pat Fulmer
who continues to enrich
the joys of
Casa de Alegria

Are you looking for a perfect retirement venue or interested in visiting (or living in) paradise?

This story of a southern couple's search for and discovery of an ideal place for the final third of their lives provides charming and useful insights about the quest for perfection.

Peter L. Brill, M.D., Director of the Third Age Foundation and Co-host of the *Third Age* Radio Show: "*An authentic search for passion, purpose and joy signals an emergence of the Third Age. Many get lost in this journey of decreasing interest in money, power and status...Bob and Pat provide a candid and interesting travelogue that can inspire us in the search to find our own happiness.*"

Précis: Like many Americans approaching retirement, Bob Fulmer and his artist wife, Pat, spent several years searching for perfection. They explored exotic locations with beautiful scenery in low-cost foreign destinations, but concluded that their lake house in the North Georgia mountains was about as Third World as they could handle. Williamsburg was lovely but too tranquil. They fell in love with destinations along the Pacific Coast Highway and finally decided to spend a sabbatical year in Santa Barbara. Before their first summer was over, Pat announced, "You can go back to Virginia, but I'd like to stay in Santa Barbara."

"The odyssey of searching for the perfect place to retire will interest baby boomers and others thinking about the ideal place for their "third age" when pressures for learning and earning no longer dominate decision making. In the tradition of Peter Mayle (*A Year in Provence*), Frances Mayes (*Under the Tuscan Sun*),and Barry Golson (*Gringos in Paradise*), Bob and Pat spent the next two years getting to know "almost 600 new best friends", adjusting to life on "America's Riviera," and trying to restore *Casa de Alegría* without it becoming *Hoyo de Dinero* (the pit of money)."

Organization: *The first three chapters cover "The Search for Perfection." The next three present a subjective review of "What Made Santa Barbara Ideal" Chapters 7-13 are about "Finding and Making a Home in Paradise." The last two chapters reflect on "Insights and Lessons Learned" through the journey.*

Table of Contents

Preface..8

Chapter 1: The Perils of Seeking Perfection: Our failed efforts to find a perfect place to live in the U.S. and abroad.............9

Chapter 2: Making Lemonade in Paradise: We rent a Santa Barbara house for a blended family Christmas during a record cold snap and make the best of the calamity when plans for a California move fall apart 20

Chapter 3: April in Paradise: Our first month in a modest condo proves to be a second honeymoon as we explore the town without the usual concerns and pressures........................35

Chapter 4: 600 New Best Friends: We discover Santa Barbara Newcomers, a benign cult with interesting new friends and opportunities for learning about our temporary home..........47

Chapter 5: We Love A Parade and Party: The summer is a blur of frenetic activities with people who grasp at any excuse to enjoy a parade or party..59

Chapter 6: Life Beyond Newcomers: We begin to look beyond Newcomers to find the Shangri-La of teaching and Santa Barbara's commitment to the arts and social justice. We also discover a dark side to paradise.....................................72

Chapter 7: Losing a Bidding War in a Land of the Rich and Famous: We experience real estate sticker shock, look at 72 houses, enter the bidding wars, and almost give up on buying a house in one of the country's hottest real estate markets........84

Chapter 8: A New Century in Paradise: We greet a new century on a luxury yacht, and I encourage Newcomers to write a book about "A Perfect Day in Paradise" while becoming a bicoastal professor...97

Table of Contents

Chapter 9: Queen Isabella or Dulcinea? We choose between a grand Spanish lady (Queen Isabella) and Dulcinea—a more daunting but affordable challenge. We wind up negotiating with clowns to buy a house John Irving would love...........110

Chapter 10: A Makeover for Dulcinea: Our realtor gives us wise counsel plus introductions to Hector, his family and friends who will help us restore a fallen Spanish lady........124

Chapter11: Traumas of Transformation:The frantic pace quickens as we, our architect and 'Uncle Beto' are traumatized by the challenges, bureaucracy and complexities of transforming our derelict hacienda.............................135

Chapter 12: *Casa de Alegría* or *Hoyo de Dinero*: Pat becomes a buyer for Grandma's Enterprises and leads the devious duo to keep the house of happiness from becoming a money pit....150

Chapter 13: Two Weddings, a Funeral and a Bandito: Our work crew becomes extended family as we cope with key transitions in their lives and our own...163

Chapter 14: Lifestyles of the Nervous and Stressed: While the rich and famous may live near our "new" house, we were running out of time, patience and money as we rush to be ready for a Newcomers' celebration of the project's completion...179

Chapter 15: Different Paths to Paradise: Santa Barbara residents may live in differing degrees of luxury, but anyone who manages the price of admission gets to enjoy the same glorious climate, culture and scenery in a welcoming, democratic community...195

Chapter 16: Walk by the Ocean.... As We Slowly Grow Old: Santa Barbara is a place where everything's better. Each week, we walk by the ocean with a diverse group of folks who have discovered their secrets of success. And the memories continue to "grow sweeter each season as we slowly grow old.".......210

Acknowledgements..222

Preface

The baby boomers, 78 million of them, have been right behind me all of my life. We've stayed just ahead of the demographic pig moving through the python's digestive tract. Now, the only lesson we have left to teach is how to live out the last chapters of life. Born during World War II, my generation has shouldered the awesome responsibility of showing our younger siblings the way to face life's major challenges. From how to aggravate parents to facing life's serious dilemmas, we've been there to provide misguided advice and flawed examples of how to make major decisions.

As you read, think about where and how you wish to spend the final portion of your life. I hope our odyssey will help point the way to making a different, equally perfect, decision that works for you. The book isn't intended to encourage more people to move to Santa Barbara. It is getting a bit too crowded and pricey, so come and visit, but choose Ventura, San Luis Obispo, or better still, return home and come back often. I hope the book will help make your visits more enjoyable.

Feel free to join the 29,000 daily visitors who already fill our restaurants and enjoy the festivals and parades along with everyone who has paid the price for permanence. The City needs the economic infusion of your occupancy taxes and purchases to keep everything pristine and pretty. Maintaining perfection and providing superb services are expensive, so bring lots of cash and have a wonderful time. We're willing to share the American Riviera, at least for a while. You'll be rubbing shoulders with some of the folks you meet in this book and with other visitors from throughout the country and the world. The foreign visitors are often part of the millions of viewers in 40 countries still watching the wretched soap opera, "Santa Barbara."

This is the story of how two Southerners did the homework for their final assignment and re-discovered some of the pleasures of being just ahead of the boomers. As they say in the South, *"Ya'll come."*

Chapter 1
The Perils of Seeking Perfection

On a magnificent autumn day, while in my early 30s, I first thought about finding a perfect place to live. Growing up in Alabama, I had never even considered the possibility of perfection, but after making a speech to a trade association, I walked from the beautiful Williamsburg Inn, through the restored colonial village, to the historic campus of the College of William and Mary, the second oldest college in the U.S. It's the *alma mater* of Thomas Jefferson, James Monroe, a long list of governors and several still unindicted politicians.

After asking for directions from one of the friendly and attractive students, I made my way to the College of Business, confidently presented my business card to a harried receptionist, and asked to say hello to the Dean. Surprisingly, I was ushered into the office of Charles Quitmeyer where he learned that, should an appropriate opening occur, I would consider becoming a member of his faculty.

It didn't work out then, but I never forgot how beautiful the College of William and Mary was on that autumn day. Two decades later, while teaching at Columbia's Graduate School of Business, complaining about the stress of living in New York City and working at a fine, but not genteel, university, a successor dean called to ask if I would be interested in an endowed chair at the College of William and Mary. "Would I be interested? Are you kidding?" I couldn't wait to schedule a visit and tell my wife, Pat, about the good news.

In the excitement about how perfectly life was working out, I failed to think about a few basic facts that should have been factored into my overly facile decision-making. Twenty years had passed since the initial impression that William and Mary would be the perfect place to conclude my professorial career. I was a tiny bit older now.

Pat quickly pointed out a couple of points I had overlooked, "Since we've been married, we've been in Atlanta or in New York City. In case you haven't noticed, these are somewhat larger places than Williamsburg. When our children were young, they might have enjoyed growing up in the calm tranquility of a small colonial village, but as college students or graduates, they like cities. You might also remember that you are no longer married to the wife who thought that Williamsburg was the most charming town in America."

Somehow, I had failed to hear Pat's frequent reminders about how much she loved New York City—or how she hated growing up in a southern town of 12,000.

Actually, I did listen, but not very well. I was convinced that Williamsburg was such a wonderful place we would be sublimely happy. With lower real estate prices, we could buy a great house, make tremendous friends, and travel in the summers. Life would be, finally, just perfect.

We were living on New York's East side during the days of Tom Wolfe's *Bonfire of the Vanities*. I must have used a couple of Sherman McCoy's best lines a few hundred times. Almost every month when the bills came in, I would groan and exclaim, "We are hemorrhaging money!" Alternatively, I would remind Pat of Sherm's thesis, "It is absolutely impossible to live in New York City on $900,000 a year." (Back in the 1980's, even the Columbia's football coach didn't make quite that much.)

The move to Williamsburg brought challenges. We had trouble finding a place that would enable us to postpone the capital gains taxes from the sale of a two-bedroom co-op. We finally found a large house on 94 acres, but my colleagues were concerned about the long drive to work. I was unfazed by the "intimidating" twenty minute, sixteen-mile commute, as it wound through beautiful Virginia countryside.

Upon arriving on campus each day, I walked through the 18th century on my way to think about the 21st. Neither traffic nor parking was ever a problem. For the most part, it was a tranquil, pastoral kind of life. For the first year, it was so quiet and peaceful, I often thought that I had died and gone to heaven. By the second year, however, I began to worry that perhaps I had simply died. It was *so* quiet and peaceful!

Redefining Paradise

By year three, we were traveling whenever we could. By year five, we were looking for another perfect place to conclude my career. I was even willing to consider taking an "honest job" in business or the non-profit sector. By then, I had reached my mid-fifties and alternatives were not available as frequently as they had been for the past thirty years. I looked at situations in London, San Francisco, and Washington D.C. that didn't quite work out.

Then I was inspired by some of direct mail's most famous and successful promotional copy. In promoting *International Living,* Bill Bonner described his idea of paradise as follows:

> *You look out your window, past your gardener, who is busily pruning the lemon, cherry, and fig trees...amidst the splendor of gardenias, hibiscus, and hollyhocks...The sky is clear blue. The sea is a deeper blue, sparkling with sunlight. A gentle breeze comes drifting in from the ocean, clean and refreshing, as your maid brings you breakfast in bed. For a moment, you think you have died and gone to heaven. But this paradise is real. And affordable. In fact, it costs only half as much to live this dream lifestyle...as it would to stay in your home.*

I showed this to Pat and we were both excited. Well, I was excited, and Pat was anxious to get out of Williamsburg. If Bonner's concept was possible, all we had to do was to find that perfect paradise with great climate, beautiful scenery, ocean views and a low cost of living. These simple characteristics become the criteria in our search for perfection.

My reasoning was, "Once we find the right location, we can drop out of the rat race and parachute into paradise. I'll retire early and write the books I've been thinking about, and you can spend every day painting. All we have to do was to find that 'perfect place'. What's more, the search will be fun."

As we were thinking about our first trip to a potential tropical paradise, we received a Christmas card from Frank and Gail Saunders. Frank had been Associate General Counsel at Allied Signal. He had negotiated a contract for Allied Signal to "outsource" its training and development programs to a small consulting firm I represented. After signing the contract and beginning a friendship, we met Frank's spirited wife, Gail, who, in addition to her role as a human resource specialist at AT&T, shared an abiding interest in art with my wife.

The Saunders were successful DINKs (Dual Income, No Kids), so we were shocked when they suddenly opted to leave corporate jobs. They were younger than we were! Frank volunteered to take an early retirement package offered in a corporate downsizing. The Saunders sold their assets, invested the proceeds in high-yield stocks and bonds, and resolved to live on the income this generated. They choose to live on Paros, one of the quieter Greek Islands, as they turned forty.

Through "voluntary simplicity," Frank and Gail found that they could get by on about ten percent of their former income– in a way they found better and more rewarding. By assuming responsibility for improving their cottage, Frank negotiated a reduced rental, learned new, gratifying skills and got in better physical condition than he had enjoyed since playing college football. Gail expanded her skills as an artist. They were the envy of their hardworking former colleagues.

Greek to Us

Their Christmas card invited us to visit them in Paros. The invitation may have been a polite riff on the Southern cliché,

"Ya'll come to see us"—which everyone understands to be just a friendly good-bye. But we were confident that the Saunders genuinely wanted us to visit and began making plans for a trip that would involve a five-day visit in Greece.

The spring weather was almost perfect when we arrived. Their favorite *kafenion* (café) had calamari straight from the Mediterranean pinned on a clothesline in the courtyard. They were the freshest and best I had ever tasted. We went swimming that afternoon in a beautiful lagoon with the clearest blue water I had ever seen and were the only four people around. In complementing their idyllic life, I may have sounded a little bit too euphoric. Frank warned us, "Stress is still something of an issue." My face must have shown a tinge of disappointment, because he explained, "Every day we struggle to decide where we want to watch the sun set."

And the sunsets were beautiful! It was true, however, that their cottage was pretty basic. Electricity was not totally dependable. It was a hassle to neatly fold bathroom tissue after use and store it in a separate container because the septic system had significant limitations. By day three, we began to miss movie theaters, bookstores and even television. You have to have a special kind of independence and a strong relationship to enjoy this much cultural isolation. By the time we packed our bags for departure, we were still happy for them, but no longer envious. By comparison, Williamsburg was a sophisticated center of culture.

But the basic idea still made sense. We had waited longer than the Saunders to make our move and had enough assets to finance a more comfortable retirement if we could just find the right inexpensive place. With this in mind, we spent a couple of years visiting locales that were billed as that perfect haven. I began to worry that we were just too picky. Costa Rica had infrastructure problems and petty crime was becoming a problem. Cape Town was beautiful, but we had missed the opportunity for the best values in coastal real estate. Moreover, crime was a tremendous concern. The most rapidly growing business was "armed response." Our friend Andy reported, "We have a high fence topped by razor wire, two Rhodesian Ridgebacks, and an alarm system that connects to a band of mercenaries armed with AK-47s, and we're still nervous."

13

In Turks and Caicos, coastal real estate was almost affordable and the diving was great. Still, it was terribly flat and, with 90 degree temperatures in early January, we couldn't help but wonder how pleasant the summers would be. Most of the Caribbean was expensive and not totally hospitable to expatriates. New Zealand had gorgeous scenery, but we were beginning to understand that we liked living around people who appreciated attractive architecture and indoor comforts as well as outdoor pleasures. The cities of New Zealand were as expensive as the United States, and Kiwis aren't tremendously excited about having Yanks retiring to their beautiful country.

We continued to study travel guides and books about the expatriate experience. We would keep looking until we found that perfect place and were convinced we would know it when we saw it. One day, we were driving in the mountains of North Georgia where we owned a lake house. If you looked past the rusted pickups and NRA signs, the scenery was lovely and we still spoke enough of the local language to get by. Suddenly, in a moment of epiphany, I turned to Pat and said, "You know, this is about as Third World as I want to get!"

Danger on the PCH

Neither of us is fluent in anything other than southern English––a dialect still recognizable in most U.S. states, with the exception of Vermont and New Hampshire. I had great memories of graduate study in California, so we started looking for excuses to travel up or down the Pacific Coast Highway (PCH), one of the most beautiful drives in the world. It wanders through scenic seaside villages, classic American towns, past picturesque beaches, thick woodlands, and fabulous farmlands —much more magnificent scenery than the red clay hills and scrub pines of my childhood. Majestic cliffs rise over a restless, churning sea. Quaint old fishing towns (now, upscale tourist meccas with carefully preserved charms), are set in tidy coves. This is a land of visual abundance. The road is often curvy and crowded, but the greatest danger is that the trip can be addictive.

A non-stop drive from San Francisco to Los Angeles can be made in five and a half hours provided you're willing to travel on I-5, eat or refuel at Flying J Plazas and endure monotonous, boring scenery. To make the trip on the PCH takes twice as long, but is worth the extra time, especially if you can spend a night or two along the way. One of the compensations for academic pay is the flexibility to add a day or two on an official trip. Whenever I had an academic conference or a consulting assignment in San Francisco or Los Angeles, I would schedule our flights into the meeting city. Then after completing the work assignment, we would pick up a rental car, drive down (or up) the coastal highway and fly out of the other city.

According to travel writer Josh Sens, "The drive down California's coastal route is much like young love: romantic, impractical, and filled with dizzying twists and turns." We didn't qualify as "young love" as we made a half dozen exploratory trips up or down the PCH during the 1990s. We were in our mid-fifties, so unless we manage to live past a hundred, our trips wouldn't even qualify as middle-aged flings. Yet we were becoming addicted to making this enchanted trip. Sometimes we would stop in Carmel or Monterey. We loved the entire California Coast. Soon, however, the major attraction became Santa Barbara, a place Pat described as being "so beautiful it almost makes my eyes hurt."

Sandwiched between the magnificent Santa Ynez Mountains (the city's backdrop) and the Channel Islands (twenty or so miles off of its coast), Santa Barbara's architectural style is a blend of Spanish, Mediterranean and Moorish. Gleaming white stucco buildings with red terra cotta tile roofs, courtyards and wrought iron create the image favored by the town. The Mediterranean climate and south-facing beaches with over 300 days of sunshine, each year have earned Santa Barbara the nickname, "America's Riviera." While less than two hours from Los Angeles airport, we would still usually spend at least one night in Santa Barbara.

Santa Barbara took advantage of a 1925 earthquake to 'reinvent' itself. With strong leadership provided by Pearl Chase and downtown merchants, the city enforced strong zoning requirements that required a consistency of architecture and a harmonious appearance to the business areas of the city. There are no billboards in town or on the main freeway. Although its population is only 92,000, Santa Barbara has good

15

museums, a resident symphony, an opera company, botanical gardens, lush parks, and several theater groups. Restaurants are so plentiful that if everyone in town wanted to eat out on a particular evening, they could all, theoretically, find a table. As a popular, but pricey, tourist destination, hotels, motels and bed and breakfasts abound. We were frequently able to get excellent prices by stopping at the Visitor Center where unbooked rooms were available at half price.

The Addiction Grows

The problem with any addiction, even one as benign as cravings to spend more time on the California coast, is that addictions grow progressively more demanding. Bigger and bigger fixes are required. We began to look for excuses to make trips to the West Coast. I submitted papers to obscure conferences that just happened to be in this desirable area. California consulting projects became more attractive and interesting. I took on an assignment with a Mike Milken project that provided several trips to the West Coast.

The Academy of Management is the professional society for professors in my discipline. (Imagine an August meeting in New Orleans with ten thousand management professors!) A modest notice in an Academy publication grabbed my attention like word of a new pusher excites a junkie. The ad that changed our lives was direct and unobtrusive. It simply read:

> *Strategy consulting firm seeks executive director for a client-sponsored multi-disciplinary research program. The ideal candidate will have academic and corporate executive experience along with an ability to communicate to both audiences.*

Interested parties were encouraged to write to the Strategos Institute in Palo Alto, California.

Now *this* was intriguing! At the time, relatively few professors had executive-level corporate experience and reasonably good academic credentials. Good academics were typically too immersed in their own scholarly research to have the time, inclination or flexibility to work full-time in a corporate setting. A true academic would feel sullied by the mundane, day-to-day minutiae of corporate practice and politics. I had managed to immerse myself in both worlds with relatively minor scar tissue. After directing Executive Education at Emory University for six years, Allied-Signal had recruited me to head up their worldwide management development. It was a great opportunity that led me to create the Executive Education Exchange, negotiate the spinoff with Frank Saunders, and teach four years at Columbia University.

My major professor had once commented, "Peter Drucker will never be considered a serious scholar because his books have sold far too many copies." I never had that problem, although my writing was sometimes considered too applied for good scholarship. Still, I had been elected as a Fellow of the Academy of Management and held a couple of endowed chairs. Moreover, I actually knew who was behind the Strategos Institute. *Competing for the Future* by Gary Hamel and C.K. Prahalad was my favorite strategy book and one that I regularly required students to read. Hamel and Prahalad had also written several award-winning *Harvard Business Review* articles. Gary's writings were insightful, opinionated, and often acerbic. I believed he might become the leading strategist of the day.

Gary was working on a new manuscript that Harvard Business School Publishing thought would be their most successful book ever. They were certainly giving it more attention than they had provided for my book, *The Leadership Investment*. He had recently left the London Business School to set up a consulting firm, called Strategos, on the West Coast. Obviously, the Strategos Institute was going to be the research arm of the consulting firm. What an opportunity that could be!

The possibility of being paid to work with the leading thinker in my field was so exciting that I immediately adapted my resume, got a couple of business and academic leaders to write letters of support, added a couple of recent practitioner-focused publications and expressed the package overnight. I actually had trouble sleeping for a couple of nights until I received a telephone call inviting me to visit early in January.

Even if nothing else worked out, this was an opportunity to spend a couple of weeks in California. I would submit grades early in December. We could get a flight out immediately

17

afterwards, rent a house in paradise and then drive up the PCH for my interview early in the New Year.

Family Planning

Pat and I each have two sons from previous marriages. We had tried for twenty years to create a 'blended family' like the Brady Bunch. When we first met as recent divorcées and found that our sons who were close to the same ages, we thought this was a fortunate coincidence. We didn't anticipate that this similarity in ages might lead to competitiveness, jealousy and conflict—on our part as well as theirs. As our children became adults and grew past the trauma of our divorces, we began to enjoy significant signs of rapprochement. We did a house swap in Miami and invited the kids and friends for a week. We all survived. A couple of years later, we rented a house in Key West and everyone had a wonderful time. Perhaps we could introduce our family to Santa Barbara and see if they shared our perception that it came close to perfection.

We booked flights for ten people leaving from five locations and started looking for vacation rentals. Our friends, Frank and Gail Saunders, had returned from Paros after losing a long battle with the IRS. With their nest egg too depleted to continue an idyllic lifestyle, they rented a small apartment in Santa Barbara while searching for employment after a ten-year hiatus. Frank reported by phone, "Santa Barbara is a wonderful place to live, but a terrible place to look for employment. Our most recent work experience is a decade old. Prospective employers find the story of our early retirement charming, but not reassuring. I would consider being a greeter at Wal-Mart, but Santa Barbara won't allow Wal-Mart in the city."

After months of exploring every lead imaginable, Frank found a job with the California Department of Labor paying half what he earned a decade before. As a consummate optimist, Frank was sure that in a couple years there would lead to a job commensurate with his experience and qualifications. Before starting to work in Santa Clara, he provided us with a lead for a vacation rental firm called Coastal Hideaways. We went to their website and found the following ad:

Welcome to this home-away-from home getaway, a majestic mountain retreat tucked away on a private road in the Santa Ynez foothills. Close to the Botanical Gardens, Museum of Natural History, Santa Barbara Mission, and a short drive to downtown.

This quiet, secluded, single level, four-bedroom house has been meticulously redecorated throughout...with two master bedroom suites. All with oversized picture windows overlooking the beautiful landscaped outdoor entertainment space; unsurpassed sweeping mountain views and a glimpse of the Pacific.

We knew enough about real estate to understand that "a glimpse of the Pacific" would mean that if we stood on a chair in the living room at four o'clock in the afternoon, we might see, between the branches of a tree, a glimpse of blue that *could* be the ocean. Never mind: there would be almost enough room for everyone, the price was reasonable, and it was available for the last couple of weeks in December.

Frank assured us that the trip expense should be tax-deductible. "You're coming to California to interview for an important assignment. Your consulting firm needs an annual meeting. I will come down for the board meeting and prepare the minutes. Everything should work out perfectly." Did I mention that Frank had lots of experience in dealing with the IRS?

All of our flights were scheduled to arrive around six o'clock and within 90 minutes of each other. Needless to say, it didn't work out that way. Everyone finally got to LA shortly after nine o'clock in the evening. Brad and Keiko (our Japanese daughter-in-law) were already in Los Angeles and had a van. They met the first plane and killed time until the later flights arrived and we picked up our rental car. The logistics weren't perfect, but went as smoothly as Steve Martin and John Candy going home for the holidays. We were ready to introduce our family to America's Riviera. We couldn't afford to live there now, certainly not without a job, but we might be able to move closer, plan for the future and, at least, have a couple of weeks in what we were coming to recognize as our vision of paradise.

Chapter Two
Making Lemonade in Paradise

Los Angeles was shockingly cold, but. I was sure Santa Barbara would be much warmer. As we caravanned up the Pacific Coast Highway, it was too dark and foggy to see the beautiful coastline. Three hours later than planned, we called and agreed to stop by the agent's home to pick up the key. Her condo was "just off the 101", and it only took us forty minutes to find her condo, pick up the key and directions before continuing on to Santa Barbara.

It wasn't getting any warmer! The fog and cloud cover plus a little drizzle made for a bone-chilling cold and rendered it impossible to read street signs. We found the Mission Street exit, made our way to the historic Santa Barbara Mission and finally located Mountain Drive, a narrow, twisting lane that surely was laid out by a very intelligent mountain goat. The road changed names with disconcerting frequency. Finally, in desperation, we flagged down the driver of the only other vehicle we saw, and he graciously provided the information that was missing from our directions. The last four miles of our journey took almost an hour to travel.

When our "majestic mountain retreat" finally appeared, we were too tired and cold to complain about anything—well, except for the temperature. The outside thermometer read 37 degrees--almost a record low for Santa Barbara. Wind gusts were approaching 40 mph. The pilot light for the furnace had blown out. My technical expertise is limited to a reasonable facility in changing light bulbs. Fortunately, Pat's younger son, Brad, had a year's worth of engineering before switching to film studies and was finally able to get the furnace going. We assigned rooms, blew up an air mattress and finally everyone stumbled to bed early in the second day of our grand adventure.

The night proved long—and cold. Even though the furnace was going full force, we were freezing. There seemed to be as much cold air coming into the house as heated air. We used all of the blankets and quilts in the house, added towels for another layer and the couples snuggled for additional warmth. As soon as the rental office opened, we called to ask if there was a problem with the heating system. "Oh, I should have told you," the agent replied. "The house was musty when I checked it out, so I left a couple of skylights open to air things out." Once that little oversight was corrected, the house became pleasant and so did its inhabitants.

The State of State Street

Everyone layered up with sweaters and jackets and made our way to State Street, the main drag for downtown Santa Barbara. We decided to start at the Museum of Art and amble down the street until it ends at Stearns Wharf. The art museum was impressive, especially for a relatively small city. In what was once the city's post office, the museum houses permanent collections of American, European and Asian art as well as contemporary photography. I was impressed that our children had developed a real appreciation for art. Obviously, those tuition investments at private colleges had some impact. My sons didn't get any genetic aptitude for the arts from me. Before marrying an artist, I used to quote Al Capp: "Art is often produced by the untalented and sold by the unprincipled to the utterly bewildered."

At the beginning of our walk, the shops and the people were clearly upscale. As we moved further down State Street, the people became younger, the stores or restaurants became funkier and the number of panhandlers increased. By the time we reached the Dolphin Fountain, sculpted by local artist Bud Bottoms, we were moving quickly and definitely ready to eat.

21

The wharf was undergoing extensive repair after being partially destroyed by fire a few months earlier. At the Harbor House restaurant, frequented more by tourists than locals, we enjoyed superb views and friendly waiters who helped fight off the seagulls who wanted to share our meals. Our entire group arrived within five minutes of the designated time. The possibility of a subsidized meal still had universal appeal.

Some of us were still shaking off the effects of what might have been hypothermia. Others were experiencing jet lag, and everyone was ready for a quiet evening in a warm house. We picked up a video, bought some groceries and got home in time to actually see the sun set over the ocean—without even standing on a chair.

Everyone pitched in and helped prepare spaghetti with meat sauce, an organic salad made from local produce and fresh lemonade with lemons from a tree in the back yard. We did the dishes, watched our video and turned in early. The forecast called for temperatures in the mid-30s again, but the furnace was working much more effectively with the skylights closed.

Courting Contentment

The next morning was crisp and clear. After a hardy breakfast, we made our way to Santa Barbara's historic courthouse. I agreed with whoever it was who called it "the most beautiful government building in America." Well-tended gardens and lawns surround this working courthouse that seemed strangely familiar to me. A wedding party was gathering in the carefully-landscaped Sunken Garden. Our first stop was to take an elevator to the 85-foot "El Mirador" clock tower for views of the city, coast and mountains. After looking at amazing vistas in every direction, we worked our way down to the first floor.

Pat soon reminded me of why the Courthouse looked so familiar. It was the backdrop for sixty or seventy episodes of the *Owen Marshall, Counselor at Law* television series back in the 1970s. "If I recall correctly," she said, "the series starred Arthur Hill and featured exterior shots of the building in every episode."

I was very impressed by her powers of recollection (and concerned about my own failing memory) until I spotted the notice near the reception area providing the information that Pat had just "remembered". We also read that the building was dedicated as the culmination of the rebuilding effort following the earthquake of 1925. As previously mentioned, Pearl Chase led this effort and insisted on a consistent architectural style throughout the downtown area. This consistency isn't obvious in this particular building, which blends several architectural styles to create a setting that is palatial and dramatic. Travel writers call it "storybook Spanish California."

Chase's strong will and good taste are still evident throughout the community and much appreciated today. One of the courthouse docents told us that Ms. Chase was especially proud of the way Moorish and Spanish architectural details came together in the courthouse. She convinced the city fathers that an appropriate celebration for the completion of Santa Barbara's rebirth would be to invite famed architect Frank Lloyd Wright to review the renovations and innovations as part of a festive gala. The invitation was extended, arrangements negotiated and, on August 14, 1929, the great man appeared and silently viewed the newly refurbished downtown. After a band concert in the sunken garden, Wright was glowingly introduced and asked to comment on the achievements of the community. Striding to the microphone, Mr. Wright turned to Mrs. Chase and began, "Madam, you have succeeded in restoring an architectural style that never existed!"

In the afternoon, we rented bicycles and pedaled along the beachfront, on past the East Beach Townhouses to the bird sanctuary. Someone suggested that we try to make our way to Butterfly Beach. This was the eastern end of our ride and was directly across from the classy Four Seasons Biltmore Hotel. We weren't comfortable leaving our bikes with valet parking so we checked out the deserted and chilly beach, then rode back by the previous sites and on to the wharf and the Harbor where we briefly visited the Maritime Museum.

Since the shadows were starting to lengthen, we decided to take advantage of Santa Barbara's discounted twilight movie special to see "A Beautiful Life." On Wednesday, Pat and I agreed that we could quit playing scoutmasters and sent everyone off to explore on their own and to do some Christmas shopping.

Unitarian Prelude

On Thursday, someone spotted an attractive young woman in our back yard, wearing a robe and carrying a towel. After allowing plenty of time for her to get fully dressed, we explored and discovered that there was a basement apartment to the house with only external access to the downstairs bathroom. The apartment was occupied by an associate minister at the local Unitarian church—which, as we learned, isn't actually called a church. Its official name is "the Unitarian Society of Santa Barbara." Rev. Carol, explained, "Unitarians don't want to offend anyone, and this group felt that the use of the word 'church' might bother their Buddhist or Jewish friends."

We enjoyed meeting and talking with Carol and, since it was Christmas Eve, most of our group agreed to attend her candlelight service. She was just as impressive in her clerical robes as the more familiar terrycloth version. Shaun, who had enjoyed less exposure to organized religion than our other children, excused himself from attending. "I might do or say something embarrassing. You know how I always get Newt Gingrich confused with the Grinch who stole Christmas."

With more exposure to conservative southern Protestantism, my children joked that we were going to a "Unitarian play church." "Oh, no," I assured them, "you don't have to handle live snakes for it to be a real church."

Christmas dawned with a promise of our warmest day to date. We slept in, prepared a leisurely breakfast, opened a few presents discovered under a drugstore Christmas tree and started the all-consuming task of preparing a traditional turkey dinner. Even with all hands on deck, I was amazed at the amount of time required to prepare and clean up after a dinner that only takes a few minutes to consume. We probably would have lingered longer over the meal, but some of our group needed to observe a religious ritual involving televised football games. The rest of us collapsed into a food induced coma.

Carol had suggested that we visit the nearby Santa Barbara Botanic Garden. On Saturday, anticipating temperatures in the mid-sixties, we set out to explore the seventy-eight-acre property's almost six miles of walking trails, which wound through the garden's regional planting schemes and micro-climates. The gardens encompass naturalistic meadowlands, craggy canyons, a tiny redwood forest; and historic Mission Dam built in 1806 by Native Americans under the direction of mission Padres. It featured over a thousand species of rare and indigenous California plants. We enjoyed the views and variety of vegetation, but complaints soon erupted. One family member observed, "I'm tired of seeing dead weeds and chilling with old folks…and exhausted from this forced march!" Of course, wearing flip-flops may have caused the trail to seem even longer than it did for the rest of us.

Weekends in Santa Barbara bring a profusion of "Open House" realty sign sprouting like mushrooms after a spring rain. We saw this as an opportunity to spend an inexpensive afternoon while getting to know the community better. While observant family members stayed to watch Bowl games, three of the party joined us to explore the housing market in Santa Barbara. Some of the home owners actually wanted to sell their residences. Others were willing to consider selling if you offered several times as much as the same house would cost anywhere else. We were intrigued by one house on what was called the Upper Eastside and a couple of condos in East Beach. They were attractive, interesting, and far too expensive.

In the second week of our visit, temperatures moved into the high sixties and seventies. We walked on various beaches, went whale watching, rode rental bikes again and explored a thoroughly charming small city.

At this point, the ten of us had spent more time together, in relative peace and tranquility, than ever before. We were delighted, but didn't want to push our luck. When Jeff suggested a one-night road trip to Big Bear Lake, we thought it was an excellent idea. All of the younger generation signed on, and we looked forward to seeing Frank and Gail Saunders who were driving down to close out their Santa Barbara apartment and take care of other details. Frank was not overly impressed with his new colleagues and dreaded a long commute from their Santa Cruz rental to his office in San Jose. He reported, "We're both happy, however, to finally have some income and health insurance."

Farewell to Family and Friends

We needed to make a quick trip for groceries, and Gail told us about a great little store on Milpas street that she called TJ's (which stood for Trader Joe's). I discovered that Santa Barbarians save time by using initials instead of proper names. For example, we had to drive on APS to get to TJ's. As it turns out, all eight syllables of Alameda Padre Serra are too much of a time commitment for local residents.

APS could be described as the backbone of the American Riviera. Frank was having some problems with his vision as well as a recurring headache, so he insisted that I drive. Pat and Gail were exclaiming about the beautiful views, but I was focused on avoiding oncoming drivers, who seemed much more confident in navigating the twists and turns than I would ever be. I remember saying, "The views may be great, but I can't imagine living in this part of town. Driving home would be like commuting on the Six Flags Adventure Park roller coaster."

Trader Joe's was an incredible little grocery store with lots of organic products at reasonable rates. I sagely observed, "This place must be owned by a California family with lots of cousins who are surfers or gardeners—or perhaps a small band of communal farmers from Oregon. Clearly, Trader Joe's is a small West Coast startup whose stock would be a wonderful investment. Do you remember Peter Lynch's advice to buy the stock of companies you like?"

My investment insight was impressive until it was tested. Upon inquiring of the store manager, I found that TJ was part of huge German discount-grocery chain best known in the U.S. for basic, functional stores often located in less expensive neighborhoods. Oh, well, so much for Peter Lynch—and my investment acumen.

We made our purchases and safely navigated the return via APS, prepared a simple dinner and enjoyed New Year's Eve by catching up with the Saunders' recent adventures over a couple bottles of local wine. Thanks to our "glimpse of the Pacific" window, we got to enjoy the Santa Barbara fireworks at midnight.

The next morning we said goodbye to the Saunders. Gail was driving since Frank still had a severe headache. We started the cleaning and packing process. Around mid-afternoon, one carload of our people arrived back from Big Bear and the other returned a couple of hours later via LAX so folks with inflexible schedules could get back to work. Everyone was exhausted from the drive and sore from exercising new muscles. Sarah (who had never seen snow before) and Shaun had discovered that riding an inner tube down snow-covered slopes was easier to master than downhill skiing. There were no broken bones and only minor bruises to talk about during our last evening in Santa Barbara.

Our interlude in paradise was coming to a close, and it was a bittersweet time. We had been together enough to appreciate each other and to understand that we would never again enjoy the kind of relationship associated with parenting young children. Fortunately, we liked our sons as adults and enjoyed being together in one of the most beautiful places we knew. The record-breaking cold of our first week made us more appreciative of the warmth and beauty of the last few days. The temperature was 72 degrees on the final morning when six people crowded into Brad's van and started toward Los Angeles. Pat and I prepared to head in the opposite direction, north on Highway 101, for the interview that was the official reason for our visit.

The Strategos Stratagem

The drive to Palo Alto was a six-hour, utilitarian trip, straight up the 101 for 377 miles, then on to CA 85, and I-280, to the Sand Hill exit. Pat was excited, but calmer than I. We arrived just after sundown, checked into our hotel, and enjoyed a quiet dinner. I reviewed some material for my interview before turning in for a restless night of anticipation.

My father, a minister who was even more anxious about time than I, once explained his obsessiveness, "We need to leave for church early enough for me to change a flat tire and still arrive before the invocation." I didn't expect a prelude or invocation, but left early enough to compensate for getting lost a time or two—a good idea, since the Strategos offices were hidden at the back of an office complex so discreet that no street signs or office numbers were visible.

Even with geographic confusion, I still arrived ten minutes early. This provided an opportunity to meet some of the staff and form some initial impressions. The offices were well-appointed but not luxurious. Everyone appeared intelligent, hard-working and reasonably friendly.

There was a tiny bit of anxiety and uncertainty in the air, to which I added my own apprehensions about meeting Gary Hamel. I am accustomed to being around people who are smarter than I, but when I meet someone who is a lot smarter, I sometimes become hopelessly intimidated and inarticulate. I was pretty sure Gary would be impressive.

Grace, one of the first people I met, requested that I not mention the specific position they had asked me to consider. "Gary is brilliant and peripatetic. He has a million ideas, most of them good. Some ideas will survive and others will be forgotten." She warned, "He's having some trouble staying focused on completing the new book because he has so many opportunities—and he hasn't gotten around to telling the staff about your potential role."

That was disconcerting, but I wasn't disappointed when Gary arrived just after ten o'clock, a California vision of "dress for success." His carefully coiffed dark hair was thinning and beginning to show a distinguished bit of gray on the sides. He wore round Lafont Trajan glasses, a light blue Turnbull & Asser Egyptian cotton shirt with darker blue stripes, and a red ribbed Mezzocollo Huron cashmere sweater. Of course, I am not impressed at all by labels or expensive brands, but I believe he also wore a Dunhill belt and Ermenegildo Zegna loafers. Not only was I outclassed intellectually, but my very best suit now felt like something from Jed Clampett's closet.

Gary could not have been nicer. He asked about my recent monograph on the state of executive education and talked about his vision for Strategos Institute. He explained why he needed someone with more academic and executive experience than the consultants on his team. We talked about his expectations, and he suggested that we work out a preliminary four-month consulting arrangement where I would make a couple of trips per month to learn more about their business model and to develop a detailed business plan for the Institute. If this worked out, he suggested that I consider getting a two-year leave of absence from William & Mary or resigning my professorship and moving permanently to California. We shook hands on Tuesday afternoon, and I looked forward to returning in a couple of weeks.

A Prayer for Frank Saunders

Bad news arrived at the end of our first week back in Virginia. Frank Saunders had received the results of medical tests that explained his recurring back pain, headaches, and vision problems. Brain cancer had metastasized into his spinal column, and he was expected to live only two or three months. Ever the optimist, Frank was counting on a miracle and grateful that his state-funded medical insurance had been in effect for almost a month at the time of his diagnosis. I arranged my next trip to the West Coast so I could spend time with Frank in Santa Cruz before going to work in Palo Alto.

It had been less than three weeks since we had said good-bye to the Saunders in Santa Barbara, but it was obvious that Frank was very sick. He was just starting chemotherapy and experiencing great pain. He enjoyed talking about their life in Paros and was excited about my opportunity at Strategos. Always optimistic but never religious before, Frank surprised me by asking for my prayers. He had read about some research that prayer might actually improve the chances for recovery. "I'm thinking about launching a national campaign around the theme, 'Hey brother, can you spare a prayer?' What do you think?"

Gail was more realistic about his prognosis and encouraged me to visit any time I came to California. While still excited about the work with Strategos, I was depressed while driving toward Palo Alto.

Most of this visit involved reviewing plans for a February conference of Institute members in Barcelona and developing an orientation program for prospective members. The Institute already had support from global leaders such as Dutch/Shell, Emerson Electric and Nokia. Barcelona is one of our favorite cities, so I bought a ticket for Pat and we went a couple of days early to look at Gaudi architecture, eat Catalan food and act like tourists.

Since Gary was scheduled to make a $70,000 convention speech in Chicago, he appeared in Barcelona via a trans-Atlantic videocast—the first I had ever seen. Once the video feed was established, Gary walked into his Palo Alto office wearing an Armani jacket with blue jeans. He sat behind his desk and spoke eloquently for 45 minutes on a variety of subjects, then answered questions from the audience in Barcelona. He was provocative, insightful and charming.

Upon returning to Williamsburg, I made a few telephone calls to corporate contacts, inviting them to a free one-day overview of the Strategos approach to collaborative research. I was absolutely shocked that people weren't clamoring to attend. By early February, I had only a dozen people committed to the conference. I needed to get back to California to finalize the program and check on Frank Saunders, but was embarrassed that neither Gary's fabulous reputation nor my charming personality generated a SRO (standing room only) response.

I flew out on the weekend, picked up a car at the San Jose airport and drove to Santa Cruz to visit with the Saunders. Frank had lost a lot of ground in the four weeks since we were together. He was frail, emaciated, and in constant pain. Their rustic rental house was shabby, cluttered and sad. Gail took me aside to talk about how brave Frank was and how hard it was for her to think about an inevitable life without him.

Frank proved the late Senator Paul Tsongas was wrong. While undergoing treatment for cancer, Tsongas had famously resigned his Senate seat and commented, "I never knew anyone who on his deathbed said, 'I wish I had spent more time at the office'."

Frank's perspective was, "I treasure our memories of Paros, but I worry about leaving Gail without the financial resources that we would have if I had stayed on the corporate treadmill." The visit was difficult and depressing.

California Calling

On Monday morning, I met Gary at Buck's famous café near his home in Woodside. For the uninitiated, Woodside is the epicenter of the affluence associated with success in Silicon Valley. There are dozens of wealthy towns where the rich and successful of modern technology can park their late-model pickup trucks with leather seats in front of houses that suggest that there's no such thing as too-conspicuous consumption. None has quite the cachet of Woodside.

I pulled my rental Neon between a spiffy pickup truck and Gary's Jaguar and wandered inside. We discussed the Barcelona meeting and the forthcoming event for prospective members over Woodsider omelets. Gary asked me to meet him in Boston in about two weeks to talk with some folks at Harvard Business School Publishing about his proposed collaboration with their senior leadership guru.

After calling everyone I knew and many that I didn't, almost 30 names were on our participant list by the time I arrived in Boston. At the Harvard Business School, everyone shared my respect for Hamel. They were, however, showing concern about the lack of progress on his manuscript and the difficulty of getting the giants of leadership and strategy together for some productive collaboration. This was clearly the message they wanted me to deliver.

Other meetings went well, and at sunset, I made my way to the Ritz-Carlton, near the Boston Commons, where we were to meet in Gary's suite. Around midnight, I left with a list of people to call and things to do before and during our next meeting in mid-March, including Gary's suggestion that I start looking for a place to live in Palo Alto.

On the flight back to Virginia, another potentially brilliant idea occurred to me. What if we could also rent a condo in Santa Barbara and spend weekends there? I remembered a couple of places in East Beach that we had seen during our brief December exploration of real estate. Maybe, just maybe, one of the sellers would agree to a lease-purchase arrangement since the condo market was in a bit of a slump. If the seller was holding an empty unit and still servicing a mortgage, there might be an opportunity. As soon as I got back to Williamsburg, I called a realtor and explained my proposal. She promised to make the offer and to get back to me in a couple of days.

Registration for our March conference dropped from thirty to twenty. I managed to hide most of the desperation in my voice as I continued to call other prospects. Eventually we had a total of twenty-four people who attended the program. Pat and I flew out together a day before the meeting in order to see Frank and Gail. It was clear that the end was near. Frank was conscious only on an intermittent basis. From a robust 220 pounds, he now weighed less than half that. We tried to be helpful to Gail, but left after a short visit.

The Strategos orientation session went well, and I enjoyed facilitating it. After our corporate guests had made their way to the airport, Gary called me into his office and renewed his offer of a one-year contract for me to work with the Institute. There were still a few details to be worked out since he was negotiating a joint venture with one of the major professional services firms. My responsibilities might involve liaison with that organization. Gary promised to resolve the details within a few days. While the ambiguity was disconcerting, the potential affiliation struck me as quite positive.

When Pat picked me up that evening, she reported, "I found two nearby apartment complexes that are nice enough for us to live in for a year although both are a little reminiscent of graduate school." I was touched that Pat wanted to leave Williamsburg so much that she was willing to significantly compromise our standard of living. I started to tell her about the possibility of a Santa Barbara retreat for weekends and holidays. I wanted, however, to offer a definite surprise, rather than a tentative hope and there was no response to my offer.

Three days later, the Santa Barbara realtor called to say that the offer for a lease-purchase of a townhouse at East Beach had been accepted. We agreed to make lease payments for twelve months and could exercise an option to purchase the unit at the original price during that time. She expressed the forms to my office, and I turned them around immediately. A couple of days later, my request for a year's partial leave was approved by William and Mary.

A week later, I received the call from Strategos I had been waiting for—at least I thought it was the call I was waiting for. Gary wasn't available, but Grace communicated for him.

The Stages of Loss

"We're really sorry, but regrettably, the joint venture negotiations have fallen apart. The funds Gary was counting on to finance your work won't be available. Consulting revenues are down because of the faltering economy."

My stomach and mind were in turmoil as she went on, "We are truly sorry if you have been inconvenienced in any way." Within a matter of moments, I went through all of Kubler - Ross' stages of loss. Initially, my reaction was *disbelief*. "This couldn't be happening! Everything was going so well."

Next, I became incredibly *angry*. "What kind of jerk would ask me to request a leave of absence, rent a condo in Palo Alto and then not even have the courtesy to call and break the news himself?"

I didn't want to appear desperate or needy, but I couldn't resist a little *bargaining*. "Is this definite or just a delay for a couple of months?"

"There's still interest in the concept. Unfortunately, the financial turmoil is significant. Gary's book is behind schedule and completing the manuscript has to be his primary focus for the next several months." I was deeply *depressed* as I hung up. *Acceptance* was going to take a little longer.

Fortunately, we had not mailed the lease papers for the Palo Alto apartment. I had hedged by keeping a partial schedule at

William and Mary for the spring term and a few days of consulting were already booked. Perhaps we could turn this negative into something positive.

My mother loved the Norman Vincent Peale proverb, "When life hands you a lemon, make lemonade." She lived by that philosophy and was the only person I know who could make the author of *The Power of Positive Thinking* seem like a cynic. Until this moment, I thought the quote was a bit sappy. I preferred Frank Saunders' adaptation, "When life hands you a lemon, just ask for tequila and salt, and give me a call." Perhaps we could turn this lemon into something positive without becoming dependent on tequila.

Turning to Pat, I shared the bad news and then added, "Why don't we treat this as a sabbatical and spend the year in Santa Barbara?"

This suggestion may have endeared me to her, more than my proposal of marriage or the couple of times I had actually apologized for something. In a year, we might conclude that Santa Barbara is vastly over-rated or we might decide that this was where we would eventually spend our retirement years.

Post-script: As I edit this chapter, I am sitting on a balcony looking out at the Pacific Ocean and the Santa Cruz Island just off the Santa Barbara coast. By my side is a pitcher of lemonade made from lemons grown on our very own tree. It is the best lemonade I have ever tasted.

Chapter 3
April in Paradise

Nothing we do is ever simple. Even projects that appear straightforward wind up with overlapping levels of complexity. Some of this is because stuff happens. Some of it may be due to being overly influenced by a time management course that emphasized the importance of grouping tasks together for greater efficiency. It makes sense to stop at the dry cleaners while coming back from grocery shopping, but if you add the hardware store, the gas station and the post office, you may find that the ice cream has melted. Still, I try to coordinate everything in a search for perfect scheduling and execution.

We were simply going to spend a year in a rented Santa Barbara townhouse. The unit was available on April 1, but we planned to take care of a couple of other things first. We needed to get some basic furnishings to the townhouse. I had a week-long seminar with a New York client. Shaun, Pat's son (and Sarah's father), was getting re-married. We would need transportation in Santa Barbara. It would take some coordination, but everything should work out.

Since we would be returning regularly to Williamsburg, we decided to transport the basic furnishings from an Atlanta house we had owned for twenty years. As I headed off for a "Key Manager" seminar with Bertelsmann Music Group

(BMG), Pat left for Atlanta to determine what we should take to California. BMG was one of my favorite clients. Participants for this program came from around the world. They were young, intelligent and hip.

When we started working with BMG a decade earlier, their culture was intimidating. One participant team reported, "BMG may stand for "Big Mean Germans" but we recommend a strategy to become known for the 'Best Music Globally'."

The group was a creative combination of diverse nationalities, but had a heavy concentration of Jews and Germans, working together productively—although when a delegation from corporate headquarters in Gütersloh came to the Broadway offices, one junior executive would announce over the PA system, "Germans on the floor! Germans on the floor! All Jews and homosexuals, go to your offices immediately!" Not only did the Jewish comic keep his job, he was invited to our program for high-potential leaders.

The seminar was going well, but each evening I received reports from Atlanta about some of the challenges Pat was facing. Since this was a temporary move, we were trying to be minimalist, economical and creative. We had decided to pack up our old station wagon and drive it to California. An Atlanta friend recommended a private contractor he had used for a couple of moves. "Stan the Moving Man might be just what you need," he told us. "He owns a medium-sized truck, has good experience, and he's available in early April."

The trip was over 2,220 miles and would take at least forty hours of driving time. Stan was willing to take the job and gave us a price that was extremely reasonable. Pat had a few reservations. "His clothes were dirty. He chews tobacco. He doesn't have any teeth, and he smells bad."

I reminded her, "We aren't interviewing Stan as a prospective suitor for your sister. Do you think he's honest and competent?"

"I think so," she responded. "He actually seemed like a very nice person, but I don't know if his truck will make the trip."

We decided to check on a rental truck and to continue our negotiations with Stan. The next evening, Pat reported that Stan had agreed with our recommendation to rent a newer truck. She offered to pick up the cost of a return flight, but Stan insisted that it would be less expensive for him to return the truck He also sheepishly confessed that he had never flown and didn't want to trust his safety to a pilot he didn't even know.

As soon as the seminar ended, I rushed to the airport, boarded a flight to Atlanta, took MARTA to the stop nearest our house, and arrived just after Stan finished loading the last items into the truck and gone home for the evening, ready to leave early the next morning. We also had an early departure as we needed to be in Gulf Shores, Alabama for Shaun's wedding. After loading the station wagon in the dawn's early light, we started the six-hour drive to the Gulf.

A Wedding on the Beach

Gulf Shores is sometimes called "The Redneck Riviera" because it possesses a pristine stretch of glistening white sand beach, now marred by chock-a-block condo complexes, teeming chain eateries and boisterous visitors. Shaun was a typical entrepreneur who had lived there since high school. He didn't need college to open his own beach service business and always had a new venture brewing that "absolutely could not fail." He was marrying Susan, whom we didn't know well, but she made him happy and was a welcomed addition to the family. After arriving and checking into our rented condo, we went for a quick run on the beach, showered, changed clothes and met most of the wedding party for a rehearsal dinner. They were planning their own ceremony on the beach, a relatively informal event with friends, family and a local band.

My family is pretty straight-laced and uptight. Pat's family was a bit more relaxed. This was Susan's first marriage, so she was lovely in white—even though she was six months pregnant. Everybody, including the grandmothers, had a bit or more to drink and were uninhibitedly dancing on the sand. I tried hard to overcome childhood conditioning, but would always be limited by my father's ministerial dictum, "There is no room on the same leg for a praying knee and a dancing foot!"

37

I suspected that his church was opposed to premarital sex on the grounds that it might lead to dancing.

While we were eating jambalaya and dancing under the stars, Stan was moving our belongings steadily across the country. One of us needed to be there when he arrived in Santa Barbara. Pat insisted on driving so she could visit with a friend in New Orleans and spend some time in San Antonio. She dropped me and her mother at the Mobile airport and headed west.

Sleeping Single in Santa Barbara

My flight was uneventful. Upon arriving at LAX, I walked outside and met the Santa Barbara Airbus. They circled the airport every couple of hours, and for thirty dollars brought people to Carpinteria, Santa Barbara and Goleta. The Santa Barbara stop was just a block from our townhouse. I found our unit, unlocked the door, and realized for the first time that, without a single item of furniture, I would have to sleep on the floor or find a motel. I was too tired and cheap to look for lodging at such a late hour, so I put on sweats and lay down for a painful night highlighted by moments of actual sleep.

The next morning, I was sore and still tired, but excited to be in Santa Barbara. I left a note on the door in the unlikely event that Stan arrived, and walked across the street to the East Beach Grill. I placed my order for a Santa Barbara omelet with a young man who appeared to be in his mid-thirties. Francisco told me, "I work here for almost twenty years. When my boss retires in a few years, he will let me take over the business." I was impressed by his personality, work ethic and by one of the best omelets I had ever eaten. (As I write this, Francisco has achieved his dream of running East Beach Grill, along with a couple of other beachfront establishments. Pat and I still occasionally share a Santa Barbara omelet and enjoy seeing what a successful entrepreneur Francisco has become.)

While enjoying breakfast, I got into a conversation with a retired pharmaceutical executive in his eighties who explained, "We have a group that walks three miles along the beach, three times a week. We go down the walking trail that extends for a mile, past the Dolphin statue at the foot of State Street to the harbor a half mile away, then turn around and come back."

Confident in my ability to match the distance of someone in his eighties, I meandered along the trail, passing by the skateboarding park, wharf, and a number of apparently homeless people who were enjoying the ocean views as much as any real estate speculator.

After burning off a third of the calories consumed at the Grill, I went back to the condo, pulled out a novel and was lost for a couple of hours in Sue Grafton's fictionalized description of a town that sounded very much like Santa Barbara. I was two-thirds through *M is for Malice* when the doorbell rang. I almost expected to find a sexy private investigator at the door, but fortunately it was our erstwhile mover, Stan. He had made unbelievable time—either by driving at breakneck speed or by staying behind the wheel with almost no rest along the way.

Pat had described Stan accurately. He was tall, slender and wiry but clearly not trying to make a fashion statement. I would not be introducing him to Pat's sister. More importantly, the truck and our possessions appeared to be in good shape. I helped unload, taking special pleasure in setting up a queen size bed. We had a sofa with a couple of chairs in the living room, a harvest table with four chairs and cooking utensils in the kitchen with a computer stand and book case in another bedroom. It looked better than it had the evening before, but was still "early bachelor" chic. We had some shopping to do.

Since Stan was driving back to Atlanta, he was anxious to get started. I encouraged him to spend one night in Santa Barbara before heading out, but the best I could do was to persuade him to take a shower and a nap before getting back into the cab of what had become his home away from home.

I worried a little about Stan's safety, but was becoming more concerned about Pat who didn't answer her newly acquired cell phone. At first I was aggravated that she wasn't responding. Then, I started worrying about her being stranded by the side of the road trying to cope with a coven of Hell's Angels or lying unconscious in a heap of twisted steel. Those were the only reasonable explanations for this lack of communication. About the time she should have been touring the Alamo, I started imagining her visiting some of my favorite clubs in San

39

Antonio. I knew a little bit about bachelors in San Antonio. Did I mention that Pat's family was a little more relaxed than mine?

Too keyed up to turn in early, I decided to take the electric trolley that runs along Cabrillo Boulevard, Santa Barbara's beachfront avenue, to the harbor and transfer to the State Street trolley. The trip would cost a quarter, but after my morning walk and unloading the moving van, I was tired and felt like splurging. The City deserves credit for providing this low cost, energy efficient means of transportation, but it doesn't qualify as rapid transit. By the time I reached lower State Street, I was starving and decided to forego the rest of the tour, get off the trolley, grab a bite to eat, and head back "home."

All That Jazz

Exiting the trolley, I heard the sounds of hot Dixieland music. I crossed the street to the James Joyce Pub, which was filled with the sounds of a group called Ulysses Jazz. They could have been refugees from New Orleans' Preservation Hall. Since the pub didn't have a food menu, I had a couple of mugs of a local beer called Santa Barbara Blonde and filled up on salted peanuts, tossing at least a pound of shells on the floor. The band was impressive. Mike, one of the regulars at the James Joyce, explained, "The leader and clarinetist is a British automotive engineer and the bass player is in his thirties, but the rest of the group is pushing seventy. Four of them grew up in Santa Barbara and have been playing together since high school. They didn't make the big time, but they enjoy performing and like each other even though their lives have been quite different. One is an heir to a Standard Oil fortune and the others are just regular Joes."

I would definitely bring Pat here, provided she survived the drive to California. And that thought brought me back to a recognition that I should be heading back. I grabbed the next trolley, waited interminably at the transfer point, and finally started to East Beach. The passengers for this portion of the trip were more interesting than they had been earlier in the evening. A nice-looking, but unkempt, young man, was clutching a paper bag. When our eyes met, he lifted the bag and said, "Well, I've got a bottle of wine. Now, if I can find a woman to sleep on the beach with me tonight, I'll really have it made."

I wished him luck as he left the trolley and thought that I was fortunate to have a bed tonight, even if I was sleeping single in a bed built for two. I would really feel lucky if I were to hear from Pat and go to sleep knowing that she was safe. As I put my key into the lock, I heard our new telephone start to ring. I raced up the stairs and picked up the phone on the fourth ring. She wasn't sobbing and her voice sounded calm. I resisted the temptation to scream, "Why haven't you called sooner?"

She gave me a full report. "The cell phone isn't working, but everything has gone swimmingly. Sharon and I had a wonderful time in New Orleans, and I just got into San Antonio. My B&B is near the downtown River Walk, but I'm too tired to go out tonight. I'll do a little sightseeing at the Alamo in the morning."

"Any idea when you'll get to Santa Barbara?" I asked.

"I made a reservation in El Paso for tomorrow night. If things go well, I should be in Santa Barbara the evening after that."

This gave me two days to get things ready for her arrival and do whatever I wanted to do by myself. Without a car, my entertainment options were limited. Thank goodness for the electric trolley. I returned to Trader Joe's on Milpas Street and purchased some basics. East Beach Grill was nice, but not a place to eat every meal. Moreover, the townhouse's owner had left a limited supply of bathroom tissue.

I placed a quick phone call to check on Frank Saunders. A tearful Gail told me that Frank had died just a few hours earlier. I tried to offer condolences and assistance, but Gail and her sister had things under control. They had started carrying out Frank's request that he be cremated and asked that we attend the memorial service to be conducted in a month. Of course, we would be there. Frank had been a great friend and would be missed by everyone who knew him.

Lonely and more than a little depressed, I went for a long walk from East Beach, along a rocky stretch of sand, past the Santa Barbara Cemetery, to Butterfly Beach. The sun was setting and an evening fog made the return walk even more melancholy.

I returned to the silent townhouse and prepared a nourishing meal of organic peanut butter on whole wheat crackers, washed down by a glass of California Chardonnay. To be honest, it may have been more than a single glass. I've never been quite sure what vintage is appropriate for crackers and peanut butter and hope that the Chardonnay was an appropriate pairing.

I had been told, probably by Frank, that every day of the week except Mondays, a farmers market selling fresh produce, fruit, flowers and nuts, is conducted within a ten-mile radius of downtown Santa Barbara. The biggest and best-attended of these is held every Saturday morning, rain or shine, at the corner of Santa Barbara and Cota streets. Because Pat was an early aficionado of organic food, we have visited farmers markets around the world. This was one of the best anywhere. The market in Aix-en-Provence had more variety, but was also much more expensive. The variety of offerings was amazing. You can get almost anything at the Santa Barbara Farmers Market—from organic strawberries, avocados, oranges, and multiple varieties of lettuce to local rock shrimp to organic honey; from flowers to free-range eggs to hormone-free, grass-fed beef. There's organic cheese, olive oil, fruit juices, dried fruits, all sorts of sprouts, and nuts. The list is almost endless. Most of this is grown locally and available at totally reasonable prices. Add in a backdrop of perfect weather and background music from a sitar player, a mariachi band and a high school minstrel troupe and you get a sense of the Santa Barbara Farmers Market, where showbiz personalities without makeup, former CEOs, and ordinary mortals rub elbows, smile, and stand politely in line to wait for their turn to pay cash for next week's organic food supply.

I purchased almost more than I could carry on the trolley back to our temporary home. We would have a well-stocked kitchen by the time Pat arrived—hopefully, this afternoon or evening. I spent a few hours doing basic unpacking, cleaning and straightening. Despite being a totally liberated male, I am less obsessive about neatness than Pat, and I wanted her to be pleased with our new accommodations. By mid-afternoon, I had achieved a level of tidiness that approached perfection, put out a couple of candles, opened a package of cheddar and a bottle of wine, prepared some pasta, and started pacing back and forth to our front window to see when she arrived. I got lots of exercise and finished Sue Grafton's book before hearing our station wagon pull into the garage. I was excited to see Pat, and she was excited to finish the longest drive of her life.

Zoo Story

We shared the wine and cheese while catching up on our individual adventures. Pat was exhausted, so we finished the pasta and turned in early. As may be true with other married couples, we have different sleep experiences. Early in our relationship, Pat would ask how I had slept. It seemed a strange question, because I usually didn't remember. She, on the other hand, had been overly influenced by the childhood story of "The Princess and the Pea." She would remember at what times she had awakened and how long it took for her to get back to sleep. Perhaps, I am a deeper sleeper.

In three nights as a Santa Barbara resident, I never heard any disturbing noises. But that first night together in Santa Barbara, around two o'clock, Pat awakened me in a state of panic about a strange noise that disturbed her sleep. "Yes," I agreed, "that was a strange noise. Yes, it does sound a little like a lion, but I'm confident that this lion doesn't pose an immediate threat." I was groggy, but may have asked if she remembered that the one of the attractions of our location was that the backyard view includes the Santa Barbara Zoo.

This vista had been charming when we first saw the property. We had liked the idea of being neighbors to one of the nation's best small zoos and enjoying a thirty-acre privacy buffer— well, almost private. I hadn't considered the nocturnal nature of some of our neighbors. We eventually came to see it as charming and positive again, but it did pose a challenge on our first night together in East Beach.

The next morning, we decided to walk over to the zoo and get acquainted with our new neighbors. Some zoos are criminal in their treatment of animals. Others, like this one, provide an environment that looked superior to what they would have known in the wild. Of the approximately 600 animals in residence, the most interesting were a couple of mountain gorillas, red pandas, a famous giraffe with a crooked neck and our friends the lions. The zoo was neat and clean. Even Pat

43

approved. Lots of shady trees and beautiful landscaping made much of it look like a botanical garden—with animals.

After a couple of hours walking through the exhibits, enjoying the ocean views and feeding the giraffes, we were a little tired, so we rode the miniature train that circled the zoo grounds every half hour and got off near the zoo's entrance. This would be one of our favorite places to show out-of-town guests, so we immediately signed up for two annual memberships.

After a week in Santa Barbara, I had gone longer without checking e-mail or visiting a library than I could remember. As withdrawal pains started, we had to do something about this. Directly across from the county courthouse, we found the current location of the main public library.

The Possible Dream

The city's first library was established in 1870. It had grown from 2000 volumes to over 350,000 volumes and was housed in a building near the Courthouse and Art Museum when we arrived. In 1959, Channing Peake and Howard Warshaw painted stylized murals with scenes from *Don Quixote* at the library entrance. As the hero of the first modern novel and one of my favorite fictional characters Don Quixote was an ideal choice for the library. I had used the lines from *Man of La Mancha*'s "The Impossible Dream" in many presentations and love Cervantes' insight that "facts may be the enemy of truth."

The library was able to satisfy two of my major obsessions. On the reading front, I found several books I had not yet read, including an excellent collection of recent publications near the checkout desk. I picked up an armful of books and patiently waited my turn to use one of the free high-speed Internet connections, where I managed to handle both e-mail accounts in less than two hours.

One of the major disadvantages of our rental was a dependency on a dial-up modem for Internet access that seemed slower than a glacier before global warming. Now, I had a legitimate reason to make lots of trips to the library. On the other hand, we didn't have to worry about other utilities. That was already taken care of for us, but we did need to know what was going on in our temporary hometown. We discovered the *Santa Barbara News-Press,* the city's daily newspaper and one of the best small-town papers I had ever seen. It was owned by the *New York Times* and provided outstanding columnists, plus international, national, state and local coverage.

On Fridays, we pored over a special section called "The Scene" that covered current movies, local restaurants, music, nightlife, theater and the art world. Each day, the Local section of the newspaper contained the *"Public Square"* column identifying all of the upcoming day's events, the agendas of local government meetings, roadwork, and even a list of local residents who were celebrating birthdays. We didn't get around to attending meetings of the City Council or birthday parties for strangers, but reviewing the *News-Press* became our first order of business each morning.

A Healthy, Happy Routine

We soon developed a routine for our days in paradise. I usually got up earlier than Pat, shaved, showered and read the paper while she got dressed. It was a small paper, so I finished before she was ready and would start our super-healthy breakfast. Fresh organic strawberries from the farmers market were first into the blender, followed by an organic banana and frozen organic blueberries from Trader Joe's. Then, I would add a bit of plain organic yogurt, a little soy protein and a few cubes of ice. A few seconds in the blender, and we were ready to enjoy tasty, nutritious smoothies. Once a week, Pat would make a big batch of whole-grain spelt biscuits, which we would freeze. Each morning, I would defrost a couple of these, add a small sliver of clarified butter and bake for an additional seven minutes while our shade-grown, free-trade coffee percolated.

About the time this was ready, Pat would emerge, radiant and ready for the day, and we would enjoy a leisurely breakfast while discussing plans for the day. Usually our most stressful moment came in deciding where we wanted to have lunch. (We were starting to sound like the Saunders!) Our goal was to try all of the 400 restaurants in the greater Santa Barbara area. Despite a valiant effort, we were thwarted because, while the number of eateries stayed about the same, the names, owners and menus changed on a regular basis.

There were plenty of restaurants that appeal to the *Bon Appétit* or *Gourmet* crowd. For our almost daily fare, we preferred places like the Palace Grill who served inexpensive but superbly seasoned Cajun food at lunch. Their dinners were equally as tasty but much more expensive. Joe's Café is one of the oldest restaurants in Santa Barbara. It opened during Prohibition as a popular speakeasy. I especially liked their calamari steaks. We tried the Enterprise Fish Company and the San Ysidro Pharmacy Grill because we heard that Jonathan Winters would occasionally wander in and try out new material or re-create some of his classic roles, like the oldest living flight attendant. A neighbor reported seeing Winters sit down, unannounced, at the pharmacy sandwich shop with an elderly matron. Seeing her shock, he introduced himself by saying, "Don't worry, my dear. I will not attack you. Mr. Pencil doesn't write anymore."

In late afternoon, we often walked on the beach. Sometimes we turned east by the beach volleyball courts to a rocky route past cliffs to Butterfly Beach. We loved this walk until we came home with tar on our feet. When clean feet were important, we turned right and followed the walking path along the beach, past the wharf to the harbor. There, we would turn around and amble back. On weekends, we enjoyed the farmers market, hiking in the San Ysidro Mountains and listening to Ulysses Jazz. It was the first time in my adult life without classes, appointments or telephone conferences. April in Santa Barbara was fantastic. I could get used to this.

The 1952 musical *April in Paris* is a romantic comedy starring Doris Day and Ray Bolger, who meet on the way to Paris and fall in love. Paris is always a beautiful city, but can be rainy, chilly and not nearly as romantic as our first April in Santa Barbara. Despite T. S. Eliot's warning, "April is the cruelest month," we found the opposite was true. We were having a second honeymoon and getting used to this version of paradise.

Santa Barbara wouldn't qualify as "low cost," but otherwise it was as close to perfection as we could find. Even if we couldn't make a permanent move, this experiment could let us know if our initial impressions were correct. Perhaps after a few more years of working, we might be able to afford the price of admission.

Chapter Four
600 New Best Friends

May is marvelous in Santa Barbara. In fact, Santa Barbara weather is almost always marvelous. Pleasantly warm days are usually followed by comfortably cool nights.

The ideal Mediterranean climate can be attributed to a unique geographic phenomenon. Everyone knows that the Pacific Ocean is on the western edge of the continental United States—everyone except those lucky people who call Santa Barbara home. For forty miles on either side of the city, you find the coast by heading south. This alignment moderates the ocean currents flowing past this portion of the coast. North, away from the Coast, the Santa Ynez Mountains shelter the area from more extreme inland heat and cold. The Channel Islands, twenty to thirty miles offshore, break the force of ocean storms and quiet the surf. The result is a comfortable year-round average temperature of 64 degrees, with an average maximum of 74 and an average minimum of 56 degrees with 300 days of sunshine each year. Small wonder that St. Peter is rumored to tell former Santa Barbarians, "I'll let you in, but you probably won't like the weather."

There is always something to celebrate in Santa Barbara. Toward the beginning of May, we started seeing articles about the Cinco de Mayo celebration. I didn't do well in high school Spanish, but I was pretty sure this was either a celebration

47

about the sinking of a mayonnaise ship or a huge weekend party around the fifth of May.

It didn't take much research to find out that the extended party was a celebration of the 1862 victory of 4,000 ill-equipped Mexicans over 8,000 well-equipped French invaders. As you might suspect, the battle took place on May 5, but you don't have to know the town (Puebla) where the battle took place to join in the festivities. Today, the French have been forgiven and fiestas are planned in Mexico and in many communities around the world where Mexicans live. Even *gringos* who have little idea why they are coming to a Cinco de Mayo celebration are happy to commemorate the day and join in the fun. Santa Barbarians welcome the day to feast on Mexican food and celebrate Hispanic tradition and achievement.

We headed toward the food booths at Plaza de la Guerra where we watched dance performances and mariachi bands while sampling *carnitas* (fried pork) sandwiches and *carne de cabra* (goat meat) tacos with hot tortillas in a cardboard basket, and a plate with lettuce, tomato and raw onions. I added some hellishly hot *pico de gallo* with big hunks of raw *serrano* pepper while Pat wisely found some milder salsa.

There were exciting parties for the well-connected, but we weren't invited to any. We knew absolutely no one in Santa Barbara. Gail Saunders would be returning in a few days for Frank's memorial service, but we felt like the outsiders we were. We had tried unsuccessfully to find good friends in Williamsburg and weren't sure if we had the energy to make much effort here. After all, we were only renting for a year.

Remembering Frank

Our routine of organic fruit smoothies, beach walks and exploring the restaurants and sights of Santa Barbara was still satisfying. Almost every day, we found something new to explore or enjoy. We relished calling our family back in the South and bragging about how much fun we were having. It wasn't clear how much they enjoyed hearing about our adventures, but everyone managed to schedule a visit before our lease expired.

We had been in Santa Barbara less than a month and had already recognized that it was going to be hard to leave.

We talked a couple of times to Gail Saunders, who reminded us that Frank's memorial was to be in Elings Park, but that name didn't appear on our city map. Finally, someone told us that locals still call it Las Positas Park. Partially built on land reclaimed from a city landfill, the park had just been renamed in honor of Dr. Virgil Elings. Perched on top of one of Santa Barbara's tallest hills, this 230-acre park has panoramic views, sports fields, tennis courts, and an amphitheatre where we were to meet Gail and a few of her friends.

The day of the memorial dawned cloudy and gray—a pronounced shift from the previous glorious climate Santa Barbara had enjoyed. We were just beginning to experience a local phenomenon called "May Gray," which would, in a couple of weeks, morph into "June Gloom." Cynics may complain, but remember that geographic peculiarity mentioned at the beginning of this chapter? When those warm desert winds hit the cold Pacific waters, they generate a billowing fog that sweeps inland. The summer temperatures stay cool partially because of this fog. The result is that throughout late May and June, until the ocean warms up enough for this occurrence to end, each morning dawns dark and foggy with an almost mystical feel. Fortunately, the fog almost always clears by noon, leaving beautiful, warm afternoons that are cloudless, fifteen degrees cooler than the inland, and followed by chilly nights that are wonderful for sleeping.

The "May Gray" was appropriate for the occasion. As we made our way to the amphitheater, we were surprised to see over 100 people with white, helium-filled balloons marking the place for the service. How had the Saunders gotten to know so many people during their short stay in Santa Barbara? Not only had these people shown up for the memorial, many had brought food to share with those of us who were not so thoughtful. The highlight of an otherwise uninspiring service was when each person took a balloon and released it along with a silent, special memory of Frank. Just as Gail scattered the ashes and we released our balloons, the sun broke through, dissipating the haze and revealing the incredible view of city and ocean.

As we began to fill our plates and meet other people, I was surprised to hear that some of them believed Elings Park was the best place in town to view the sunset. I was reminded of Frank's comment in Paros that "deciding where to watch the sunset is now the most stressful part of our day."

Who Are These People?

Since we didn't know anyone but Gail, our "get-acquainted question" for the day was, "How did you get to know the Saunders?"After a dozen people replied that they had met them through an organization called Santa Barbara Newcomers, we wanted to know more about this group. Without exception, the immediate response was something like, "It's the most wonderful organization you can imagine to help you meet other newcomers and to get to know Santa Barbara."

Berkeley Meigs, a curvaceous, attractive redhead, was more specific. She told us that the mission of SB Newcomers is to help 'newbies' make friends and learn about the many social, cultural, and civic opportunities in the Santa Barbara area. "We have about forty committees composed of members who volunteer their time to organize about seventy get-togethers and events each month," she enthused. Without pausing for a breath, she went on, "The organization has 600 members who range in age from twenty years to eighty-plus. It includes folks who have moved to Santa Barbara within the previous two years from as near as Ojai and as far away as New Zealand."

This sounded pretty nice. If we were going to stay in Santa Barbara, I would definitely be interested. As I mulled this over, Pat responded with animation, "It sounds like a great group. Maybe we ought to become members. When is your next meeting?"

Berkeley explained that prospective members were invited to an introductory session, conducted on the first Monday of each month. "They are always at the Fess Parker Doubletree Hotel on Cabrillo. We even provide refreshments. We hope you can make it on the seventh."

Over the years, I've slowly learned not to correct Pat's tendency to get overly excited about prospective new activities.

On the drive home, we argued about the appropriateness of attending the June meeting, given our short-term focus. Pat was impressed with how enthusiastic people were about the organization, and I was a little put off by their gung-ho outlook. Most people from the South genuinely believe that California is "the land of fruits and nuts." I was far too sophisticated to get involved in a West Coast cult. We decided democratically, and after losing by a narrow margin, I grumbled, "All right, I'll go, but I'm not going to join, and I won't drink their Kool-Aid!"

Pat had already decided that we simply wouldn't mention that we would be spending just eleven more months in Santa Barbara. "Lots of folks probably decide to move away after being here for a while. I'll bet some people get tired of living here and decide they want to try somewhere else."

"Sure," "I groused, "all this perfect weather and beautiful scenery must get depressing after a few months. That's why we see so many moving vans heading out of town."

We Go To the Dogs

A few days remained before the first Monday in June, so we checked the newspaper's *Scene* section. What was this Saturday event called "The Big Dog Parade?" We had noticed a Big Dog Sportswear store on lower State Street that featured oversized shorts and shirts. The concept had started with a group of friends who wore large, colorful shorts on a river-rafting trip and attracted lots of attention. Soon the phrase, "Man, those puppies are big!" became a motto, and the Big Dog sportswear brand with the familiar St. Bernard logo was born. The brand's first store opened a few months later, in 1984, on State Street. The parade started as a simple block party with Big Dog employees and some friends celebrating near the flagship store. Over the past few years, it had grown into a spectacle capable of shutting down the entire city for a weekend. Organizers were expecting the parade to attract 1,000 dogs and up to 15,000 humanoids to downtown Santa Barbara for contests, revelry, and good old-fashioned parade fun.

We made our way to the parade route just before it was scheduled to begin. Obviously this was going to be a bigger deal than we had anticipated. People were already lined up, three or four deep, with many having "marked their territory" the previous evening by leaving plastic chairs at good viewing locations along the way.

Finally, we found a place with a decent view of hundreds of dogs dressed in fetching costumes, often matched with those sported by their owners. Canine ballerinas, devils, clowns, kings, cowboys, and biker dudes meandered down the street. Several bands and floats featuring dogs in various motifs competed for awards in various categories. We also enjoyed watching the spectator dogs watching the parade. A golden retriever stationed near us was well behaved until a collection of other retrievers marched by with their owners. Perhaps he was barking at a long-lost sibling or cousin. Pat was convinced that he was humiliated because his owner didn't care enough to enroll him in this after obedience-school activity. I've never been good at knowing what pets were thinking, but I did wonder if he harbored resentment about a promise of getting "tutored," and finding out that the vet had an altogether different agenda.

After the parade, many of the enthusiasts headed for more fun at the Canine Festival in Old Chase Palm Park. Reportedly, "thousands enjoyed rows of vendor booths, kid's activities, live music, yummy food, and celebrity guests." I was beginning to suspect that the parade was a clever marketing ploy to advertise the company's T-shirts and multi-generational active wear when I spotted a notice that "all the proceeds from the parade events will go to the Big Dog Foundation, a nonprofit charity for dogs, children, and dogs that help people."

We were looking forward to the Newcomers orientation on Monday. At least, it wouldn't be difficult to find the meeting place. Just a couple of blocks from our townhouse and across the street from the Pacific Ocean, Fess Parker's Doubletree's circular main building with three floors and seven two-story mission-style buildings on twenty-four landscaped acres make up Santa Barbara's largest hotel complex.

Fess Parker had moved from being TV's Davy Crockett and Daniel Boone to become a major developer. In addition to this hotel, Parker's operations also include 1,500 acres of vineyards in Los Olivos for his winery, inn and spa. At the tasting room and visitor center, you can buy wine, coonskin caps and bottle toppers inspired by Parker's television characters.

Parker built the Santa Barbara property in 1986 on a site that had included two Southern Pacific locomotive roundhouses. When the 1925 earthquake almost destroyed them, the ubiquitous Pearl Chase convinced the railroad to rebuild in the Spanish style for which Santa Barbara was becoming famous. The railroad's main building was also influenced by a bull ring in Seville. The hotel's circular rotunda maintains the feel of Southern Pacific's design and is Santa Barbara's most popular facility for conferences and large meetings.

A Benign Cult

We left home in plenty of time to be among the first arrivals. Since we were walking, I didn't have to worry about changing a tire, but I wanted to be able to check out the crowd and identify emergency exits in the event we needed to escape from a brainwashing initiative.

We found the meeting room on the second floor of the hotel. An elegant, middle-aged couple (actually they were about our age, but we still like to maintain the fiction of middle age) registered our attendance and invited us to enjoy decaffeinated coffee or lemonade and cookies. There was no Kool-Aid in sight. They introduced themselves as Bob and Alex Nourse and were co-chairs of the Welcoming Committee. Since my registration indicated that I "had been" a professor at William and Mary, Nourse mentioned that he had taught at Western Ontario and the Harvard Business School before going into the retail business. We found out later that he and Alex had built The Bombay Company into a multinational chain. As we moved to the refreshment table, Pat made me admit that they didn't sound or look like cult leaders or potential terrorists.

Other folks started trickling in and all looked respectable. Better still, most were in our age category. Many had retired early, just retired, or sold a business. We wound up sitting by Mark and Barb Palmer from Chicago. Like us, they were empty nesters. I was about to ask some intrusive questions about their backgrounds when someone rang a bell indicating it was time for the meeting to start.

Our friend Berkeley, from Frank's memorial service, was presiding. She was president-elect of the club and was just as enthusiastic as she was at our previous conversation. In fact, some of her presentation sounded familiar.

"Welcome," she began, "to one of the best newcomer associations in the country. We are 44 years old and with 600 members, we are also one of the largest. Over forty committees plan some seventy activities each month." She added that these committees cover a range of activities from athletic (beach walking, tennis bicycling, hiking, golfing) to outings (sailing, visual arts, performing arts) to eating out ('out to lunch', gourmet dining and cooking), wine appreciation, and club socials that take place at members' homes three or four times per month.

"Annual dues are $75 per couple. Members receive a monthly newsletter announcing and describing each event and activity, with details on how to sign up and where to meet. Postage for those twenty-thirty page newsletters is our biggest expense. Members receive this on the last week of each month, and at nine o'clock on the first Tuesday, start calling to reserve a place for a particular event," she told us. "By ten o'clock, some activities will already be filled."

Berkeley closed her comments with a phrase that still literally gives me a little thrill. "Joining this organization provides you with an opportunity to make 600 new best friends."

The next speaker was a slender brunette. What was it with all these slender people? This wouldn't be happening in the South. Was it possible that these 'Stepford Newcomers' disappeared people who became too hefty for Santa Barbara's aesthetic standards? Her name was Ellen Lilley and she was the Activities Vice President with responsibility for coordinating all of the club's events.

Ellen explained a unique characteristic of Newcomers, "The membership is always changing; and the activities change according to membership interests. Certain committees may cease to exist and be replaced with another based on the interests of members." She pointed out that this ebb and flow of activities made the organization adaptable to the wants and needs of the membership base. "If there is an activity we would like to see represented, all you need to do is volunteer to head up a committee focusing on that activity."

Short Term Investing

At the end of the two-year membership, newcomers should know the city and have enough friends to 'outgrow' the organization. "Consequently, membership is limited to two years—unless you work on a committee or become an officer." Ellen went on, "One of the secrets of our success is the experience of working together on committees. It helps you know each other and deepens your relationships."

Pat had already pulled out her checkbook and was ready to sign up. I must confess that my own skepticism was beginning to diminish. Spending $75 to meet a few hundred interesting people while gaining a unique perspective on what Santa Barbara had to offer looked like a pretty good investment.

Ellen then opened the floor for questions, and we got to see Santa Barbara democracy at work. The first inquiry came from a younger woman, probably in her forties, who said, in a challenging manner, "It doesn't seem right that a single person should have to pay as much to belong as a couple since the two of them will be getting twice as much benefit."

As Ellen attempted to explain that the dues simply cover the cost of mailings and other incidental expenses, a single man raised his hand and suggested, "Why don't we join as a couple? That way, it will only cost us $37.50 each."

If I were writing fiction, these two strangers would fall passionately in love, have a moonlight wedding on the beach with their 600 best friends in attendance and live happily ever after. Unfortunately, she decided not to join. He became a member and developed a romantic relationship with another newcomer that lasted until she moved out of town a couple of years later.

Yes, people do leave Santa Barbara for various reasons. Younger newcomers often find jobs that pay better in locations that are less expensive. Unfortunately, a few older newcomers
55

find their house payments are just too much to manage on retirement income and become "equity refugees" looking for locations where their home equity, built up over twenty or thirty years, will be enough to pay for a house and eliminate or reduce the need for hefty monthly payments.

At this point, we were invited to introduce ourselves, in two minutes or less, by providing our names, where we had moved from and what we had done professionally before coming to Santa Barbara. We learned that Mark Palmer had held leadership positions with IBM and Sun Microsystems before taking on a turnaround challenge for a firm called Tri-Mark. (I assumed, incorrectly, that he and two other people named Mark had started the firm.) He had just negotiated the sale of this business to PeopleSoft and was looking forward to a long, leisurely retirement in Santa Barbara.

Fortunately for us, not everyone was a former CEO. Tom and Judy Nelson, who sat just in front of us, were former high school teachers from Los Angeles. She was interested in arts and crafts, and he drove the Santa Barbara sightseeing trolley on weekends. Everyone was interesting. We enjoyed their introductions and the prospect of getting to know them better. As we mingled around the refreshments table, Pat gave our check for annual dues to Bob Nourse, and we made plans with the Palmers to attend our first Newcomers event next week—a 'social' in the prestigious community of Hope Ranch.

Hoping to Pass in Hope Ranch

To enhance our charade of being new, permanent Santa Barbara residents and to sound informed at our first event, we decided to do the kind of research that made us good students. We went looking for information about Hope Ranch with a pre-Google Internet search and a review of materials in the public library. Finally, we turned to a realtor with our inquiry.

My assumption that the property had once belonged to Bob Hope was mistaken. I had imagined Hope, Fess Parker, and Ronald Reagan driving up from Hollywood and discussing what they wanted to do when they stopped making B movies, but the actual history was much older.

Thomas W. Hope emigrated from Ireland to become a cowboy in Texas. The 29-year-old Hope moved on to San Francisco, married Delia Fox and operated a San Francisco rooming house until he could purchase two thousand sheep. Hope drove them to Santa Barbara where he leased 6000 acres from the Cieneguitas Indians until 1861 when he borrowed $8,000 to purchase the entire parcel. In 1887, his widow sold the western half of the ranch to California's "Big Four"—Mark Hopkins, Charles Crocker, Collis P. Huntington and Leland Stanford—for $250,000, the beginning of today's Hope Ranch..

Prices continued to escalate, and when we arrived, there were 700 residences, with smaller Hope Ranch properties selling for just under a million dollars. Impressive estates jumped quickly to three to five million dollars, with much, much higher price tags for the magnificent oceanfront properties.

We prepared our *hors d'oeuvres* for ten and rode to the social with the Palmers. We cruised down the palm-lined main road past the prestigious La Cumbre Country Club. Sparkling Lake Laguna Blanca lay between us and the well groomed golf course. Turning toward the ocean, we came to an imposing estate owned by a former Phillip Morris human resources executive, George, and his wife, Marlene. Of course, both of them were slim and attractive.

Mark wasted no time in asking George how he had managed to acquire such an impressive ocean-view estate as a former human resource executive. Mark didn't say it, but his unspoken implication was, "Phillip Morris must pay their staff people too much. I know line managers who couldn't afford this spread."

George responded by praising his financial planner. Mark unabashedly asked how to contact this person. I liked Mark's moxie, but decided it was time for us to mingle and sample the variety of finger foods that each attendee had provided.

We tried to meet all of the sixty people in attendance, but managed to remember the names of only a dozen in addition to a few we had met at the orientation session. There were lots of professionals and business leaders but also a smattering of teachers, nurses and artists.

On balance, it was an attractive, positive group. The women were elegantly coiffed, attractively dressed, looking younger than their years. There were a few signs of chemical or surgical enhancements, but I couldn't help but wonder when grandmothers had started being sexy.

The basic costume for men was dark sport coats, light slacks and shirts bearing the insignias of their teams. I was pretty sure that, before the event ended, there would be some competition between the polo ponies and the alligators.

To be honest, everyone wasn't thin. A couple of guys had stomachs large enough to have their own zip code, and many of us probably resolved every January 1 to "lose ten pounds this year." Everyone was ecstatic about being in Santa Barbara and part of Newcomers. I kept thinking of the Stepford comparison, but my cynicism was wearing thin.

On the ride home, we compared notes with Mark and Barb, who agreed that we had made a good $75 investment and the group was well-organized with excellent leadership. During the first month of membership, the "new" newcomers could attend any event, so we looked over the newsletter and picked out six or eight activities we wanted to sample in June. Some were with the Palmers. Some were on our own. We didn't have 600 new friends yet, but we were off to a good start.

*To check my memory, I recently asked Mark, who is more organized and an earlier adopter of electronic calendaring, to review his records. He sent the following summary:

"The first year in Santa Barbara we had over 100 events with Newcomers or with people we had met through the group. Events included Socials, Lifestyles, wine tasting, Square-dancing, Mahjong, hikes to Inspiration Pointe and Rattlesnake Canyon, a chili cook-off, roller-blading, gourmet dinners, birthday parties, weddings, potlucks, Gaucho basketball games, Fiesta, the New Year's Eve parade of boats, trips to the zoo, the Botanical Gardens, the Music Academy, the University Club, several plays, CALM house, Casa Dorinda, and more. We never had such a talented and diverse group of friends.

Chapter 5
We Love a Parade and Party

Our first summer in Santa Barbara was a blur. We enjoyed a welcoming coffee, a hike up Jesusita Trail, play reading, a visit to the animal shelter, dining out, happy hours plus parties and parades—lots of parties and parades.

The summer could have been a drunken blur except for two constraints. Because of liability issues—and good judgment, Newcomers enforced a two-glass maximum on wine. More importantly, even after all these years, I was still influenced by my fundamentalist father's sermons on the evils of demon rum or anything alcoholic. He would sometimes proclaim, "If I were starving of thirst in the desert, I wouldn't drink water from a beer can for fear that it might influence someone to take up a life of drunkenness and debauchery!" I never experienced that kind of influence, but I liked the Newcomers' philosophy. So, in lieu of the blurring effect of excessive alcohol consumption, the blur of that summer was largely from the frenetic pace of activities. But I would work on my inhibitions.

Like most people, we enjoy a good parade. In New York, we stood in chilling rain to watch the Macy's Thanksgiving Parade (before realizing that we could have a much warmer, better view in front of our television set). We traveled downtown to

Greenwich Village to see the extravagant Halloween Parade in chilling rain, and had watched portions of the St. Patrick's Day parade, also in chilling rain, until we tired of watching drunken Irishmen watching drunken Irishmen march up Fifth Avenue.

The Longest Day

Santa Barbara has a host of great parades, and in this town, we never had to worry about standing in a chilling rain. We had observed the Big Dog Parade by ourselves, but made plans to share the tribute to summer's longest day by meeting a group of newcomers in front of the art museum at high noon. We had never been to a Solstice day parade and weren't sure what to expect. Another former New Yorker explained, "This is just a PG-13 version of Greenwich Village's Halloween Parade."

And so it was. Nudity has not been allowed since a local madam managed an innovative form of product placement in the parade. Today, no advertisements, live animals, or motorized vehicles are allowed. We purchased plastic chairs, a bargain for three dollars, at Longs Drug store, wrote our names on them, and on Friday evening, marked our territory just as we saw old-timers do with the Big Dog Parade.

Because of Pat's interest in the early goddess religions, we knew that the celebration of the Summer Solstice is a very ancient practice, dating back to pre-Christian times. "Midsummer" was originally a fertility festival with many customs and rituals associated with nature and with the hope for a good harvest in the coming fall. In *A Midsummer's Night Dream*, Shakespeare memorialized a Solstice celebration tale of love and trickery where the faeries came out to celebrate with the creatures of the forest. The original Summer Solstice parties were clothing-optional and lasted until the wee hours of the following morning.

About a decade earlier, Pat's art had made a dramatic shift when, on a trip to Greece (including our visit to Paros); she discovered a pre-Greek goddess figurine that prompted her to start reading about this concept in archeology, mythology and the early history of western religions. We were both surprised to learn that the pre-Greek goddess was not an aberration but actually a mainstream deity before most of recorded history.

"I had never questioned the image of God as a male and was shocked to imagine the implications of a change in gender," Pat explained. "Everything you think about God shifts if you imagine a feminine deity and this gender bias has probably negatively influenced the status and self-image of women." She began to put those feelings on canvas in a series of paintings that portray modern women as images of deity—all with roots in ancient mythologies and filled with symbols from the earliest of goddess religions. For the past couple of years, she had been trying to organize her notes into a manuscript to describe the way a simple change in perspective could create significant changes in an individual's life and worldview.

Our friends weren't concerned about fertility or the harvest aspects of the solstice, but just before noon, armed with wide-brimmed hats and sunscreen, we located the contingent from Newcomers (all fully clothed, thank goodness) and found that our chairs were just as we had left them. Maybe the chairs weren't worthy of stealing, or perhaps Santa Barbara is a trustworthy place.

With almost 100,000 other observers, we watched nearly a thousand participants, ranging from seasoned performers to first-time exhibitionists who took part in the Mardi Gras-type parade. We enjoyed the extravagant floats, whimsical costumes and dancers, but the highlight was getting better acquainted with new friends and making appreciative comments about the attractive young people in the parade.

I never properly appreciated youth until I was bumping up against sixty. Early in my career, I had traded on being the youngest this or that, but suddenly, I was too old to be the youngest anything—perhaps not 'suddenly,' but events like this parade jolted my lagging awareness into a sudden realization that senior citizens were now our contemporaries.

After the parade, a dozen newcomers walked over to Alameda Park for an eclectic collection of live world music, delicious foods and beverages from local restaurants and non-profits, an arts and crafts show, and a large drum circle formed by parade participants and anyone who wanted to join in the beat. I could have done without the drumming but enjoyed getting a closer look at floats from the parade on display in the park.

By three o'clock, we were tired, full, and sunburned, so we headed home for a quick nap before a solstice party in the evening.

A Rite for Writers

That same month, the Santa Barbara Writers' Conference was scheduled at the Miramar Hotel—an oceanfront facility with two bars, two pools, and security guards on little golf carts who went around the bungalows at last call to make sure the drunks got back safely. Pat thought that this popular conference might help with her quest to turn some of her research notes into a manuscript, and I needed to go back East for a seminar. Hopefully, Pat wouldn't need the golf carts.

The Workshop was modestly described as "the nation's preeminent conference for writers interested in improving their craft, primarily through workshops that focus on critiquing each writer's work." Ray Bradbury, author of *The Martian Chronicles* and *Fahrenheit 451,* was to open the conference and had been a mainstay of every session since SBWC was founded in 1972. Charles Schultz, creator of the Peanuts comic strip and franchise, was also a perennial presenter. Pat enjoyed five crammed days with more than 400 writers and wannabes trying to learn from each other, hearing from more successful authors, and interacting with publishing world professionals.

Pat took great notes, as she always does, received encouraging feedback from the non-fiction faculty, and especially enjoyed the conference-wide sessions with the likes of Sue Grafton, Eva-Marie Saint and Jonathan Winters. After running over the allotted time with his non-stop comedy patter, Winters informed the chair of the session that he "preferred to work alone," insinuating that he could get by just fine without being reminded of the time.

Despite the encouragement and writing tips, Pat didn't get to devote much attention to her writing after the conference. When the program ended and I got back to Santa Barbara, it was almost time to start getting ready for the Fourth of July celebrations.

Four on the Fourth

We were definitely improving our partying muscles with constant workouts, but Independence Day would be a challenge with four separate events to attend. The celebrations started, naturally enough, with another parade, this one presented by the Spirit of '76 Association. This parade began near Micheltorena and State Streets, and then traveled down State to Cota. Our brief appearance confirmed the presence of several high school marching bands, dignitaries in vintage automobiles and plenty of people dressed in red, white and blue. After the parade, the celebration continued in the Old Town section of Santa Barbara, with eats, drinks and music followed by a patriotic rally at Chase Palm Park.

We skipped the official post-parade events to attend a party hosted by new friends, Don Bushnell and Julie Lopp, at their upper State Street home. Their house is charming but not huge. Yet, they were expecting about sixty people for hot dogs, pretzels, beer and lemonade. Don was the recently retired founding dean of the human and organizational development Ph.D. program at the Fielding Institute. He was charming, playful, and still innocent after several marriages. Although Don was a long-time resident, he became eligible for Newcomers when he talked Julie into moving to Santa Barbara and setting up housekeeping. She was an irrepressible entrepreneur and former musical comedy performer who had a steamer trunk full of costumes that kept her from ever being overlooked at a party. They were always fun to be around, and we assumed that their friends would be interesting too.

We weren't disappointed. We recognized a third of their guests from Newcomers, another third seemed to be people whom they knew from the Unitarian Society of Santa Barbara (USSB) and the remainder included friends from Fielding and new neighbors. Their well-tended croquet lawn was in use and Sousa marches were playing on the stereo. We grabbed our first hot dogs in five years, poured something cold to drink, mingled in the shade and added to our list of new best friends.

The highlight of the party was a performance by Jim Henderson, a veteran Hollywood writer, who did a rehearsal of his comic reading, "The American Politician," from Don and

63

Julie's bedroom balcony. He was to deliver it again at the Symphony's patriotic concert later in the afternoon. Complete with the clichés, hyperbole, and the self-aggrandizement expected of Independence Day political speeches, Henderson managed to insult politicians of all stripes while keeping us laughing so hard I was blowing beer bubbles from my nose— not a pretty sight, as Pat quickly pointed out. Some of the sissies who had lived in Santa Barbara for several years were ready to call it a day, but most of the Newcomer guests were going with us to the Symphony concert.

The Santa Barbara Symphony has a tradition of presenting a free July 4th concert at the Courthouse's sunken garden. Everyone sat on quilts or plastic chairs that survived previous parades to enjoy patriotic favorites played by an orchestra that was far too good to be based in such a small city.

Almost a hundred new inhabitants had reserved an area with a great view of the symphony members, who were framed by a gorgeous 'triumphant arch' above the Courthouse steps. Conductor Gisele Ben-Dor led the group in a variety of marches, hymns, and other music selected for this stirring salute to America, with, of course, Jim Henderson's oration. At this time, I believe that Gisele was the only female conductor of a significant symphony in the United States. She told the audience about asking her ten-year-old son if he might want to become a conductor someday. "Of course not," he replied. "That's woman's work."

When the Santa Barbara Symphony moved toward the close of its program with a medley of military marches from each of the armed forces, I was thrilled to see the diversity of people from all walks of life being recognized as veterans from each branch of service. As the stirring strains of their marches were played, representatives of today's military; Caucasian, Hispanic, African-American, and Asian, along with aging veterans of Vietnam and Korea, were applauded. But the most inspiring moment came when octogenarians from World War II stood proudly in their dress uniforms and saluted the gigantic flag behind the symphony. I wished Dad could have been here. Some of these folks may have helped him liberate Europe.

With lumps in our throats and considerable fatigue, we found our car and drove back to East Beach. But the day of celebration was far from over. We didn't want to miss the big fireworks display. We could have watched from our condo complex, but around eight o'clock, we walked a mile or so along Cabrillo to West Beach to a reserved seating area with a couple of tables for—guess what?—another Newcomer opportunity. To provide variety, we ordered hamburgers, instead of hot dogs, with lemonade and waited for the grand finale to a full day of celebration.

The July 4th firework event is co-sponsored by a private organization, appropriately named SPARKLE, and the city of Santa Barbara. We enjoyed our food and beverages while listening to musical entertainment provided by Ulysses Jazz until the fireworks began at nine o'clock.

Back in a July 1776, John Adams wrote a letter to his wife, Abigail, that Independence Day "ought to be solemnized with ... Illuminations from one End of this Continent to the other from this Time forward forever more." Santa Barbara, along with over 300 other communities across the country, still follows his advice. According to the American Pyrotechnics Association (yes, there really is an American Pyrotechnics Association), some 225 million pounds of fireworks, costing almost $350 million, are used to honor Independence Day each year. We were close enough to the Santa Barbara fireworks to get a little ash in our hair as we enjoyed the carefully crafted twenty-minute program. There were gigantic sparklers, wheels, Roman candles, golden rain fountains, and cakes (an assembly fused together to fire in a rapid sequence)—all designed to prove "by the rocket's red glare, that our flag's still there." In fact, the program ended with a pyrotechnic representation of the American flag. We've come a long way since fireworks were invented in China more than a thousand years ago.

Party On!

It took us a couple of days of relaxation to recover from all of the Fourth's festivities. Then, we were ready to attend a special reception for patrons of the Santa Barbara Museum of Art that the Visual Arts Committee had managed to expand to include a group of Newcomers. Docents were on hand to provide tours of the museum holdings and provide more information than we had garnered on our previous visits. The wine and cheeses were nice enough, but we were especially pleased to meet three older residents who convinced us that it might be possible to live forever in Santa Barbara.

Estelle Meadoff was probably in her mid-80s and had lived in London's Mayfair Hotel for a quarter-century before moving to Santa Barbara a few weeks earlier. We thought that she was sophisticated, cosmopolitan and intelligent even before we learned that she had been born in Memphis. Estelle and Pat immediately began comparing Memphis memories, and I wandered off to talk with a distinguished, diminutive gentleman who was impeccably dressed in an exquisite bespoke suit that helped him look like a retired captain of industry or a deposed aristocrat from one of the Balkan countries.

I soon learned that Rudi was 92 years old, lived in a nearby retirement community called Villa Santa Barbara, walked two miles every day from his residence to the beach and back, and had been a tailor for almost sixty years before retiring. He had grown up in Poland and managed to leave just before the Nazis arrived. He had come to this country penniless, worked at his vocation, reared three children, and moved to town after his beloved wife of 65 years died. Although he still missed her, he confessed to enjoying being part of a distinct minority—that of able-bodied males—at the Villa Santa Barbara.

As the reception was winding down, we looked for the chair of the museum board to express our appreciation at being included in the event. Almost immediately, we could tell that Mercedes Eichholtz was indomitable, outspoken and clearly someone of importance. Later, we learned that she had been married for several years to Supreme Court Justice William O. Douglas before meeting the love of her life, Robert Eichholtz, one of the country's leading tax attorneys. Together, they had amassed an amazing art collection. Little did we know that this impressive woman would become our next-door neighbor and that Estelle would become one of Pat's closest friends.

Toward the middle of July, we attended the third annual Great Gatsby Newcomer Party at Berkley Meigs' oceanfront estate in

Hope Ranch. We were instructed to dress completely in white, bring a jacket or sweater (since late afternoon breezes from the ocean could be chilly), and, of course, *hors d'oeuvres* or dessert for ten people. Perhaps this Tuesday social wasn't as elaborate as Scott Fitzgerald's description of the grand affairs that "attracted entertainers, socialites, and even ordinary people," but Berkeley, like Gatsby, was "a perfect host(ess), generous and hospitable." I managed to find an almost white sport coat, shirt and pants and enjoyed mingling with people who were becoming good friends, all garbed in white dinner jackets, polo outfits or shorts and tee-shirts. We played croquet on a court that almost reached a bluff overlooking the Pacific, sampled a wide variety of *hors d'oeuvres,* sipped wine (white, of course), and watched dolphins frolic in the surf.

In addition to its panoply of parades and parties, summer in Santa Barbara is filled with a series of ethnic festivals. We had missed the Jewish Festival in May and the Caribbean celebration in June, but we were ready for the French Festival later in July and were looking forward to the Greek Festival that followed a few days later. In case anyone might feel left out, there was a "Multi-Cultural Festival" scheduled in mid-August and, of course, a month later, the celebration of Mexican Independence Day.

In late July, we visited Oak Park where we found smiling families dining at sidewalk cafés with checkered tablecloths and umbrellas. Romantic couples were toasting each other with wine from Reims-Épernay and artists wearing berets were painting at their easels or doing quick caricatures. The air was filled with music, laughter, and the tempting aromas of French cuisine. It could have been Aix-en-Provence—but it was Santa Barbara's 22nd Annual French Festival. Admission was free for this observance of the Bastille Day, where 20,000 people celebrated in Oak Park during the weekend while even more Parisians were celebrating their revolution some 8,000 miles away. We enjoyed the sights, sounds, foods and *joie de vivre* of France without experiencing jet lag, worrying about exchange rates or being humiliated because of our linguistic failings. The Fête Française featured dozens of chefs preparing Gallic cuisine—from crêpes to Cajun dishes, served with *café au lait* and wines from Bordeaux, Burgundy, or Champaign.

We managed to make room for a couple of decadent desserts and wandered between the free entertainments provided on three stages, including cancan, Moroccan belly dancers, operatic arias, Cajun and classical groups, along with cabaret music in the tradition of Edith Piaf and Maurice Chevalier.

Already we were beginning to realize that you can't go anywhere in this town without seeing people you know. (How does anyone in Santa Barbara have an affair?) We saw Ellen Lilley (Newcomers' Activities VP) watching a wandering mime. Fortunately, the handsome man by her side was her husband, Bob. We joined them briefly and then went on to observe two jugglers and listen to accordion players who performed throughout the park. Oak Park isn't Les Tuileries, but as transformed on this particular evening, *c'est magnifique!*

Forward to Fiesta

The Local Heritage Newcomers group arranged a late July event where Erin Graffy de Garcia, a popular columnist for the *SB Independent* weekly newspaper, was to "describe the history of Old Santa Barbara Days and get us ready to party"— as if we needed assistance. Erin deepened our understanding of Fiesta—which, she pointed out, is more accurately called Old Spanish Days. She explained, "Old Spanish Days in Santa Barbara represents many things to many people. To some, it's a commemoration of an important period in our town's history. To others, it's a good excuse to drink lots of tequila and dance in the streets." Now, she had our attention!

Erin went on to inform us that Old Spanish Days had started in 1924, and that one of the goals is to preserve the songs and dances of the previous century. The theme of this 75th anniversary celebration was "Legends of Old Spanish Days."

Each year, two young women are selected as Junior and Senior Spirit, based on their *flamenco* skills and ability to represent the spirit of Fiesta. Erin explained that "this year's Senior Spirit, Chantilly Lopez, was known as 'the fiesta baby' because she was born during Fiesta, twenty-two years earlier, and is part of a family that has participated in Fiesta for six generations."

This comment made us a little nervous, as one of our pet peeves about Williamsburg was how frequently people introduced themselves by mentioning how many generations their family had been in the state. I remembered the moment when I knew our future as Virginians was in jeopardy. Almost innocently, Pat had asked a colleague "Is it positive or negative if your family has stayed in the same area for a long time?"

Erin encouraged us to take part in the carriage decorating and margarita party scheduled on the day before the Fiesta parade. We looked forward to hearing more about the event from the perspective of the Parade director, Bill Lewton, and dutifully marked our calendars.

August began with scorching heat affecting most of the country. Reading the paper, we saw that the hot temperatures had been blamed for 150 deaths nationwide. In Santa Barbara, however, the month began with "morning fog followed by sunshine along the coast, with highs of 75 degrees and evening lows of 57 degrees." Safe from the heat wave, we read on to learn that the world's most famous intern, Monica Lewinsky, had been slightly injured when she lost control of her SUV while en route to Santa Barbara. As we started out on our morning walk, we found that hundreds of people had invaded our territory and that a beach volleyball competition was taking place all across the sand.

We had stumbled into the Karch Kiraly Classic, named after the Santa Barbara native described, at least locally, as "the world's greatest volleyball player." After considering Kiraly's three Olympic gold medals and 150 beach championships, we chose not to quibble about that designation. Actually the competition was more popularly known as the José Cuervo tournament. Evidently, José was a beloved, earlier volleyball champion. In fact, we heard several people bragging, in song, that José was a good friend of theirs.

We watched the tournament for a few minutes, until we discovered that 75 degrees in direct sunlight is much warmer than it sounds. Neither of us thought that there was much likelihood that we would be challenging Karch and his partner in next year's competition, so we moved on to a less demanding stroll along the beach.

69

On the first Thursday in August, we walked a along Cabrillo to the Carriage and Western Art Museum of Santa Barbara in Pershing Park, near the waterfront. We found the country's largest collection of old horse-drawn vehicles, all painstakingly restored. Everything from polished hearses to police buggies to old stagecoaches, mud wagons, and circus vehicles were on display, and most were to be part of the Fiesta parade. Commercial growers from Carpinteria (about ten miles south of Santa Barbara) had provided thousands of fresh-cut flowers, which we were to use to decorate the various carriages.

Before starting to work, we reviewed the Museum's collection of saddles that once belonged to such famous people as the Cisco Kid, Will Rogers, Clark Gable, and Jimmy Stewart. We also fortified ourselves with wonderful fruit smoothies and lemonade provided by the Fiesta Committee—especially the Fiesta specialty—salty lemonade that went down very easily and left us more gregarious than usual. Unfortunately, I don't remember much about the presentation or the work itself, but I think we all had a wonderful time.

The Price of Partying

On the walk home, Pat looked up at me, with what might have been a romantic smile, and asked, "Have I ever told you that you are charming, handsome, clever and irresistible to women?" I modestly replied that I couldn't recall her mentioning this before. Without hesitation, she retorted, "Well then, where in the world did you ever get such an idea?"

The next day, a much quieter group of newcomers lined the streets to join some 60,000 others to watch the country's largest equestrian parade. Some awoke with flu-like symptoms; headache, nausea, chills, sore eyes, etc. We debated if it was a Spanish variation of "wine flu" or if pollen from the flowers had given us headaches. In either case, we took great pride in pointing out the beautifully garlanded carriages that we were pretty sure we had helped to decorate.

All morning, horse trailers arrived at the parade's starting point. We watched as *charros* slide silver-clad saddles onto their mounts and wranglers fit their halters. Women in fancy dresses decorated their rides with ribbons and bows.

Toward mid-morning, they started wending their way through the park and lining up on Cabrillo Boulevard and Castillo Street. Crowds were already starting to gather. Despite the apparent informality, the horses, classic carriages, vintage wagons, and riders merged together in a seamless ballet, along with the dozen or so floats and several marching bands. We especially wanted to see 88-year-old Hattie Feazelle ride by. She had been in every Fiesta Parade since the whole shebang started in the 1920s, and still sits a horse with confidence and skill. Maybe people in Santa Barbara *can* live forever.

We didn't manage to see all 800 horses in the parade. Soon we began to understand why the invention of horseless carriages had been hailed as an ecological breakthrough. Several of us decided we had seen (and smelled) enough horses for one day and walked back to De la Guerra Plaza, across from City Hall, to enjoy the colorful Mexican market, feast on Spanish and Mexican-American foods, shop for crafts and enjoy live entertainment that continued all day.

We passed on the goat tacos this time and tried a unique, but popular, Santa Barbara cut of beef (a "bottom-butt top sirloin") known as *tri-trip*. We sampled it barbecued with lettuce, tomato, and avocado, washed down with a Corona or two. Yes, my father would have been disappointed, but, he was 2000 miles away. In my late 50s, I was making real progress on my inhibitions. By mid-afternoon, we were partied out and ready to head home.

All in all, this was proving to be one of our best summers ever. Although I love my work as a professor and consultant, I was beginning to dread making several trips back to Williamsburg for classes at William and Mary. Eight weeks after joining Newcomers, we had met more interesting people and formed more promising friendships than we had in eight years in Virginia. The climate and scenery initially intrigued us, but richness of cultural life and fascinating people should have been on our list of what makes for perfection.

I wasn't surprised when Pat snuggled up to me one evening and whispered, "I know, you may need to go back to Williamsburg, but I would really like to stay here."

71

Chapter 6
Life beyond Newcomers

Once our Santa Barbara time horizon extended beyond a year-long experiment, the world began to shift in exciting and frightening ways. Would our townhouse be suitable for the long term? Could we find affordable alternatives? Now that we no longer saw ourselves as tourists or as imposter newcomers, what would we do when our membership in our favorite organization ended?

As our consciousness shifted, new opportunities began to emerge. In the midst of July's party marathon, Otis Baskin, Dean of Pepperdine's Graduate Business School, called with an invitation to have lunch in Malibu. Any opportunity to challenge conventional economic wisdom that "there is no such thing as a free lunch" is worthwhile, and it would be fun to catch up on Pepperdine and Otis' challenge of gaining accreditation from AACSB (now The Association for the Advancement of Collegiate Schools of Business).

Pepperdine Redux

I had worked at Pepperdine many years earlier while finishing a graduate program at UCLA. As the 25-year-old chairman of the business department, I was asked to develop a curriculum for an MBA program. After reviewing AACSB's guidelines, I presented my recommendations to President Norvel Young, who approved the concept and asked me to teach Pepperdine's first graduate business course. In response to the recommendation to seek AACSB accreditation, Norvel shook his head sadly and said resignedly, "We could never meet those standards." It only took 35 years to prove the usually optimistic Norvel wrong.

From what I could tell, Otis was a perfect choice to lead Pepperdine through this important challenge. He understood academic excellence, shared Pepperdine's religious heritage and understood the constraints this involved. I had grown up in the Church of Christ and felt comfortable in the school's culture while pursuing a Ph.D. in the mid-1960s. My father had agonized over my graduate ambitions because he "never knew anyone who got a doctorate without losing his faith." I had scoffed at Dad's naïveté. How could graduate study in business affect one's religious beliefs? But my father was wiser than I knew. It is difficult to keep insisting that you have already found 'ultimate truth' while learning the critical thinking required for conducting research or analyzing data.

When Pepperdine moved its primary campus from South Central Los Angeles to Malibu in 1970, its culture became more open—too much for some of its primary religious constituency in the Southeast, but maybe not enough for me. I wasn't sure what to expect at this meeting with Otis, but I looked forward to my lunch and to discovering the reason behind this invitation. (Okay, no lunch is really free.)

We met at Taverna Tony's in Malibu, where Otis introduced me to Andre van Nierke, a charismatic South African, who was Associate Dean for Executive Programs. They were interested in our plans to stay in California, and moved quickly to discuss Pepperdine's strengths (a business school alumni base of over 20,000 graduates since my first course in 1966, a strong orientation toward applied learning for working professionals, and a faculty committed to teaching excellence). Weaknesses were a wide variability in the quality of students, little visibility in the wider academic community, and a faculty with limited interest in research but jealously guarding the status quo.

"We have to change the culture, but need to do it incrementally," Otis explained over our stuffed grape leaves
73

appetizer. "I am insisting that a faculty me member who wants to be considered outstanding will have to have written something for publication every year—even if it's just a short article for a newspaper." Evidently, this edict had generated a great deal of protest from the faculty.

"We both know that this is an embarrassingly modest requirement that would be considered ludicrous at a second- or third-tier school," Andre added, "but that's our starting point."

By the time my moussaka was served, Otis got to the point of our meeting. He asked me whether he could "hire your résumé on a part-time basis" to help Pepperdine's business school establish credibility with AACSB and to provide a reference point for its faculty. I was flattered by the implied compliment, but needed a little more detail.

Before Otis had signaled for the check, we had agreed on a half-time arrangement starting in August. I wouldn't teach in the fall, but would spend two days each week at the West LA campus where the business school was headquartered; attend a Workshop for the beginning of a new Executive MBA class; conduct my own analysis of Pepperdine's strengths, weaknesses, opportunities and threats; then prepare a set of recommendations for the business school. I also agreed to teach an EMBA class in January. Although the compensation was significantly less than my half-time assignment at William and Mary, I liked the challenge and looked forward to working with someone who just might be a great dean. As it turned out, Otis, along with Kirby Warren at Columbia, were the two best deans in my lengthy career. Pat was pleased by the news—especially the part about additional income. Theoretically, you can live inexpensively in Santa Barbara, but it isn't easy.

A Pepperdine Starr

Our friends were less sanguine about the development. Many of them remembered when Ken Starr had given and then withdrawn his acceptance as Dean of Pepperdine's law school to devote more time to serving as chief persecutor in the Clinton scandal. In 1998, when Starr's decision *not* to become a Pepperdine dean was announced at commencement, the graduating class applauded enthusiastically.

Based, I suppose, on his spending $40 million to prove that Bill Clinton enjoyed a blow job from Monica Lewinski, his previous work for Big Tobacco and subsequent representation of Blackwater, the deanship was offered to Starr again in 2004, after I was teaching there. When I heard the news that Starr was to become the law school's dean, I told a senior administrator, "If it weren't for health insurance, I would resign on principle!"

"But he will open lots of doors for us," I was informed.

Yes, but what's behind those doors?" I asked. "If Pepperdine plays its cards right, it could become known as the Bob Jones University of the West!" For some reason, my popularity seemed to peak around 2004, but for a time, Pepperdine provided the Shangri-La of teaching.

Of course, in 1999, I didn't know that all of this was going to happen. My first day of work brought a pleasant surprise: I had been given a spacious corner office, a part-time secretary and a title as "Virtue Distinguished Professor of Management." I was touched, believing that this title was recognition of my sterling character, but soon learned that it honored a donor with a righteous name.

Dean Baskin pointed out that Pepperdine had been lucky with the names of key donors. "Shortly after I arrived," he said, "we named the business school in honor of George Graziadio, founder of Imperial Bank. George is proud of his Italian heritage and likes to point out that his name comes from '*graci*' meaning 'thanks' and '*dio*' meaning God—and that's pretty much what I said when he made his very significant gift to the school—thanks be to God!"

Despite having served as director of two more highly ranked Executive MBA programs, I was impressed with several aspects of Pepperdine's commitment to executive education. In September, I spent four days with an entering class and the entire teaching team with whom they would study during the next 18 months. Students were given an overview of the program's content, worked through some interpersonal dynamics with the behavioral professor who facilitated the workshop, and "created a collaborative learning environment."

75

Committing to an almost impossible dream had led to events that made the dream more feasible. I now had a California job and further exploration of our new hometown revealed more attractions than the obvious aesthetic charms.

2000 Points of Light

Back in Santa Barbara, we were still on a terrific treadmill with Newcomers. In addition to the parties, socials and other fun, frivolous events, we were starting to notice a more serious side to the community. Each month's list of activities included a chance to get better acquainted with one or more of the charitable causes in the city. When George H.W. Bush spoke of "a thousand points of light," he sold Santa Barbara short. Almost two thousand Santa Barbara County non-profits were already in full swing addressing local, national and international issues.

While millionaires abound in this community, it would be a mistake to assume that everyone is rich. The median annual income for a family of four was under $58,000, $6,000 less than the state average. Santa Barbara County ranks 33rd out of 58 California counties in child poverty. The homeless population continues to rise and immigration issues are pervasive. Affordable housing is a political and social issue, with many nurses, firefighters, and teachers unable to find local housing and having to commute from Ventura (45 minutes south) or Santa Maria (an hour northeast). Despite Santa Barbara's glamorous image, an increasing disparity between rich and poor continues to develop. There are ample opportunities for social justice outreach. Over six hundred non-profits directly address cultural and social justice concerns, while hundreds more focus on education, the arts, historical preservation and the environment.

In Santa Barbara, multiple charity balls or other philanthropic events are held almost every week. Many groups hold their fund-raisers on the same day every year so key donors won't forget when to pull out their best clothes and checkbooks. Each day's mail brings multiple solicitations, all from worthwhile causes. Making small contributions to various causes can lead to your contact details being shared with other charities. If you give more than $10,000 to an organization, that group will definitely stay in touch, but is less likely to give your name to others. Going through our daily mail (today there were seven solicitations) leaves little doubt that we are stuck in the minor leagues of non-profit support.

The Santa Barbara Foundation holds a central position of leadership in the local world of philanthropy. Its president, Chuck Slosser, was a development officer at Pepperdine until he recognized that a religious conversion would be needed for advancement there. The Foundation coordinates the charity activities of 38 local family foundations. Members of this group, known as the Roundtable, meet regularly to go over scores of requests from groups throughout the county and to distribute about $60 million each year to about 350 nonprofits.

Local television station KEYT, *Santa Barbara Magazine*, *The Independent* (weekly newspaper), *Montecito Journal*, the *NewsPress, CASA* and other local media consistently support and publicize the community's many good works.

The Santa Barbara world of charitable giving includes at least four distinct categories. At the apex of the pyramid are a few very wealthy, deeply committed philanthropists. Michael Towbes, Paul and Leslie Ridley-Tree, Katherine and Stewart Abercrombie, Andy and Dolly Granatelli, Sarah Miller McCune and Baroness Leni Fe Bland appeared to be part of what could be called the "Old Guard" of the Santa Barbara charitable scene.

No one is more ubiquitous than Michael Towbes, Chairman of the Towbes Group (real estate management and development) and owner of Montecito Bank & Trust. He seems to attend every event and support every important cause. He encourages his bank to give a million dollars to the community each year. Shortly after we moved to town, Towbes helped the Santa Barbara Foundation acquire the local classical music station, KDB, with proceeds from a 1031 exchange involving the sale of a shopping center he donated.

Towbes is typically low-key and enjoys working behind the scenes. Other major contributors have a flair for flamboyance. If you ask anyone at a Santa Barbara nonprofit about their all-time favorite redhead, most would mention Lady Leslie Ridley-

77

Tree before Lucile Ball. She moved to Santa Barbara a decade earlier with her husband Paul and brought the energy that had built Pacific Air Industries, a leading supplier for firms like Douglas and Boeing. Shortly before our arrival, they became Lord Paul and Lady Leslie Ridley-Tree "when a distant Irish relative died and Paul inherited the title." Art and education were their greatest passions, and the couple established more than 120 scholarships at different educational institutions. (Sir Paul died of lung cancer in 2005, but Lady Leslie continues their philanthropic heritage.)

A very important second tier is composed of popular local celebrities like Jeff Bridges, Tab Hunter, Kenny Loggins and John Cleese, who are frequently associated with major causes. Fannie Flagg, Jonathan Winters, Fess Parker, Rona Barrett and Bo Derek are also active in the community. When we first moved to the area, Michael Jackson would sometimes donate trips for children's groups to his nearby Neverland estate in the Santa Ynez Valley, but that prize mysteriously declined in popularity shortly afterwards.

A third essential tier of the philanthropic pyramid is made up of individuals who are wealthy by any standards other than Santa Barbara's, but are not competitive with the "Old Guard." Obviously, money doesn't guarantee happiness, but it does help define your place in the pecking order. One of the denizens of this tier observed contentedly, "Money isn't that important. I know people with forty million who are just as happy as folks with fifty million." In Santa Barbara, a person with forty to fifty million might still worry about being adequately appreciated in the social galaxy. A successful entrepreneur from Ohio lamented wistfully, "In Dayton, I was considered to be a big deal." Disappointed with the way he was received at UCSB, he gave a couple of million dollars to the University of Dayton, where he was properly appreciated as a big deal and got a very nice write-up in the *Dayton Daily News*.

Despite the importance of celebrity and very wealthy contributors, Santa Barbara's nonprofit engine is fueled by middle-class wage earners and retirees. According to Erin Graffy de Garcia, the author of the tongue-in-cheek book *How to Santa Barbara*, the number one rule for social success is philanthropic involvement. "In Santa Barbara, there is an unwritten understanding that to take your place in the community, you must be an integral part of a local nonprofit," she writes. "If you aren't able to donate *beaucoup* bucks, not to worry: *All* your spare time will also suffice."

Most of the nonprofits know that new arrivals, especially recent retirees, often want to become involved in community activities that make their new home a better place for everyone. They regard the Newcomers Club as a great source for finding talented people to help serve their new community.

Perhaps I'm not very observant or too far down the food chain to have a vantage point, but I never sensed much posturing within Newcomers. Multi-millionaires and affordable housing residents alike bring their plates of *hors d'oeuvres*, serve on committees and contribute as they can. We checked out the Santa Barbara Art Museum, the Ensemble Theatre, Planned Parenthood, and the Santa Barbara Food Bank. All were doing good things, but Pat decided to join the Board of the University of California, Santa Barbara (UCSB) Art Museum, and I joined the Board at the Unitarian Society of Santa Barbara (USSB).

A Church with a Past

We had been introduced to the Unitarian movement by Forrest Church, senior minister at All Souls in New York and son of former Senator Frank Church. Having grown up in a denomination with a conviction that they were the only "true church," it was refreshing to find a group that looked for areas of agreement rather than seeking points to argue. I agreed with a young Chicago politician who wrote in *Dreams of My Father* that his grandfather had become a Unitarian because, "They look for what's right in other religions...it's like getting five churches for the price of one."

Since 1876, the Unitarian Society of Santa Barbara (USSB) has been an important voice for social justice and liberal values. During our initial visits, we heard about Minister Emeritus Lex Crane's exposé of the John Birch Society in the 1960's; the Congregation's provision of sanctuary for Salvadoran families during the 1980's; support of the homeless shelter that led to the formation of a short-term residence for homeless families; and leadership and seed money to start the Mind/Supermind

79

lecture series that continues through Santa Barbara City College. Pat and I got to participate in the beginning of a Food Bank that continues to serves low-income families.

We visited USSB a couple of times during that first summer and found some interesting members. Overall, however, the group was dispirited and reeling from a series of setbacks. Membership had peaked at 750 members during the tenure of a charismatic minister who hosted a regular television program, wrote columns for the *News-Press* and provided leadership in a number of social action arenas. After his departure, the discovery of sexual improprieties generated national attention, traumatized the congregation, led to a dramatic decline in membership and contributed to a prevailing state of malaise. Some members were upset that a person whom they admired had disappointed them. Others were to learn that their relationship with the minister was not as unique as they thought. A final contingent may have wondered why they received no amorous advances: "What am I? Chopped tri-tip?"

The whole ordeal resulted in a schism among members, led to general sense of depression, and ended with a painful parting (called a negotiated settlement) with the next parish minister and her associate minister (our friend Carol from chapter two) shortly before our move.

On our first visit, we were welcomed by John Warnock, a local litigator, who found out about our previous involvement at All Souls in New York. "Oh," he said, "you need to meet the Sterns. They moved from New York about a year ago and are always singing the praises of Forrest Church."

Ted Sterns was a former real estate executive and Kay had recently served as president of the Public Relations Society of America. They were probably the best-organized, most analytic couple we had ever known. They gave us great advice when we started looking for houses and introduced us to several people who became close friends. When, at our first meeting, Ted discovered that I was an academic, he immediately suggested that we meet Don Bushnell and Julie Lopp. Of course, we already knew this couple from Newcomers and their Independence Day party. In Santa Barbara, you seldom need six degrees of separation.

By September, everyone was excited about the arrival of Rev. Jim Grant, an athletic sixty-something dynamo from North Carolina. As transplanted Southerners, we were especially pleased to hear a minister without an accent.

Jim's specialty was working with "troubled congregations." He explained that he was already "pre-fired" in that at the end of two years, he had to move on even if the congregation wanted him to stay. With this agreement in place, he was free to say and do whatever he thought was necessary to restore the vitality of the congregation. He succeeded admirably, added a hundred members during his two-year ministry and laid a foundation for potential future growth.

I was intrigued by references to "our place in the Unitarian-Universalist movement." In one sermon, Jim explained that Unitarians had believed in the undivided unity of God and the humanity of Jesus rather than his divinity. Universalists, on the other hand, believed in universal salvation and thought that the teachings of Jesus and other prophets should conform to the laws of science, reason and philosophy. "Since the two groups merged in 1961, the historical distinctions aren't that important, but it may be helpful to remember that the Universalists thought God was too good to send them to hell, while Unitarians thought *they* were too good for God to send them to hell. Today, UUs wonder, 'what is hell'?"

A Welcoming Congregation

After the service, we were talking with Don and Julie in the courtyard when Julie pointed out a difference in the fashion sense of our friends from Newcomers and the USSB crowd. "You know, most of the Newcomers can be pretty spiffy, but Unitarians must take dowdy pills," she observed. "There is no way this many people could be so dowdy without taking some kind of supplement." (A few weeks later, when the ladies' auxiliary announced plans for a Unitarian Fashion Show fundraiser, I couldn't help but ask, "Is 'Unitarian Fashion Show' an oxymoron?")

With a twinkle in his eye, Don added to Julie's observation, "I've often said that that you might be a closet UU if, for a dressy affair, you wear a simple black dress, pearls and Birkenstocks—and your wife thinks you look great!"

Pat immediately corrected him. "Don't you mean... and your 'husband' thinks you look great?"

"No," Don retorted smugly. "You obviously haven't discovered how liberal this group really is."

This repartee had the earmarks of a practiced routine, but it provided insight into our new spiritual home. Actually, it felt good to realize that Anna and Deb or Perry and Ross or Birdie who used to be called Brian were welcomed just as warmly as we had been. We wouldn't be coming here to worship; we would be coming to "build community, reason together and respect the interconnected web of all existence."

The Dark Side of Paradise

A few days later, as we rode our bikes to Trader Joe's, we passed three or four cluttered old campers just off the railroad tracks. We had noticed them before, so on our return, we stopped and found several people in a final stand to fight off homelessness. They had given up looking for an apartment or a house in this extremely affluent city because finding anything they could afford looked impossible. Crumbling hotels on lower State Street that once offered reasonable monthly rental were being renovated for wealthy tourists.

This camper compound was one of Santa Barbara's few growth neighborhoods. The streets of Santa Barbara seemed to be filling with permanently parked campers and recreational vehicles, which were becoming last-resort housing for the working poor, disabled veterans or older folks on fixed incomes. Tax cuts for the wealthy may have "lifted all yachts," but the bounty hadn't trickled down to Jim, who was receiving $750 each month in disability benefits. As he leaned against his rusty camper, he said in a matter of fact tone, "There's just no room for anybody but the rich around here anymore."

Kim, who has been living in her camper for a couple of years, added, "To make enough to pay what they want for rent here, I'd always be working, so I'd never be at home anyway."

On Sunday at USSB, we saw Marty Blum, a City Council member, and asked about this problem. She was concerned and had thought about the subject as she explained, "The problem is that the RV's are substandard housing and can cause problems when they gather in places. The City has over 3000 dwelling units for low income folks, so we need to get these people on our housing lists and provide a safe place to park."

I thought this was an excellent long term solution, but wondered about the short term. Marty agreed and explained that the City had begun a relationship with the New Beginning Counseling Center to supply outreach workers in order to get these folks back on their feet. "This is called the City's Safe Parking Program," she said. It has been recognized as innovative, and we are proud of it."

We didn't have better suggestions and felt good that the City had a relatively enlightened approach. Like most of the more fortunate residents of Santa Barbara, knowledge about the proximity of poverty made us nervous. At some level, we know there the right set of unpleasant of circumstances could cause most people to start checking on the price of used campers. We felt a bit guilty as we pedaled back to our comfortable condo to think about facing the daunting challenge of finding more permanent housing for ourselves in a market that defied logic and reason.

Chapter 7
Losing a Bidding War in a Land of Rich and Famous

Tony didn't want me to mention his name, but after finishing his second glass of Sauvignon Blanc and securing a promise of anonymity, he confided that his net worth was close to ten million dollars. That puts him halfway up the top one percent of Americans, according to data from the Federal Reserve, but hardly enough to get much respect in an affluent town like Santa Barbara. He commutes to Los Angeles each week to keep his business active and logs 50-70-hour work weeks because he doesn't think he has enough money to ease up.

"At ten million, you're nobody in Santa Barbara," Tony complained. "A few million doesn't go as far as it used to. Maybe in the '70s, it could mean 'Lifestyles of the Rich and Famous' and living in a big house with a butler, but no more. People in Milwaukee or Cleveland might think of me as rich. They would seek me out for boards. But here, I'm a dime a dozen."

Tony and his wife were renting at El Escorial, not far from our townhouse. We had bumped into them on weekends at East Beach Grill or on our walks along the beach and spoken only briefly, so I was surprised when he asked me to join him for lunch on Saturday at Stella Mare's, a short walk around the bird refuge from our condo.

We must have mentioned that we were beginning to look at houses and were shocked to find how much a decent house could cost, because real estate was clearly on his mind. Quickly, he warmed to the subject. "I remember when a million dollars might buy a mansion or a waterfront estate. Not anymore—at least in this town. We've looked at million-dollar bungalows and two-bedroom condos. To buy a decent house here will take half of my net worth!"

"You must have expensive tastes," I replied. "Our townhouse isn't bad and you could buy several like it." I knew Santa Barbara was among the ten U.S. places with the most expensive housing and that houses cost four to five times the national average, but I was sure we could find something nice for a reasonable price. "It's just a matter of looking long enough and being patient," I said, somewhat naively.

"Mark my words," Tony predicted, "In the next couple of years, you'll see the average house price here hit a million dollars—and the 'average' is a 1950s ranch-style piece of crap. The experts are saying that prices will go up over twenty percent this year alone. Next year, you won't be able to afford the place you thought would be a stretch right now."

I let Tony pay for lunch. After all, he did invite me. His analysis depressed me and made me frightened about the prospects for our dream house in paradise. Fortunately, the next session of Newcomers' "Money Talks," (a committee commonly referred to as the "Ernie and Bernie Show," since it was coordinated by Ernie Marx and Bernie Krakower) was entitled, "You and Santa Barbara Real Estate: All the Possibilities." Almost perfect timing!

The Potential of SB Real Estate

Three real estate and mortgage specialists were lined up to address the fine points of residential real estate and "creative financing approaches" that they said would "show the benefits of owning real estate in one of the most unique and beautiful areas in the country." The session was predictable. Surprise, surprise! They thought local real estate was a great investment.

85

Ed Heron, Branch Manager of Coldwell Banker, did have some impressive numbers. "The California Economic Forecast Project recently reported that the median home price in Montecito (a tony offshoot of Santa Barbara, just to its south) increased almost 30 percent last year and will probably do the same in 2000. Coldwell Banker believes that the median price in Montecito will be over $1.5 million by the end of the next year. We're finding buyers who have cashed out of the market or a business and want to park a lot of that wealth into Santa Barbara real estate," he concluded.

"Perhaps we should buy something tonight," I thought. "By tomorrow, we won't be able to afford anything." Instead, I checked my apprehensions with Mark Palmer who agreed that Tony and Ed were on target. He and Barb had moved into a large, tree-shaded rental in Montecito. Unfortunately, it lacked the one attribute that Mark thought was essential. "It's okay for now, but you can't see the Pacific," he complained. "Why would you move to a place like Santa Barbara and not enjoy its most important attribute?"

"Well, there is the almost perfect climate," I reminded him, "and don't forget about all of the wonderful people you've met, like Pat and me."

"That's true," he admitted, "but I will enjoy everything more if we can see the waves as we read the newspaper and have our morning coffee."

I didn't argue with Mark, but was beginning to get cold feet before actually putting a toe in the water. We were scaling back expectations for what we might be able to purchase.

The next day, Pat and I rode our bikes past the Clark Bird refuge to one of the best ocean views in Santa Barbara and, on a square foot basis, the city's most expensive real estate. The Santa Barbara Cemetery doesn't allow bicycles, so we parked just outside to take a leisurely, scenic stroll. Many of the cemetery plots have striking views of the Santa Ynez mountain range on one side and the ocean on the other. Ghosts of former residents can wander through a marble temple or a rough-hewn stone mausoleum. The landscaping is exquisite with ancient cypress trees, exotic palms and a variety of flowers.

Architect George Washington Smith designed the principal Moorish building as part of Santa Barbara's revitalization in 1926. Yes, people were dying to get in, and someday, we, too, might 'enjoy' a small plot of ocean-front property.

Beach Musing

We were in no hurry for this final move, so rode on to Butterfly Beach, and went for an extended walk past the Biltmore Hotel and the Coral Casino. There, we discovered a condominium complex where several of the buildings enjoyed ocean views and were literally steps from the beach. We decided to explore and walked in with confidence and a sense of belonging to discover that this gated development had excellent security with a guard who directed us back to the beach. Bonnymede looked like an exclusive, private resort with a large pool, hot tub and tennis courts in a quiet, peaceful setting. We didn't see any 'for sale' signs, but signs were probably considered tacky. Resuming our walk, we meandered by an even more exclusive beachfront enclave of private residences. The air was a little rarified, so we turned around and headed back.

The fog was beginning to roll in toward the beach, creating a pleasant, magical mood. As we approached Bonnymede, we noticed a willowy, attractive older woman walking on the beach. She was tall, elegant and nicely dressed for an evening constitutional. What was there to lose? We spoke, and I asked how we could learn if units were for sale. In a cultured Southern accent, she replied, "Strange that you should ask, but I am thinking about selling my place. The commute to Charleston is becoming a bit of a burden. Why don't you call me in the morning so we can discuss this in greater detail?"

She gave us her telephone number and disappeared into the fog. I had bought two houses in synchronistic situations, and felt that this might be the opportunity we were seeking since condos still hadn't enjoyed the appreciation of houses.

We called to set up an appointment early as we thought polite. Prices were increasing almost daily and this could be our future home. Susanna could have just stepped out of the pages of a vintage issue of *Vogue* as she greeted us and showed us around her two-bedroom condo.

The furnishings were tasteful and expensive. She was dressed in an outfit that might be a few years old, but would never go of style. She was still beautiful in a timeless, elegant manner. Pat described her as having "great bones." Unfortunately, her condo did not. Beyond her English antiques, the unit was a small, basic box.

With comfortable, yet perfect manners, she served us tea in fine bone china cups and told us a little about her life. She was in her mid-eighties, had actually been editor of *Vogue*, and for the past two decades had divided her time between Charleston and Santa Barbara. It was such a pleasant moment that we hated to ask about price. Eventually, she told us her expectations. The timing and price were quite reasonable by Santa Barbara standards, but we needed to think about the constraints of living in an even smaller place than East Beach.

"We could rent an office and studio in town," Pat suggested. It wasn't a bad idea, but we already felt constrained in a larger condo. Reluctantly, we called Susanna to thank her and to pass on what would have been a great investment. Prices in Bonnymede doubled over the next few years.

Eastside Story

On Sunday, we joined the throngs of folks wanting to get in on the Santa Barbara real estate gold rush and tried to see how many open houses we could attend. We both had watched aging parents trying to adjust to losing driving privileges and wanted to be as close to the vibrant, attractive downtown area as possible. When I described our preferences and limitations to Ed Heron at the "Money Talks" session, he suggested this probably meant restricting our search to the Eastside, which runs from east of State Street to the base of the Riviera—the foothills that run along the northeast side of the city.

Ed pointed out, "The Upper East is a wonderful walking area. The land is flat to gently sloping so a brisk walk to downtown is feasible and fun, as is a stroll through the nearby Mission rose gardens. Residents enjoy the convenience of being minutes from the city stores, museums, theaters and most of downtown. Many homes have great mountain views and some have peeks of the ocean."

We clipped newspaper descriptions of Eastside houses that might fit our wants and wallet, then began checking them off one by one. We almost got through our entire list without seeing anything promising. Fortunately, we had saved the best prospect for last and had just enough time to check out one more possibility.

> *Victorian gem located in desirable upper East! All the charms of Victorian architecture in totally updated, gracious home built in 1892. The original Balsh House features hardwood flrs, copper plmbg 16 circ electric system, 10' ceilings, stained glass window. Great for those who work at home with 5 phone/computer lines. Perfect for writers, professors and artists.*

This ad sounded like it was written for us. The house was in walking distance of downtown, a couple blocks from USSB, and most importantly, just a little more expensive than our townhouse. We weren't crazy about Victorian architecture, didn't especially like the way the previous owner had upgraded two baths and the kitchen, and thought the neighborhood wasn't ideal. Yet, it was the best value we'd seen. We agonized for a few days, went back twice and finally asked Ted and Kay Stern for their opinion. They walked through the house, quietly noticing the tiny closets and inadequate kitchen and bathrooms. They sat with us on the floor of the empty living room and asked a series of penetrating questions, never offering their own opinion, but helped nudge us toward a decision to wait and look for something that we would know was right for us.

A couple of weeks later, we read about a house in a better part of the Eastside and just forty percent more than the Victorian we had decided against. The ad read:

> *Pass thru the historic gates of Junipero Plaza and enter a beautiful garden or take a few steps to the Mission Rose Garden. This 3BR, 2BA home has been completely remodeled. The new kitchen is a chef's delight, and custom touches include Italian tile in the kitchen and baths, a Jacuzzi tub in the master bath surrounded by tumbled marble, and custom hardwood floors.*

Despite the poetic tone, this was the basic three bedroom ranch house Tony had described—but it had been purchased and remodeled by a broker with excellent tastes. The floor plan was simple, with tiny bedrooms off a single hallway. The kitchen was barely large enough to accommodate two people. We loved the location and liked the décor, but were concerned about spending twice as much as the price of our condo and getting less space—without a glimpse of the ocean.

We thought about adding a room above the garage and asked for advice. The realtor recommended Peter Becker, "a tall, friendly, James Stewart type who graduated from UCSB and studied architecture in Colorado. He specializes in residential work and has a historic office on Mission Street."

A Sheltie named Sam greeted us at the door of an attractive space that looked like it was built a century earlier. He (Peter, not Sam) was happy to explain the building's history. "You may know," he began, "that Santa Barbara was home to California's first major movie studio, the legendary Flying A. This was the last remnant of that studio. When I learned the building was for sale, I flew in and bought it immediately."

Peter knew firsthand how difficult it was to modify historic buildings or even those in historically significant areas. "I probably know more about building codes than most people, but found it extremely challenging to get even basic modifications in this structure," he told us. With disarming candor, Peter explained that we had three major issues to address: "Junipero is close to the Mission so you will need approval from the ABR (Architectural Board of Review) for any changes. The construction could be seen from the Mission, so they will have lots of questions and concerns. Secondly, your proposal would increase the height of the house. If neighbors complain that the addition would interfere with their views, this could kill the project. Finally, the cost of the delays, getting the permits and the actual construction would easily push the costs of the finished house to double your budget."

He would be happy to work on the project, but wanted us to know the headaches involved. We appreciated his honesty and made an offer contingent upon getting the appropriate approvals.

We breathed a sigh of relief when our offer was rejected. It would be expensive and difficult to make the changes we wanted. And the bedrooms would still be tiny.

The Chase for Pearl's Place

Our hopes for finding a perfect place on the Eastside were fading when, driving down Anacapa Street, we noticed someone putting up a "For Sale" sign in front of a fairly attractive Craftsman house. We skidded to a stop, hopped out of the car, and asked about the house. "This is a great opportunity," the broker enthused, "I am just having a walk-through for realtors. The house doesn't go on the market until tomorrow, but come back in an hour, and I'll give you a sneak preview." He handed us the following description with a couple of attractive pictures:

> *1904 Edwardian landmark, the 'Chase House,' lifelong home of Pearl Chase, huge interior space with two staircases, parlor, sun porches, country kitchen. paint free original redwood woodwork— a grand old home in great condition! Gracious 2 story w/apprx 3250 sq ft + legal 1 bed 1 bath rental house. Many classic features including hardwood floors, crown moldings, 3 fireplaces, 2 kitchens (one outside), & formal dining room. Great value & bright, sunny location on 0.38 acre.*

This sounded almost too good to be true. We were already big fans of Pearl Chase, and living in her house would be a thrill— maybe even a little prestigious. While Craftsman architecture was not our favorite style and the yard was not particularly beautiful, this was a definite possibility. We drove a few blocks to Mimosa, an elegant, if slightly dowdy, neighborhood restaurant specializing in casual French cuisine. Over the years, I've probably eaten there fifty times and almost always order a house specialty, pork scaloppini. We also like the fact that we are sometimes the youngest patrons in the place. As an aging actor once commented, "I love Santa Barbara. It's the only place where people still call me 'kid'."

The Chase house cost more than we had hoped to pay, but this would be true for any property, without wheels, that captured our interest. By local standards, this house was reasonable. Lunch at Mimosa was tasty and the service was efficient.

We were back in front the Chase house ten minutes earlier than the realtor suggested. We waited across the street so we could be absolutely punctual. The last departing agent came over to our car, offered her business card, and told us confidentially, "This house is priced twenty percent below the market. There will probably be several offers coming in tomorrow, so if I can help you in the negotiating process, just give me a ring."

We were grateful for the advice, and walked across Anacapa to look at what we were almost certain would be our Santa Barbara home. Everything in the brochure was accurate, but somehow the total effect wasn't as grand as we had imagined. Nevertheless, we huddled briefly and told the listing agent we would make an offer as soon as the house was officially for sale. He also believed there would be multiple offers and recommended that we comeback by nine o'clock the next morning with our agent prepared for a round or two of bidding.

Dutifully, we talked about the situation with our realtor, and agreed to make a "stretch offer" that was ten percent above the suggested price. At noon, we learned that our offer was barely in the top half of six already received. If we wanted to try again, the owner would consider other bids until seven o'clock. We couldn't justify going high enough to stay competitive, conceded defeat again, and dropped out of the bidding war.

As friends were moving ahead in the housing steeplechase, our townhouse was looking better and better. The Sterns had gotten "a real steal" for an uninspiring house on a beautiful lot in Montecito. They were planning to give the house to a charity, move it to the charity's location, take a tax deduction for the gift, and build their dream home on the property. It was a brilliant plan, and we couldn't help but be envious.

The Palmers had purchased a large 1950s ranch house on the edge of Montecito with a "drop-dead" view of the Pacific. According to the Newcomer grapevine, they had paid $1.7 million for the property, and planned to tear down the existing house in order to build their dream home. It was an ambitious plan, and again, we couldn't help but be a bit envious.

Fortunately, we had several Newcomer events to divert our attention and, in one instance, to actually help drown our sorrows. The Wine Appreciation Committee had announced a special tasting of ten Scottish single malt whiskeys. I signed up quickly for this event and walked eagerly to Fess Parker's Doubletree. I planned to get my money's worth and didn't have to worry about driving the three blocks back home.

Steve Watson from Southern Spirits explained, "The word 'whiskey' comes from the Celtic '*uisgebaugh,*' meaning 'water of life'." This assuaged my guilty about the prospect of getting soused. I was making real progress in overcoming inhibitions.

After the tenth generous tasting sample, I staggered home, happily singing Scottish, or maybe it was Irish, lullabies. I discovered that Pat was interviewing contractors Hank and Peggy about a modest refurbishing of our condo. It made sense for us to improve the quality of our living space and hopefully improve the resale potential, but I needed to notify the owner that we would be exercising our option to purchase, which hopefully was reflecting the rapidly growing real estate prices.

The Mystique of Montecito

Even with limited real estate data available to us, two trends were strikingly evident. We weren't going to find a house that we truly liked within our price range. Moreover, we kept hearing how Montecito was the 'in' place to live. Tony wanted to live there because "a 93108 zip code is the most prestigious." There are beautiful mansions largely hidden behind imposing gates and stone walls, but many houses were relatively simple. The shopping area was essentially a strip mall, albeit with pricey stores and restaurants. We didn't think it was nearly as attractive as downtown Santa Barbara. Many of the houses were close to the railroad tracks. We already knew what it was like to hear the early morning train whistling through the area. I asked Ted to explain why he thought Montecito was the best part of Santa Barbara.

"We spent most of our life in Los Angeles and didn't like the glitz of Rodeo Drive, the garish Beverly Hills mansions or the Bel-Air palaces that scream "look at me," he answered. He described Montecito's understated elegance as 'less is more.'

93

"We like the English gardens and the quiet genteelness that comes from having nothing to prove."

As usual, Ted had done his research. "For over a century, people with money and taste have been coming to Montecito." He went on. "There are eight square miles of neighborhoods and expansive estates. Early in this century, people with names like Rockefeller, Carnegie, Fleischmann, Cudahy, DuPont, Swift, McCormick, and Deere visited the hot springs to "take the waters" for their health. Many fell in love with the area and developed fabulous estates here."

Ted recommended T.C. Boyle's book, *Riven Rock,* which "provides a great picture of the different strata of society in the area during the early 20th Century." Almost a century later, we theoretically had a range of housing alternatives from easy-care condominiums near the beach to large estates on many acres.

Ted and Kay had lived in Europe and liked the dignified Cotswold-like feeling of many of the streets, especially those in the Hedgerow area—named for the tall hedges that fronts each property and the mature eucalyptus trees that form arches over many streets. The Sterns even found the commercial areas charming. In the upper village, near their house, was a book store, post office, hardware store, gas station, drugstore, coffee shop and deli and the ubiquitous real estate offices. In the lower village: more galleries, restaurants, a bank, supermarket, nursery, and, of course, more real estate offices. "Coast Village Road is a long way from Rodeo Drive," he said happily. "This isn't a place for the faint of wallet, but you should take a look."

Our different take on the commercial areas aside, we respected Ted's insights and asked him to recommend a realtor who knew the area. He introduced us to Greg Leach, whose father appropriately hosted "Lifestyles of the Rich and Famous." Greg showed us a couple of listings so we would appreciate his typical clientele along with two we might be able to handle, at least for a couple of years, provided I took another job, sold our other property, and took on a huge mortgage. The first was just around the corner from the Sterns, on Hot Springs Road.

"Las Sombras" features a circular driveway to a classic 1917 Spanish hacienda. Prime Montecito location with many architectural features including hand-hewn beamed ceilings, wood floors, four fireplaces, French doors with decks over a barranca *(ravine) & romantic gardens. Charming guest house with separate entry.*

We were intrigued. Despite being located on a busy street, the house had a privacy barrier provided by lush vegetation. It needed a major remodel, but nothing bigger than we had undertaken before. Houses with Spanish or other foreign names, like "Las Sombras," are automatically worth a hundred thousand dollars more—especially if the name is carved in a pillar next to the wrought iron gate to the property. We needed a little time to recalculate our finances and assess our appetite for another renovation project. Greg had one more possibility to show us that might be a consideration.

Estate sale for 1960s single level home. Walk to beach & Biltmore, attractive 3BR, 4BA home with large picture windows & high ceilings. Spacious lot with gardens. Prime location, partial ocean view. Fantastic potential.

At this point, we had looked at more than 50 houses. Most we eliminated quickly. The process had helped us understand that peculiar brand of English utilized by real estate professionals. Roughly translated, *"Fantastic potential"* means "there's a hell of a lot of work to do." And there was! Still, the location was wonderful and we had done well with estate sales in New York and Atlanta. The price was the highest we had even considered, and renovations would easily add another thirty percent. We would need to modernize the kitchen and bathrooms, repair water damage from a leaky roof, fix that roof, and completely redo the landscaping. Everything else was in decent shape— and it would be wonderful to walk to Butterfly Beach.

Tacos and Temptation

We thanked Greg for showing us around, promised to call him back, and headed home to wrestle with our choices—or lack thereof. It was dinner time, so we rode over to Milpas Street and a tiny taco shack that had become Santa Barbara's most famous eating establishment. Frommer "highly recommends" it. Montecito resident Julia Child had described it as her favorite local restaurant. While visiting his nearby ranch, Ronald Reagan sometimes sent a Secret Service team to pick up takeout orders. We, too, had learned to appreciate La Super-Rica Taquería's unique approach to genuine Mexican food.

As usual, there was a line waiting to place orders and another wait for the food to be prepared. At Super-Rica, everyone from Hollywood stars to local construction workers sit on plastic chairs and eat off paper plates. The tacos and tamales are relatively small and served simply with seasoned meat on fresh corn tortillas you watch being made. The owner, Isidoro Gonzalez, took Pat's order for *carne asada* and mine for the *pollo suiza*. We've never been there when Isidoro wasn't.

While waiting for our order (this is definitely not fast food), we discussed the Montecito alternatives. Pat was more bothered by the noise and pollution caused by traffic on Hot Springs Road. I was excited about being close to the Biltmore and beach so we decided to see how weekend beach traffic might affect our privacy. We didn't know contractors or workers in Santa Barbara and were frightened to undertake a major renovation on a house we really couldn't afford. The Montecito options were tempting, but the cost and challenges were overwhelming.

Like Scarlett O'Hara, we would "worry about that tomorrow." Riding home, we passed Jim, Kim and their battered campers. Knowing that we actually had choices made it easier to accept our place in the local hierarchy. We were grateful to be in such a beautiful city. Sometimes, I was depressed not to have accomplished more. Most of the time, however, I felt sheepish, even a little guilty, about having been so lucky.

Talent and hard work play a role in success, but so does being in the right place at the right time. We wouldn't have our limited choices if I not explored the spinoff at AlliedSignal and balanced two jobs for most of my career. We wouldn't have the equity to explore any Santa Barbara options if Pat had not utilized her aesthetic sense for increasingly challenging renovations in Atlanta, New York and Williamsburg. We resolved to accept our place in Santa Barbara's hierarchy, while enjoying great friendships in the same climate and scenery as the rich and famous.

Chapter 8
A New Century in Paradise

The century in which we were born was drawing to a close. We had never lived through a transition to a new century, much less a new millennium. Doomsday scenarios were prevalent, apprehension was almost universal, and signs of potential disasters were being carefully analyzed. Something had happened to the calm, leisurely days of our first weeks in Santa Barbara. I was commuting to Los Angeles every week for Pepperdine; we were going to be part of a new Newcomers administration; and were thinking about a collective effort to write a book about the pleasures of moving to paradise. We had passed on our Montecito options, still hadn't purchased a house, and were about to launch a minor renovation on our East Beach townhome. We didn't have time to run out and buy sixty pounds of dried beans, twenty gallons of filtered water, or seven laying hens to prepare for the Rapture or Apocalypse.

In late November, Shaun, Susan, Sarah and Jack came for their first visit to California as a family. Sarah was still a delightful eight-year-old, but new grandson Jack was a rambunctious, colicky three-month old who had not discovered how pleasant it could be to sleep through an entire night. One afternoon, Pat volunteered to take Susan and Sarah shopping, and Shaun agreed to take care of Jack for a few hours while I prepared the syllabus for a new class at Pepperdine. Shaun had hoped to get a little rest while Jack was down for a nap. That was not to be. Almost as soon as the shoppers pulled out of our garage, Jack started to cry. Shaun rocked, walked, dipped and even sang a bit. I was equally unsuccessful. As I retreated and tried to organize a coherent plan for my course, I couldn't help but admire Jack's stamina and lung capacity. The crying moved into a robust tantrum, and I could hear Shaun pleading, "Please, Jack, just what do you want me to do?"

Jack didn't answer, but continued, non-stop, at the top of his well-developed lungs for most of the three hours the female contingent spent at Paseo Nuevo, Santa Barbara's largest, downtown shopping area. When they returned to find Jack finally napping on his father's chest, just as Shaun started to enjoy a much-needed siesta, Pat commented, "How nice, they must have slept the whole time we've been gone."

We did not have the dishes, utensils, space or energy to prepare a traditional Thanksgiving dinner, so we signed up for the Unitarian Society's community Thanksgiving meal. The price was reasonable, the food was excellent, and the convenience was superb. Shaun and Susan enjoyed meeting some of our new friends, or were polite enough to act pleased, and Sarah charmed the adults. Rev. Jim and Betty Grant served as unofficial host and hostess, and made everyone feel that we were enjoying a holiday celebration with extended family. Don Bushnell suggested, "It's good to spend part of the holiday with families who seem less dysfunctional than your own."

Our contemporaries frequently comment, "Nothing is better than that moment when your children and grandchildren arrive for a visit—but waving good-bye after an exhausting visit is a close second." After an enjoyable visit (and good-bye) with Shaun and his family, we returned from the airport, poured more coffee, spread out the *News-Press* and tried to catch up on what was happening in our (hopefully) no longer temporary, hometown.

Funky Development

The *Opinion* section doesn't usually get much attention, but I was intrigued by a proposal for the redevelopment of an industrial area near the beach that was sometimes called the

"Funk Zone." A local architect, Michael Arth, had a detailed proposal calling for "the creation of an environmentally sustainable pedestrian-oriented development in what was a somewhat blighted area near the Santa Barbara waterfront." Almost three hundred dwelling units were proposed, including a mixture of row houses, condos and apartments, with special emphasis on low and moderate-income housing. A sixty-room hotel, a hostel, and a small number of bed-and-breakfasts were proposed. The result would be the creation of a compact, low-rise, mostly residential neighborhood where people could live on safe, clean, auto-free *paseos.*

The entire proposal was creative and exciting, but we were especially intrigued by the possibility of acquiring housing, near the ocean, that was "environmentally sustainable and pedestrian-oriented." I went to my computer, waited for the dial-up modem to connect, and searched for Arth's telephone number. Even though it was Sunday, I called, introduced myself, congratulated Michael on his innovative thinking, and asked when we could move in. Arth explained that his was a totally speculative proposal, but he would be grateful if I would write a letter supporting his concept to City Hall. An enthusiastic letter notwithstanding, nothing came of the proposal, but knowing another architect might be useful if we ever managed to buy property.

Pat had chosen someone to upgrade our townhouse. The husband-wife team had good recommendations, seemed competent, and was willing to work with us on a small project. I had met them just after the Scotch tasting event, but didn't recall enough of the conversation to help with the decision— and Pat really didn't need my input.

Probably the biggest component of the project was to take out the ugly "cottage cheese" ceiling that crowned every room. We wanted to remove the aging carpeting on the first level of our unit as well as in the third bedroom that we used as an office. We planned to replace it with tile or white oak flooring. The bathroom and kitchen tile needed to be modernized. We felt installing marble countertops in both locations would increase the aesthetics and resale value. Kitchen and bathroom fixtures were old and unattractive, and we wanted to replace the tired, stained wallpaper in both bathrooms and one of the bedrooms with something that reflected our tastes. The project would add ten percent to the unit's total cost, but we were sure it would add at least twice that to the market value.

We summarized the proposed changes, confirmed our plans to exercise the purchase option, and sent everything, via e-mail, to the owner in Greece. Since the prices for townhouses were starting to catch up with the overall acceleration in real estate price, Kostas wasn't particularly happy with our decision to purchase but had no objections to our upgrading plans.

The CEO in the Next Barber Chair

Frequently, we were finding ourselves returning to one of the city's unique jewels hidden in plain sight at the epicenter of our Santa Barbara. Near the courthouse, library and art museum, La Arcada is a quaint and charming alternative to the typical shopping center. We had eaten at a couple of restaurants there and enjoyed its art galleries and retail boutiques. The vine-covered, tile-lined walkways are like an outdoor museum with a turtle-filled fountain. Life-sized statues by J. Seward Johnson, George Lundeen, and Bud Bottoms, plus the interactive Mozart Trio by Bonifatius Stirnberg, add to the pleasure of visiting La Arcada. Prominent plaques honor Myron Hunt, the California architect who designed the buildings during the post-earthquake restoration and Hugh E. Petersen, the former owner of La Arcada, who "transformed it into Santa Barbara's most beautiful courtyard."

And why not get your hair cut in the historic barber shop that is a mini-museum of early 1900 hair cutting parlors? Carlos did a good job of cutting hair, but was also something of a Santa Barbara character: gung ho, *semper fi* former Marine, perpetual candidate for the City Council, and movie extra. He told me confidentially that he had a role in the forthcoming movie, *Seabiscuit,* and he did. After being on the set and getting paid for two full days, he was on screen for all of six seconds.

Just before Pepperdine Graduate Business School December graduation, I decided to get a haircut. This was a special graduation exercise since the featured speaker and recipient of an honorary doctorate was the CEO of Raytheon Corporation. Raytheon was the largest employer of Pepperdine graduates, but I had known Dan Burnham as a young comptroller for AlliedSignal.

In my management development role during the late 1980s, I got to work with most of the firm's senior execs. Dan was the youngest, most energetic and learning-oriented of the attendees at the firm's first International Senior Executive Program. Allied-Signal's prevailing culture was, "real men don't need development." That culture had to change, but not everyone agreed. Dan obviously enjoyed learning, exploring new ideas, and didn't mind challenging his colleagues or the instructors.

Clearly, he was one of the highest potential young executives in the firm. At some point, I asked, "Dan, what are your career aspirations?" Without hesitation, he replied, "Oh, I would like to be CEO someday." In truth, the other twenty-four executives at the program probably had the same aspirations, but were not willing to be candid about their goals. Dan went on to explain, "I can't imagine working for an organization and not wanting to have as much influence as possible in shaping the future. I love my current responsibility, but having twice as much responsibility ought to be twice as much fun!"

Immediately, I wanted to write a teaching case about this unique individual. With the help of a talented graduate assistant, we prepared two cases I taught at Columbia, William & Mary and in several executive programs. Dan reminded me of a comment about a Dilbert character described as having great potential. "He's tall and has a full head of hair that we think will become distinguishingly gray at the temples in just a few years." Dan had gone on to become vice chairman of AlliedSignal and probably the leading candidate to succeed Larry Bossidy as CEO. Just before a merger with Honeywell, he accepted a call from executive search firms, was offered the presidency of Raytheon, and six months later was named chairman and CEO.

As I thought about how pleasant it would be to see Dan at the graduation exercise, I looked over, and unbelievably, there he was in the next barber's chair. Sure enough, there was a distinguished sprinkling of gray in his thick, dark hair. Dan and his wife, Meg, had purchased a Santa Barbara estate from Whoopi Goldberg (previously owned by John Deere), which they planned to use as a retirement home. Until retirement rolled around, they occasionally got away from it all at "Deer Lodge." Small world!

We enjoyed catching up. He was in the midst of a complicated turnaround situation at Raytheon, and confided that, once that was accomplished, he probably wouldn't stay on the job until compulsory retirement at sixty-five.

"But you've worked all your life to get this job," I said. "How could you walk away from it after all this time? Wouldn't you miss all the excitement and challenges?"

"Maybe I would," he responded, "but there is a story going around about a retired CEO who was asked the same question. 'Actually,' admitted the former CEO, 'I do miss my people.'

'That's nice,' the questioner replied. 'I think it's wonderful that you miss all the great people who worked for you.'

'No, no, you don't understand. I miss *my* people—I miss my chauffeur, I miss my pilot, I miss my executive assistant'."

We laughed, and Dan told me that while he had always enjoyed his work and the challenges it brought, he was also realizing that there was more to life than work. "I think it might be fun to be successful as a grandfather, and I know it would be fun to spend more time with Meg, looking out over the Santa Ynez valley and sipping a good local *pinot*—although Meg has warned me that I shouldn't expect her to fill the void created by the loss of my corporate support systems."

Doubtless, Dan would be as successful at retirement as he had been at everything else. He was certainly successful the next day at delivering the best commencement speech I had heard.

In every way, it was a powerful, professional graduation exercise. President David Davenport was articulate, Dean Baskin impressive, and, of course, the commencement speaker was superb. Afterwards, Pat and I enjoyed a pleasant, non-alcoholic meal at the university President's residence overlooking the Malibu coastline. We drove home along the

PCH, enjoying the scenery and savoring the varied, but almost always positive, tenor of our lives in California.

The Riviera Reassessed

The next morning, after services at USSB, a vivacious redhead, perhaps a couple of years older than we are, walked up and said, "I'm Barbara Sanchez, and I would like to help you buy a house." She had heard about our real estate misadventures from the Sterns. We had now looked at seventy houses and made five unsuccessful offers. Barbara thought she might help improve our batting average.

We sat down in a corner of Fellowship Hall with Barbara and described our interests and limitations. She listened carefully, took notes and suggested, "It sounds as though you have done a good job of exploring the Eastside and Montecito. You aren't likely to find anything that fits your parameters downtown so I suggest that you consider looking in the Riviera."

We had little experience with the Riviera, but knew that the views were excellent and the roads were dangerously curvy. I still remembered my first challenging drive along APS with Frank Saunders almost a year earlier.

"Why," Pat asked, "do you think the Riviera might be a fit?"

"Well, you've mentioned the ocean and wanting to be close to town as well as some limitations on price. The Riviera is basically an ocean-facing hillside that runs about two miles between Mission and Sycamore Canyons. The early *padres* called the area the 'mission ridge,' but for the past half century, it has been known as the Riviera because of the resemblance to slopes along the Mediterranean coasts of France and Italy.

"Most of the area does have curving streets with mature trees and foliage. Prices are slightly less than in Montecito, and many people who live here think they live in the best part of town because of the unsurpassed views of the city, mountains, sea and islands. The winter is a little warmer, and you are only five-ten minutes from most places. Why don't I do some research and to find a couple of houses you might really like? I won't show you anything that I don't think will work for you."
103

Barbara impressed us because she actually listened to what we said and instead of talking about a wonderful property she had just listed that didn't meet any of our requirements. "We're going to be pretty busy for the next couple of weeks, but we'll look forward to hearing from you," Pat said as we moved on to make plans for dinner on New Year's Eve.

A Frantic Family Christmas

Just a year ago, we had enjoyed a family "prelude to paradise." We looked forward to another holiday with better weather. Just before Christmas, we walked by beach in shirt sleeves and waved to a roller blader who passed us, shirtless and in shorts.

For the first time in 138 years, the first official day of winter coincided with a lunar perigee (the point in the moon's orbit that is closest to earth). The moon would, we were told, appear about fourteen percent larger than it usually does. We had missed the previous time this happened, in 1861, so we looked earnestly at the moon as we drove to Santa Barbara's small but charming airport to meet Pat's mother, Catherine, and niece, Lauren. The moon was bright enough to drive without our lights, but decided to use them anyway, just to be safe.

Catherine's dementia was worsening, so Lauren was traveling with her as a precaution. After a second minor accident involving the postman, she had given up her driver's license and reluctantly moved to assisted living in Dyersburg, Tennessee. An advantages of small-town living is that people understand and accommodate personal idiosyncrasies. After the second accident, Pat's mother had apologized profusely. "Oh no, Ms. Catherine," the postman had said. "I saw you coming in plenty of time and should have gotten out of your way."

Along with the holidays, the flu season was peaking. It was a time to exchange presents and flu germs. Brad arrived from Los Angeles with a slight fever and headache. Lauren was becoming a beautiful young woman, but was still a teenager with all that implies. At one point, Catherine asked in a perplexed manner, "Who is that girl?"

Pat explained, "Mother, that's Lauren, your granddaughter!"

Sadly, Catherine shook her head and responded, "No, she's not. No granddaughter of mine would act that way."

We were trying to put together a festive Christmas dinner using our patchwork of utensils and dishes, but several potential contributors to the preparation were wounded or missing. Brad was coughing and resting on an air mattress in our third bedroom/study. Catherine kept wandering out of the townhouse in an effort to find her own home. Lauren was engaged in a book and extended telephone conversations. Pat and I struggled in the kitchen and tried not to strangle each other.

Finally, everything was ready. We crowded around our harvest table, took a collective breath, and enjoyed Pat's culinary skills, especially the cornbread stuffing. As *sous*-chef, I specialized in peeling, chopping and cleaning up, and quickly decided that paying for the community Thanksgiving dinner had been a wonderful idea.

The following day, we met my sons, Jeff and Burt, at the airport and tried to re-create some of the greatest hits from the previous year. Our townhouse was out of sleeping spaces, so we rented a couple of rooms at a nearby hotel. Brad was miserable and probably contagious, so he locked himself in one of the rooms and main-lined Theraflu while the rest of us made plans to explore the nearby wine country.

Professionally-led tours were available for $125 per person, but I decided to serve as the designated driver. After a late brunch, we headed out San Marcos Pass and stopped first at Fess Parker's, winery producing premium, award-winning Pinot noir, Chardonnay, and Riesling. The tasting room and visitor center reminded us of Fess' Disney-era past. We sampled the featured vintages, but resisted buying a raccoon-skin hat.

The next stop was at the rustic Foxen tasting room, where I was assured that the Pinot Noir, Chardonnay, Syrah and Cabernets were excellent. While nibbling on cheese samples, I chatted with the friendly staff and watched my passengers grow happier and sillier. Even worse than missing the pleasures of good wine is not being part of the humor that everyone else finds so hilarious.

Despite a name most frequently associated with automotive tires, the Firestone vineyards have almost thirty years of winemaking experience and the double distinction of being Santa Barbara County's first estate winery and the largest at 250,000 cases per year. Firestone produces a wide variety of wines from Bordeaux-style blends to late-harvest Rieslings and their classic Chardonnay. The facilities were impressive and the staff was well-informed and helpful. I strolled around and perused Firestone family photographs and mementos. One picture showed proprietor Brooks Firestone's grandfather with Henry Ford, Thomas Edison, President Woodrow Wilson and a couple of other gilded-era titans—just like one of those Sunday afternoon gatherings I used to enjoy so much at my grandfather's tiny farm in north Alabama.

By this time, everyone had tasted enough and was ready to head back to East Beach for a nap. Most didn't wait till we got back to Santa Barbara. That evening, we went to dinner at the yacht harbor's unpretentious but delicious Brophy Brothers, often billed as "where the locals like to eat." It may be a place that tourists believe the locals like to eat, but the restaurant overlooks the harbor with over a thousand boats in the foreground, and the fresh seafood is excellent.

Celebrating a Centennial

The last day in Santa Barbara for our visitors was spent visiting the zoo, recycling Christmas gifts and bicycling along our favorite beachside path. Everyone had early morning flights. Since we were John Irving fans, we ended the last day before New Year's Eve with a twilight screening of *The Cider House Rules*. Early the next morning, Catherine and Lauren headed to their homes while Jeff and Burt flew to Washington to celebrate the new millennium in a historic setting with friends.

We wouldn't be around for another millennium and hoped this celebration could be truly memorable. We had purchased First Night buttons that would grant us admission to a variety of events beginning in the early afternoon and ending with a gigantic midnight fireworks display. This sounded like fun, but we had done the fireworks over the harbor for July 4. Surely we could find a memorable way to end one century and start another—something we would remember fondly in our dotage.

We were intrigued when our friend, Elden Dellania, asked if we would like to celebrate the event with him and a few friends aboard a luxury yacht. Elden is a retired FDA investigator, a real estate investor and the proud owner of a twenty-five-foot sailboat. "That sounds great, Elden," I responded, "but with all due respect, I wouldn't call your boat a luxury yacht."

"Well, if my boat isn't good enough for you, how about an eighty-five foot catamaran that boasts three levels, three thousand square feet of space, a full bar, library, media room and a few other bells and whistles? You may be hard to please, Fulmer, but I think this will meet even your standards."

While the rest of us had been trying to imagine a unique way to celebrate, Elden had met King Williams at the harbor. Williams, a former Santa Barbara diver and lobster fisherman, had answered some questions one day from a couple of guys in their sixties and wound up helping Warren Buffett's partner, Charlie Munger, build and manage a world-class sailing vessel. Munger had failed in his goal of staying "just beneath the Forbes 400 list of the world's richest people," but occasionally made his yacht, *The Channel Cat*, available for rental. Elden had nailed down the date, negotiated the rate, and reserved the yacht with his own credit card. Now, he needed to persuade a hundred newcomers to pay $115 each for *hors d'oeuvres* and four hours on the gorgeous *Channel Cat*, with dancing on the deck and a perfect perspective from which to view the fabulous fireworks display welcoming in a new century. It was the best deal in town. I had saved more than this by being the driver on our wine-tasting tour. Newcomers had grown to 700 members by this time, so it didn't take long to fill this event.

We had already purchased our First Night buttons and wanted to do as much as we could before boarding the yacht. Most afternoon events were child-friendly activities. My knowledge of science was, at best, childlike, so we walked up to De La Guerra Plaza where the UCSB Physics Circus was entertaining children and unsophisticated senior citizens with science demonstrations. The world-class Physics Department had lined up engaging demonstrations of mechanics, sound, electricity and magnetism.

It wasn't the most exciting thing we had done in the old millennium, but we felt intellectually virtuous as we rushed back to East Beach to dress for the evening.

A Millennium to Remember

Around dusk, Santa Barbara prepared to end the century in grand style and began a transformation into a spectacle of light, sound and color, with outdoor concerts, special commissioned art installations, gallery tours, musical programs, street corner musicians, staged theater productions, multimedia displays, dances, and street performers. I got dressed more quickly than Pat (a lot more quickly), so I took the electric trolley to the art museum. With the celebratory traffic, it seemed to take forever. Surprisingly, I found Don and Julie easily, and we strolled along looking at the special millennium exhibition. Don was appropriately dressed as a Unitarian professor, and Julie was elegantly attired as a sophisticated flapper from the 1920s.

At six o'clock, we walked across the street to the Arts & Letters Café, where we were to meet the Warnocks, Sterns, and Pat for a Unitarian millennium dinner. A&L (remember how Santa Barbara loves abbreviations?) serves basic bistro fare in a beautiful courtyard setting designed in the tradition of the walled gardens of Spain and Mexico. The courtyard trees were illuminated with tiny white lights and a central fountain created a backdrop of water sounds. To counteract a slight winter chill, the garden was warmed by portable heaters.

The predictably punctual Sterns were a little late because of traffic, and Pat probably wouldn't have made it if the Sterns had not seen her standing forlornly at the trolley stop in her chic evening wear and graciously provided transportation. We didn't linger over coffee and dessert, as the Sterns and Warnocks were heading to the Symphony's performance and we, along with Don and Julie, wanted to get to the Presidio chapel for a performance by Mama Pat's Inner Light Community Gospel Choir.

The chapel dates back to 1787, and its simple façade belies the rich interior that features artwork, sacred artifacts, *faux* painting and was illuminated by candles. Mama Pat was a Santa Barbara institution who came to Santa Barbara in 1978 to work as a nanny for actress Anne Francis. She quickly chartered the Church of Inner Light and began popularizing Gospel singing. The interdenominational community choir is open to aspiring vocalists of all ages and all backgrounds. Their stated purpose is "to touch hearts and lift spirits through the medium of Gospel music." Their lively, engaging music probably wasn't the purpose for which the chapel was created but, on this special evening, they were perfect for each other.

We left the concert a little early and were able to flag a taxi to take us to the harbor. Pat wanted to watch the Times Square celebration at nine o'clock. Since the Y2K bug had not afflicted Sydney or London, we assumed that we didn't need to worry, but New York would be the ultimate test.

Our sleek, white, opulent, eighty-five foot catamaran was waiting, and we were duly impressed. Once aboard, we quickly found the yacht's theater where Captain Williams downloaded the NBC Times Square broadcast for a few former New Yorkers. Afterwards, we made our way to the twenty-five foot bar, helped ourselves to hors *d'oeuvres*, and mingled with 100 new friends. Elden provided a comprehensive collection of music from the forties, fifties, and sixties. Pat even managed to get me on a somewhat unstable dance floor a few times.

It was truly a magical evening. Everyone enjoyed celebrating this momentous event in such a beautiful setting with people we were coming to love and appreciate. Long-married couples were holding hands or slow dancing to Frank Sinatra, Pat Boone and Elvis. Singles were finding partners who were looking quite fetching in the moonlight. The most common topics of conversation dealt with an almost universal sense of appreciation for the combination of events that had enabled us to be here at this moment in history.

Spectacular fireworks began at midnight. We could see the red tile roofs of our adopted city through a prism of beautiful pyrotechnics. At midnight, everyone found someone to kiss, and no one was raptured away. In the first hour of a new millennium, we optimistically wished our shipmates a happy new century, were grateful for the blessings that brought us here and walked home by the ocean, happy to have discovered our version of paradise.

Chapter 9
Queen Isabella or Dulcinea?

Barbara Sanchez was as good as her word. With excitement in her voice and an absolute conviction that we would buy one of the two houses she had selected for us to view, she explained that the quintessential Santa Barbara architectural style is Spanish colonial, with its characteristic red tile roof and stucco walls. "I want to show you two 'Spanish ladies.' One is a grand dame designed by the area's most distinguished architect on a quiet, picturesque street. I think of her as 'Queen Isabella'," she told us, "and I believe you will fall in love with her even if the asking price is fifty percent more than your target."

We gulped at "fifty percent more," but were intrigued:

> *Classic Spanish mediterranean home situated on private lane in the heart of the Riviera. Built in 1932, G.W. Smith designed old world charm with a versatile floor plan. 4 bedrooms, study, family room & 4 car plus garage. Hardwood floors throughout. Beautiful mature landscaping, unobstructed city, ocean & harbor views. One of a kind.*

Barbara warned us that the second house, while also Spanish, had seen better days. "She's more like Dulcinea, the fallen woman in Don Quixote. She has tremendous potential, but if you like a challenge, you'll love the fact that the price is actually under your target."

Checking the description, we both noted that our agent and the listing emphasized "potential." That meant there would be a tremendous amount of work to do. We also recognized that, during one of the hottest real estate markets in Santa Barbara's history, this house had been on the market for almost a year. Just how bad could it be?

> *Potential abounds for new owners with vision and sense of restoration to the original grandeur for this classic Spanish Colonial Revival villa built in 1920. Situated on a terraced half-acre among prestigious homes & estates, this villa is on Santa Barbara's lovely Riviera and near the renowned el Encanto Hotel. Basic features include courtyard living room, 5 fireplaces, 6 bathrooms.*

The two houses were within three blocks of each other, so we resolved to keep an open mind as we climbed into her car. Up a hill reminiscent of San Francisco, we turned on Mira Vista and stopped in front of an attractive house designed in what we were coming to recognize as Spanish Mediterranean—an identification aided by the brochure. The lawn was sparse because of the pervasive shade of two huge eucalyptus trees. The owners were moving into an assisted living facility. Their age and long tenure showed in every aspect of the house.

Barbara was quick to point out impressive views from the living room, the wine cellar and the solar heated pool. She let us form our own opinions of the Reagan-era kitchen (his *GE Theater* era, not his presidential period), an unimaginative layout in the upstairs bedrooms, the limited closet space, and the small, antiquated bathrooms. Still, it had "curb appeal," a great location, and was ready for occupancy. I was more impressed by the views and other positives than Pat and was attempting to think of a creative approach to financing while we drove even higher to Mission Ridge.

A Fallen Lady

Barbara warned us about meeting the owner. "Imogene is in her mid-80s and in bad health. After showing the house for several unproductive months, she's decided that there's no reason to leave while prospects poke around. You need to be prepared for a little eccentricity," Barbara said, in what we would soon recognize as British understatement. "The house has been on the market for such a long time because it shows badly, and Imogene can be a bit difficult. She doesn't want to sell the house, but she can't afford to keep it."

"Imo" and her partner, Ruth Michaelis bought the property thirty years earlier and were very happy until Ruth died in 1989. She had been a celebrated contralto with the Bavarian Opera company. Imogene also loved to sing, reportedly, "has a Sophie Tucker-type voice," had been an elementary-school music teacher in Montecito and, after retiring, composed an operetta for children that she still hoped to have performed.

"Some people called them 'the odd couple,' Barbara said. "Ruth was tall, slim, elegant and sophisticated in the European manner, while Imo was short, stocky, disheveled, and a little crude in the Arkansas manner. But they were together for 45 years. Ruth received a nice stipend from the West German government that stopped at her death. Imo's retirement and the income from her greeting cards and party business weren't adequate to maintain the property, so she started renting out rooms—something not permitted by neighborhood zoning. The house is a warren of rental units, but she made few structural changes and, as realtors like to say, 'the bones are good'."

We drove up a steep winding driveway made of crumbling asphalt to find another Spanish-style house. This one showed distinctive signs of neglect. The front yard faced south toward the ocean and contained sporadic clumps of grass and bushes (fertilized, it appeared, by dog manure), a badly pruned jacaranda tree, two imposing palm trees and a large, beautiful bougainvillea vine that covered a homemade arbor just outside sliding glass doors.

We rang the front door bell, then knocked and were surprised when a plump, energetic woman with graying hair opened the door to greet us. She certainly didn't look like someone in bad health and in her mid-80s. I had to admit that she didn't look much older than I did. We soon learned that this was Anita, a former nun who served in Berkeley during the 1960s—and was born on the very date as I. She was the owner's nurse, business manager and *majordomo* and took us to the large living room to meet Imogene, who had moved her king-sized, red satin canopy bed into the middle of that room in order to free up other space for rental. A big-screen television was stationed at the foot of the bed. The flooring may have been oak, but was too cluttered to be sure. A stack of boxes filled with greeting cards created a partition of sorts, and behind the cardboard divider, on a brick floor just inside the discolored sliding glass doors, was a cot she rented to a gentleman named Gus.

Imogene greeted us imperially, introduced us to Wolfgang and Amadeus, her pug and dachshund companions, and asked Anita, "Why don't you show Barbara and the Fulmers the house so I can see the end of *As the World Turns*?" With that, we were dismissed, and she returned to her soap opera.

Barbara demurred. "I have already seen the house, so why don't I stay here and see what's happening in Oakdale? Perhaps during commercials, we can catch up a bit. I don't think I've talked with you since the September CAMA (Community Arts Music Association) concert."

Anita ushered us out of the living room to a chaotic, L-shaped kitchen and dining area where some dirty pans were soaking in a stained porcelain sink and others were still resting on an antique gas stove. Mismatched dishes, still unwashed from breakfast, covered a dining table in front of a Bavarian bay window. On the window base sat a black-and-white television.

I was overly anxious to get out of the depressing area, so I opened a door on the other side of the kitchen. "Oh, that's just a big storage area," Anita said. Indeed, we discovered a 10 x 15-foot room that appeared to have a dirt floor, and was filled with a jungle of boxes and bags. As we tried to reconstruct our impressions later, we called this "the dirt room."

Anita led us back through the living room, where Imogene and Barbara were discussing the latest dilemmas of the Dixon family, across a wide entrance foyer and into a fairly standard bedroom. She proudly described it as "my little corner of the world," then showed us a picture of herself as a nun and answered a question that we had not gotten around to asking.

113

"I was in Berkeley at a really exciting time and couldn't help but think that everyone was having a more interesting life. The bureaucracy, judgmental outlook and dogma of the Church started to bother me a lot, but it took several years for me to 'kick the habit.' I'm still a spiritual person, but don't believe that one person or group has all the answers."

The most distinctive part of the room was another Bavarian bay window. "Ruth never adjusted to Spanish architecture," Anita explained, "so she added a few touches from her native land." We noted a simple fireplace, modest ocean view, utilitarian bath, and were surprised to discover a long, narrow area behind her room. This area served as a walk-in closet and was separated from a tiny kitchenette by a red brick archway. For an old house, the first floor had lots of storage space.

A Diva's Domain

From the foyer, Anita opened an arched doorway to a large, dramatic family-room that had been a tiled courtyard. The original owners had gone through this door and up an outdoor stairway to reach the upstairs bedrooms. Imogene and Ruth had installed steel beams that ran from the second floor ceiling to a retaining wall on the northern side of the courtyard. They covered the beams with corrugated sheets of fiberglass and added glass panels from a hothouse to form an eastern wall. The result was a shaky, but striking, light-filled area warmed by a six-foot 'heatalater' fireplace. From this room, we saw a suspended balcony that embraced the southern and western portions of the second floor and connected to thick, oak doors that opened to four bedrooms. In most places, this balcony was simply a dramatic hallway with hand-hewn banisters forming a protective ring, but near the master bedroom, the balcony extended theatrically for an extra three or four feet.

Anita pointed proudly. "They used to have great parties where Ruth would sing arias by Mozart, Puccini, and Strauss from that balcony. Ruth made her Munich operatic debut in 1932, and performed in Vienna, Bordeaux, Lisbon, Barcelona, Rome, and London and throughout the United States. After retiring from performing, she continued to teach singing at the National Opera School of Istanbul, the University of Florida, University of Southern California and the Music Academy of the West."

The most arresting decorative touch of this room was an indoor fountain featuring a replica of Brussels' famous *Manneken Pis*. The other artistic highlight was a red and black Aztec design, hand-painted on an eighteen-inch circular metal flue that extended from the fireplace's mantel to the second story ceiling. After twenty years of marriage, I could almost read Pat's mind. We exchanged glances, and she rolled her eyes in disbelief. Sometimes she can be so picky!

We walked up the worn carpeted stairway to inspect the bedrooms, stopping first at a room near the top of the stairs that was rented by Theresa, who was recovering from a serious automobile accident and spending much of her time in physical therapy. The room had a full bath and a small closet.

Hotel Mission Ridge

The next two rooms were occupied by Jenny and Franny, students at Santa Barbara City College, who shared a bedroom with a fireplace plus a spacious area they used for reading, study, computer access and light cooking. Despite the community college decor, this room enjoyed windows on two walls with views of the Pacific and Channel Islands. Come to think about it, you could see the ocean from all of the upstairs bedrooms and three of the downstairs rooms. Unfortunately, the views were marred by two telephone poles that supported a large transformer and wires from the telephone, cable and electrical companies.

We exited to a small porch as Anita apologized for not showing us the master bedroom. "It is a beautiful room, about 17' x 20', with a nice fireplace, two balconies, large windows, bathroom, kitchenette, and private entrance. The occupant is an alcoholic, agoraphobic depressive who is having a bad day. He's locked both doors and refuses to let anyone in."

His refusal was not a big deal to me. I definitely wasn't interested in this house. Although I am a fan of John Irving, I didn't want to be a character in one of his novels, and already this was starting to feel like a cross between *Hotel New Hampshire* and *The World According to Garp*. I expected to see a grizzly bear on a motorcycle at any moment.

To be polite, we walked out to examine a steep, scrubby and rocky backyard that did contain a small orchard with lemon, orange, tangerine, apple, pomegranate, persimmon, cherimoya, fig, olive and loquat trees. Dozens of pumpkins punctuated the stone terraces. "Pete loves pumpkins and has a 'sharecropping' arrangement with Imo. She provides the land while he provides the seeds and labor. During the summer, he grows tomatoes, peppers, and lettuce. We have wonderful, fresh, organic salads," Anita bragged.

We walked up the rocky hillside to examine Pete's garden plot and compost heap. When we turned to walk down the hillside, I did a double take when I realized that, while the front roof was the traditional red tiles, the back roof was covered in a thin tarpaper covering.

"What's the story about the roof?" I asked, incredulously.

"Imo was going to finish that before putting the house on the market, but she ran out of funds and decided to reduce the sales price by the cost of completing the roof," Anita explained.

We passed another porch leading to what we were assured was "a legal studio apartment." It contained a small living area, bedroom, bath and kitchenette, and had obviously been added to the original structure. Anita went on to explain, "When Ruth retired, they decided to add the studio, got permission from the city. Before it was finished, Pete reserved the unit and has lived here ever since. At Ruth's death, Imogene had to start renting out bedrooms. Some neighbors complained about the number of people living here, but the City has been pretty tolerant because of her situation. Of course, the new owners won't be able to continue renting to anyone except Pete has lived in the studio for twenty years."

I was struck by the sad predicament of growing old with limited financial resources in an expensive community and wondered if there would ever come a time when we had to resort to such desperate measures. At this point, I didn't think we would need to take in boarders, but with prices escalating every day, how could you know?

We walked back in the house to collect Barbara and found Imogene in a much improved mood. Barbara had "jollied her up" so we stood and chatted a few minutes before making our escape. As Barbara navigated down the narrow, challenging driveway and drove toward East Beach, she asked our impression of the two houses. Before I could chuckle and say something witty about "a house that John Irving might appreciate," Pat shocked me by saying, "I really didn't like the first house, but the second one has potential. It would take a tremendous amount of work, but I think it could be fabulous."

"What?" I exclaimed. "We probably couldn't afford the first house, but it looks like *Tara* compared to the hovel on Mission Ridge!" I knew this wasn't a time to be funny, and I was too shocked to think of anything that could pass as clever.

"No," Pat explained patiently, as if speaking to a very slow third grader. "The Mira Vista House is in better shape, but it doesn't have as much space or potential. There's no way to provide more closet space or extend the bedrooms in Queen Isabella." She chided me for overreacting to the menagerie of tenants as well as the neglect, mess and clutter. "Don't forget," she reminded me, "Dulcinea is forty percent less expensive."

I had to admit that the cost was a powerful argument, and that slovenly housekeeping had biased my perspective. Barbara chimed in, "I am so glad, Pat, that you could see the potential on Mission Ridge. You have an artist's eye and can see beyond the disorder and neglect. The house has been on the market for so long because most people don't look beyond the superficial."

Barbara had figured out who made the decisions in our household. She was flattering Pat and didn't care if I was offended by being called superficial. If this decision came down to a vote, I was going to lose by a two-to-one margin. I figured my best defense was to play a delaying game.

"Let's think it over," I countered, hoping to reduce the numerical advantage of the opposition. "You can draw the floor plan and think through everything that has to be done." From past experience I knew Pat would need to do a sketch, determine how our furniture would fit and decide how big the challenges would be. To be serious, we would need to come back and visit several times. I was confident Pat would quickly realize that the work Dulcinea required was overwhelming.

A Still Born Book

That would have to wait for a little while as we had the Newcomers "officers' installation" meeting to attend. Berkeley Meigs had completed her term as president and would be succeeded by Ellen Lilley. Pat would be in charge of the Visual Arts Committee and I was to join the Newcomers' Board, chair the "Money Talks" group, and launch a new committee to coordinate a book-writing project. As a fan of A *Year in Provence, Under the Tuscan Sun,* and *Gringos in Paradise,* I naively believed that it should be relatively simple to get fifty of our seven hundred members to write a few charming pages about one of their many "perfect days in paradise."

Berkeley prepared a brief announcement for the newsletter:

> *Here is your chance for immortality! Our lives may be but a brief candle, but words can build for eternity. Newcomers Club is writing a book about our impressions of Santa Barbara. You can be part of this. Pick your favorite day since moving to Santa Barbara, and describe it like you are telling your best friend or family how exciting Santa Barbara can be.*

> *You don't have to be a Shakespeare or even a Hemingway. Plenty of help is available if you want guidance or encouragement with your contribution. To qualify for the Book Kickoff Party, you need to bring* hors d'oeuvres *and a written description, outline or draft of your literary contribution. We will provide the wine, cheese, brainstorming, editorial assistance and encouragement.*

We were a little discouraged when only six people showed up for this wonderful opportunity. Perhaps the plan to get fifty individuals to write humorous or inspirational stories was overly optimistic. We ate lots of *hors d'oeuvres*, reviewed each other's ideas and decided to try once more to marshal the resources for what everyone agreed was a fabulous idea.

Privately, I thought that less than half of the submitted sketches had potential, and would require more work to get into a consistent style than it would take for one person to do it all.

Pat was very involved in helping plan "the gala event of the new millennium," an ambitious project called *La Grande Affaire des Arts*. The promotional materials asked "all talented newcomers, or those who think they might be talented, to exhibit paintings, photographs, sculpture, ceramics, weavings, glass, or collage." Musicians, writers and other exhibitionists were also encouraged to perform at this special event, to be held at the elegant facilities at the Music Academy of the West. Pat was also exhibiting her painting, *Bridget,* which portrayed our friend, Susan Anderson, as a modern version of the Celtic goddess who originated in ancient Ireland and was so powerful that the Catholic Church eventually canonized her because devotees refused to stop worshipping her. She later became one of the patron saints of Ireland.

Class Consciousness

Unfortunately, I would not be able to attend this grand event. I possessed neither artistic nor musical talent and had my first meeting with Pepperdine's 39th EMBA class in Santa Clara on the same weekend. On Friday morning, I boarded a 9:25 United flight to San Jose and arrived 64 minutes later. Class adviser Larry Hebert picked me up at curbside and took me to lunch near Pepperdine's Techmart Center. Larry was lean, muscular and handsome. He looked like a former professional athlete, which is exactly what he was.

He provided a comprehensive overview of the class and the challenges of this particular group. Most of them were in their thirties, from young, high-tech Silicon Valley firms, and at "check-in," I would learn that the majority planned to ride the boom and "cash out" in a few more years. We also had a sprinkling of students from more established firms like IBM, HP and Adobe who had a slightly longer perspective

Classes began at 2:30 on Friday afternoon and continued until ten that evening. On Saturday, they ran from eight to five o'clock. As the only professor for the weekend, it was a much more grueling schedule than most programs where three or four

119

hours was considered a tough assignment. In a perverse way, I preferred this kind of schedule because I could explore subjects in much greater detail—and wouldn't have another session for three weeks. I would usually teach four cases, do couple of exercises, and have at least one student team presentation. By Saturday afternoon, we were all exhausted, and no one complained when I cut the lunch hour to thirty minutes and dismissed the class a little early so that Larry could race me to the airport for a 5:15 flight back to Santa Barbara.

By the time I reached our townhouse, it was seven o'clock, and Pat was engrossed with a sketch of the room arrangements on both floors for the Mission Ridge property. "Look," she said, "this could work out nicely. Obviously, those hideous bay windows will have to go. The kitchen and dining area need to be separated. I think that the current area should be used as a dining area and butler's pantry."

Without pausing to take a breath, she continued. "There may be enough space in the 'dirt room' to install a new kitchen. In the portion of the old courtyard they called 'the family room,' we could extend the ceiling to the top of the second floor with the creation of a northern wall with a couple of arched eight-foot windows. We would then have a magnificent room with twenty-foot ceilings.

"We would definitely enclose the Aztec flue to create space to hang a large painting, remove the indoor fountain with the pissing boy, and enclose Ruth's balcony," she went on. "Unless you plan to sing arias on a regular basis, I'd like to make that into a closet. We need more storage space on the second floor, so I've asked Barbara to set up an appointment tomorrow for us to look at everything again to see if my ideas made sense."

"And how was your class, dear?" I responded. "I know you must be exhausted. While you were gone, I've decided which house we should buy. Would you like to hear about all the decisions I've made or would you prefer to just sign the necessary paperwork?"

In retrospect, it was not a wise response. My only excuse was fatigue. I was tired, but what bothered me most was that every suggestion she made was creative, insightful, and right on target. The only thing worse than Pat's being right was the sickening recognition that my reaction was ill-tempered and boorish. Uncharacteristically, I apologized, eventually, and we started over.

We've discovered that, after a short separation, reentry is often difficult. I suspect that we each have expectations of how the other will react when we get back together, and the actual experience rarely reflects that unspoken anticipation. I had hoped that Pat would meet me in a lovely negligee and serve a four course meal before we headed to bed. She probably wanted me to take her out for an expensive dinner and dancing, after being duly impressed with her creative ideas.

When Pat was speaking to me again, she reported that the *Grande Affaire des Arts* had been a great success."You wouldn't believe how many former businesspeople, doctors and teachers are also good artists!" she beamed. The musical program had been a highlight. Some of the singers and musicians had been very talented, and the others had just as good a time. One of the highlights was a song sung to the melody of "Getting to Know You" but with lyrics reflecting the newcomer experience. Pat was also in a good mood because her *Bridget* was the only art work pictured in the newspaper account of the celebration.

Send in the Clowns

The afternoon was misty as we drove back to Mission Ridge. I parked on the street rather than attempting to navigate the driveway. An 'interesting' wall blocked much of the street view of the house. We made our way around the old rock wall that had provided the foundation for a much newer red brick construction with several levels of "v's" presenting an unusual and unattractive façade to the street.

Imogene and Anita had a birthday party gig, but had made arrangements for us to go through the house and check the accuracy of Pat's sketches. Everything was just as jumbled as before. The intermittent rain made the house seem even more depressing.

Despite these negatives, I was starting to grasp a bit of Pat's vision. Her ideas about the former courtyard could result in a great room and still allow ample space for a beautiful outdoor courtyard.

The "dirt room" was just large enough to create a comfortable food preparation area for two. We couldn't replicate Spago's kitchen, but it would be adequate. Upon closer inspection, we found there was a concrete floor under all the dirt. When we walked up stairs, we found the master bedroom still locked, but Pat had another brilliant idea. "We don't need all of these bedrooms. What if we took the room at the top of the stairway put in bookshelves on both sides and made it into a reading room and library? We could take out the bathtub, use that space to double the size of the closet, and still have a nice half bath."

I was also in a better mood today, so I quickly agreed with the concept. "Maybe I could use this space as an office," I suggested helpfully.

"Oh no," Pat replied, "this would be an attractive space that could be seen from the great room below. (The family room was now officially the great room.) Your office is always so messy; we wouldn't want it to be visible from below."

"All right," I countered, "I'll use the area where the students have their computers, the one with the great ocean views."

Pat didn't think so. "Definitely not, I need that space, with all the light, for my studio. The light would make it hard for you to see the computer screen. I think we might be able to work something out for you in the area behind Anita's room, where she has the kitchenette and closet."

I knew it would be a mistake to say, "That sounds very considerate. You take the large area with the wonderful ocean views and spare me the pain of having to deal with the light and distracting views. The tiny, dark cubbyhole will be good enough for me." Surely, no one will be skeptical if I report that my response was, "That sounds just perfect, dear."

Of course, we were only exploring possibilities, but were edging closer to a decision. Just as we were leaving, Imo and Anita returned from their birthday party. They were wearing authentic clown costumes with baggy pants, wide suspenders, red leather 14-inch clown shoes, white grease paint, red stick-on noses, and raggedy-Ann wigs. Evidently Wolfgang and Amadeus were part of the act and sported fluffy, white tutus.

Anita took off her wig and asked hopefully, "Are you seriously interested in the house?"

"We probably are," Pat replied. "We're trying to figure out what would need to be done to fit our lifestyle and how extensive those changes would be."

Suddenly I saw us from an external perspective. We were standing by garbage cans in a misty rain and negotiating with a couple of ancient clowns—well, at least one. Anita couldn't be called ancient. She was my age.

"If we made an offer," I asked, "how long would you need to give notice to your renters and clear everything out? We have a place to live, and will want to do some work before moving in."

They asked for two months to close on a house in Santa Maria and to clean out the accumulation of decades on Mission Ridge while their tenants made new arrangements. We promised to get back to them before I left for Virginia.

When we called Barbara, she was delighted to hear about our unanimous decision, dutifully incorporated our stipulations, suggested a few of her own, and submitted our offer, a little below their asking price, just before my departure.

We were choosing the wild, tempestuous Dulcinea over the staid, respectable Queen Isabella. Would the sixth offer to purchase result in our becoming Santa Barbara homeowners? Did we really want to take on a project of this magnitude? Could our marriage survive the stresses of a huge renovation effort in an expensive, unfamiliar market?

Chapter 10
A Makeover for Dulcinea

Pat was giving some final instructions to the contractor who was handling the modifications to our townhouse, and I had almost finished packing for Virginia, when Barbara called with "some good news and some bad news."

"Barbara" I said, "things are a bit hectic around here, so if the punch line is, 'Moses says the good news is that I got the number down to ten and the bad news is adultery is still in there,' I've already heard it."

"No, no," Barbara explained, "The good news is that Imo wants to sell the house to 'the woman who paints angels.' Evidently she misunderstood what I said about Pat's goddess paintings, and I didn't want to correct her. Unfortunately for us, they expect another offer tomorrow that will probably be slightly higher than yours."

She suggested we make a second offer that was not conditional on our securing a mortgage. "The only previous expression of interest in the house came from a couple of guys who, at the last minute, weren't able to arrange financing," she explained. "By state law, you will have twenty days to change your mind on any real estate contract, and we should know by then if there is going to be a problem getting a mortgage."

"If you are comfortable with my recommendation" Barbara suggested, "I will meet you at the airport, get your signatures on the revised contract, and try to get Imo to accept the offer before we get into a bidding situation."

I put her on hold while I checked with Pat, who wanted to move ahead. She was now convinced that Mission Ridge would be a wonderful place to live…eventually.

We said goodbye to Hank, the contractor who was to remove the 'cottage cheese' from the ceilings of our townhouse while we were gone, and met Barbara at the airport. We signed the second offer while waiting to check in for our flight to Richmond.

"Oh, by the way," Barbara informed us, "I did some research on Dulcinea. She may have a more illustrious pedigree than we thought. In 1920, Isabella Goodrich Breckinridge, daughter of tire magnate, B. F. Goodrich, bought the lot next to her cousin's new home for the grand sum of ten dollars. Her husband, John Cabell Breckenridge, was the grandson of the U.S. vice president of the same name who came in second to Lincoln in the presidential election of 1860. John and Isabella, built the house immediately, christened it *Casa Alegría*, and lived there until his death in 1942." Barbara concluded, "Mrs. Breckinridge's cousin was also named Isabella, so perhaps this property is destined to become 'Queen Isabella' when you finish with the renovations."

We knew that Barbara was playing us very effectively. Still, it felt good that she was being proactive and nudging us in the direction a slight majority wanted to move. I would have felt even better if she had been able to provide photographs of the Goodrich-Breckinridges entertaining people comparable to those I had noted at the Firestone Winery.

Back to Old Virginny

In Richmond, we collected our luggage and found the car service that provided a shuttle between the airport and Williamsburg. In less than an hour after landing, we were pulling up to our Williamsburg house. It had been two months since either of us had been in Virginia.

In the interim, a winter storm with ice and snow had left a number of broken limbs and one fallen tree in our back yard. Taking care of this would be major item fifteen on the "to do" list for our five-day stay. We weren't going to miss winter (and summer) in Virginia. In California, we only had to worry about earthquakes, fires, floods and mudslides.

The first "to do" was teaching an evening class for William and Mary at the Newport News campus, 22 miles from the main campus. I stopped at Ford's Colony to pick up Bill Kauffman, a former vice president at Black & Decker, who was co-teaching the class. The previous year, we secured a small grant for a team teaching effort to "bring more relevance and pragmatism to the classroom." It was a great success, and Bill had some ideas about dividing responsibility this year.

"Why don't you handle the academics of the program since that's your background?" he suggested. "You do the boring stuff like the course design, covering the assigned readings, and of course, grading. That requires a Ph.D." Bill would be responsible for the good stuff like inviting executive speakers and making sure they addressed course themes rather than just telling 'war stories.' "I'll even handle the entire class on occasion when you can't get back from California," he offered.

"I was going to argue with you about the grading, but since you are cutting me some slack when it's hard to get here, you've got a deal," I responded. When we looked at the class composition, we saw that almost a third of our students did their undergraduate work at one of the service academies—an indication that our class would be filled with bright, confident, challenging and polite men and women.

Bill agreed, "They do everything except salute when we enter the room. I find a little respect endearing. Even without business experience, they definitely understand leadership."

Teaching at the Newport News Center was my favorite William & Mary experience. The students were a little older and typically had more relevant experience than the full-time students at the main campus. The negative was that by 9:00 pm some of them were starting to wilt. Since I had just traveled two thousand miles to get there, it was easy to be sympathetic.

Pat and I worked through all of the fifteen items on our to-do list and made plans to put our Williamsburg house up for sale. Despite our frustrations and disappointments about Williamsburg, we were a little sad to think about selling a house that we had worked so hard to make a home. This chagrin started when we locked the door and headed for the Richmond airport and lasted until we got off the plane in Santa Barbara where the temperature was thirty degrees warmer.

The Contractor and the Steel Magnolia

We were anxious to see the progress Hank and Peggy had made on the remodel of our townhouse. When we arrived, there were lots of signs that someone was getting ready to work with sawhorses, tarps and tools strewn about. Unfortunately, there were no indications of actual work having been done.

Peggy was apologetic, but Hank was defensive. "You didn't tell me you were going to get back so quickly. Another project took longer than anticipated through no fault of ours. We were just about to get started when you walked in."

This did not bode well for our working relationship. I was ready to throttle Hank, but he was younger, bigger and in better shape, so I resorted to a sucker punch. "What do you think about this? Did we not explain when we would be back?" I asked Pat. Hank had all the contractor moves down perfectly. He knew how to lie, scratch his balls and frown, but he had never dealt with a true Southern steel magnolia.

Pat batted her eyelids, smiled, and drawled (her Southern accent gets much more pronounced when she is dealing with recalcitrant males, including her husband), "Why Hank, I'm very disappointed. You must have forgotten our agreement. Here is the schedule we went over a week ago." She reminded him that, while discussing the possibility of handling the Mission Ridge renovation project, he had assured us that they would have removed all the cottage cheese from our ceilings and finished the work in our bedroom before we returned.

"But I understand," she said. "It is a scientific fact that women have better memories than men. That's why you men need instant replays in sports. In a few seconds, you forget what just

127

happened. Now, I want you to write on a sheet of paper *exactly* what you will have done in the next two days. If that isn't done, we will cancel this contract and you can forget about doing any other work for us…or anyone in Newcomers."

The written account of the conversation might sound harsh, but when delivered with a smile and a soft Southern voice, it sounded less like a threat than a promise of great things to come. Hank could see himself managing a mammoth remodeling project on the Riviera and becoming the official contractor for 700 newcomers. He would definitely work on his memory and committed to get us back in the condo quickly.

We managed to sleep one night admist the clutter in our condo, but left the next morning for Los Angeles, where we spent a night at the Sheraton and I put in two days at the Pepperdine office. Barbara called me there and reported that Imo and Anita wanted to meet with us when we got back. I telephoned Michael Arth, whose proposal for a pedestrian-friendly development had excited us a few weeks earlier, and asked if he would join us to share his assessment of the house.

When we returned to Santa Barbara, our ceilings and bedroom looked infinitely better. Hank agreed that he could finish the remaining work in ten days but unfortunately, his memory failed again, some of the work had to be redone, and we were still waiting for the finishing touches after six weeks. Hank would definitely not be adopted by Santa Barbara Newcomers.

"Do you realize," I asked Pat as we were getting ready to meet Barbara at Mission Ridge, "we may be about to purchase a very expensive, almost derelict, house without ever having seen the master bedroom?"

"Well," she responded, "we know the size, we know it has views of the ocean, and we know it will need lots of work. How bad can it be?"

I remembered our first impression of the living room and kitchen, but managed not to say anything.

The Nun's Story

Barbara met us by the gate to Dulcinea. (Neither of us enjoyed navigating the driveway, and who knew how many other vehicles would be squeezed into the parking spaces.) "They want to accept your offer, but have some concerns to discuss. They made several modifications without getting permits and that will have to be addressed before they can provide a certificate of occupancy for a new owner."

We waited a couple of minutes for Michael, and did introductions. Michael was young by our standards, probably in his mid-forties, good-looking and confident. He looked at the tired exterior of the house and commented, "She sits nicely on the lot. With the downward sloping hill, the houses on this side of the street will always show better."

"That's it!" Pat exclaimed, "That's why I didn't like the Mira Vista house. It was on the wrong side of the street."

We rang the front doorbell and, when no one answered, knocked loudly. Evidently the doorbell didn't work either. Anita finally came and greeted us enthusiastically. She led us on a quick tour of the downstairs and Michael was enthusiastic about the potential, especially for what he agreed should be called the great room. Anita was upbeat and almost bubbly. "Imo and I have been looking forward to seeing you. We've been praying that you will be the ones who buy the house."

We didn't know how to reply, so we thanked her and asked if there was any chance of our seeing the master bedroom today. Anita replied, "We have been praying for Denny too, and I think his agoraphobia is getting better. He still doesn't like to leave the room, but I told him that we have the key and we're coming in today. 'Just pull the covers over your head,' I said, 'because we need to show this room to these nice people'."

She marched up the stairs, knocked on the door, and announced, "Denny, we're coming through!" Hesitantly, we entered a spacious room and noticed a large, completely covered lump in the middle of the bed, along with a fireplace and ocean-facing windows. They might provide a nice view; however, the drapes were tightly drawn.

"The view makes Denny nervous," Anita explained as she took us into a large closet area with several windows and still another kitchenette. "Every day, we try to get him to walk a little farther. Yesterday, he walked almost to the stairway." Pat made a quick sketch of the area adjacent to the bedroom and asked to inspect the master bathroom again.

Neither of us was sure how this small, dark bathroom had earned the title of 'master,' but I knew that Pat's muse was speaking to her. After we said goodbye to Denny, she explained, "The bathroom is right next to the balcony I want to make into a closet. We need to turn the old bathroom into another closet and convert the current closet and kitchenette to a larger bathroom. The tub can stay where it is, and we'll move the wall to the other side of the tub. A large walk-in shower should go where the little stove and kitchen sink are located. The basic plumbing connections are already there."

Michael seconded Pat's recommendation about moving the bathroom, but seemed fixated on the uninspiring view of the back yard. He sat on the stairway, looking out the back window, and began making a sketch. Anita and I were impressed by Pat's ingenuity, but I was beginning to worry that this remodel might be more expensive than tearing the house down and starting over.

Anita must have been concerned that her references to all of her prayers might strike us as being overly pious, prim and sanctimonious. She did know that we were Unitarians. After informing us that she liked to collect nun jokes, she started in on one as we descended the stairs. "Two nuns who were helping with some remodeling at the convent were asked to paint a large room. They were worried about getting paint on their habits, so they decided to lock the door of the room, take off their habits, and paint in the nude. Before completing the project, there was a knock at the door. 'Who is it?' called one of the nuns. 'Blind man,' replied a voice from the other side of the door. The two nuns looked at each other, shrugged, and decided that no harm could come from letting a blind man into the room. They opened the door, and the man entered. 'Nice boobs, Sister. Now, where do you want these blinds'?"

I thought the story was funny and surreptitiously glanced at Anita's chest to see if the story might be autobiographical. Michael was still absorbed in his sketching, and Pat probably thought it didn't demonstrate enough feminist sensitivity.

We sat down in front of their family room fireplace, and Barbara explained, "Imo and wants to accept your offer and appreciates the fact that it isn't contingent on financing."

They were concerned that getting a certificate of occupancy, closing and moving to Santa Maria plus cleaning out 30 years of debris would take longer than first anticipated. "They lack the money to hire someone to tear down the arbor in front and the carport in back or remove the three unauthorized sinks." Barbara reported and then asked, "If they accept your original offer, would you extend the closing for another month and take responsibility for getting the certificate of occupancy?"

Picking Lemons

Pat and I exchanged nervous glances. We were finally getting close to a deal, but were we truly ready? "We appreciate your situation and want to be flexible," Pat began quietly. "Your suggestion seems reasonable, but we are a little intimidated by the permitting process in Santa Barbara. We don't know a handyman or contractor whom we trust, so I am not sure how we would go about getting the certificate of occupancy."

Barbara nodded sympathetically and suggested, "Let's go get some lemons from the backyard and talk about this privately."

Michael excused himself and promised to call as soon as he finished sketching what he described as a "dynamite idea that you will absolutely love." As we picked enough fruit for a week's supply of lemonade, Barbara tried to be both reassuring and candid. She told us, "Santa Barbara has more rules and regulations for renovations than anywhere you've lived. Some cynics claim that it takes nine people to change a light bulb in the city—two to fill out the forms and carry them to the planning department, two city employees to do the plan check, three members of the architectural review board to approve, and two attorneys to argue at the hearing about the pros and cons of the proposed modification.

131

"The situation isn't quite that bad, but almost," she went on. "It's easier if you are familiar with the process, but most people do only one or two big projects in a lifetime. "A general contractor can be helpful since they know the hoops to jump through, but I think you should keep things simple."

"We are all for simplicity," I assured her, "and we do need to keep costs down."

"To help you through this initial challenge, I'm going to give you a gift that you will come to appreciate." She handed us the telephone number of Hector Torres, whom she described as "a very intelligent, hard-working young man who works in the city's housing department. He starts at seven o'clock and deals with all aspects of the city's housing construction and repair, but does other projects after work and on Saturdays. "He can do the demolition and has a brother who will haul away the trash. You'll have to hire someone to do drawings so you can get permission to tear down the unauthorized additions."

"Wait a minute," I exclaimed, "Let me see if I understand this. When we have a signed sales contract, the city will send someone to inspect the house. If they find unauthorized changes, they won't give us a certificate of occupancy. We have to hire an architect to do drawings of the proposed changes so we can get a permit allowing us to do what they are requiring us to do? Will we also need a permit every time we want to drive a nail in some poor, innocent piece of wood?"

"That's pretty much the story," Barbara agreed. "The city collects a fee for the original occupancy inspection, for issuing the permit, and for the inspection to prove that you have complied with their requirement. The original architectural drawings were destroyed in the 1925 earthquake, so you have to submit a set of 'as is' renderings as well as detailed drawings for all the proposed changes."

For renovations we had done in Atlanta, New York and Williamsburg, we had never gotten permits. New York had a recommended process, but we brought in a North Carolina carpenter and his wife who stayed with us for two weeks. Between sightseeing expeditions, he built and installed bookcases, cabinets, and a *faux* divider in the foyer.

We sat on the edge of an unfinished garden pond and Pat asked, "What do you think?" She often asks my opinion after the decision is essentially made. It makes me feel masculine to pretend that my input is significant. We had now crossed an emotional line and were thinking about *how* rather than *if.*

"Well," I pontificated, "we certainly don't have any problem with the extra time they have requested." I mused out loud, thinking about the variables. "An ad for our Williamsburg house will run this weekend. If it sells, we will have no trouble with financing. Michael should give us a good price on doing the drawings. Hector sounds like a great resource for getting the occupancy permit without too much difficulty. How do you feel about taking on a huge renovation project?"

"This is the best opportunity we've seen or are likely to find in this market," she responded. "It's almost affordable but will be a huge job. Since you are commuting to Los Angeles, Santa Clara and Williamsburg to make our Santa Barbara dream possible, I'm willing to take on that responsibility."

"I think you've made a good decision," Barbara observed. Since she had done a few remodels and watched previous clients go through the process, she had a little gratuitous advice to add. "There are only two ways you can survive a project of this magnitude. You can get a divorce now or you can make an agreement that nothing you say to each other in anger during the next eighteen months will be taken seriously. Write it up as a contract, sign it, and tape it to your refrigerator door. Don't let a day go by that you don't remind yourself of the promise."

The Cable Guy

We went back in the house, where Barbara made some modifications on our original contract and collected the necessary signatures. We were simultaneously excited and frightened. As we shook hands and wished each other well, Anita added a request. "We've told all of the renters that they will need to leave in a month. We haven't figured out how to handle Denny's agoraphobia, but we'll take care of that.

As you know, Pete works for Cox Cable and has been here twenty years. He hopes you will consider letting him stay. He's
133

a very nice man; quiet, active in his church, never has guests, and enjoys working in the yard."

"He sounds perfect," I responded, "Let's go talk with him." Despite the glowing recommendation, I fully expected to find a version of "Larry the Cable Guy" from the Blue-Collar Comedy Tour: a fat guy in blue jeans, a sleeveless corduroy shirt, and camouflage baseball cap, punctuating his conversation with inane phrases like "Git 'er done!'"

We couldn't have been more surprised when a tanned, muscular man in his early fifties opened the door. He was anxious to talk with us and repeated the interest that Anita had reported, so I asked, "Why don't you tell us a little about yourself and why you like living here?"

He told us that he had grown up in Pennsylvania, graduated from college, and thought California might be an exciting place to live. He moved, got a service job with Cox and had been in Santa Barbara ever since. "After installing cable all over the county, I decided the Riviera was the best place to live. I advertised for something in this area and was delighted when Ruth and Imogene responded. Most of my free time is spent working with my church, working in the yard, or surfing."

"We're glad you want to stay" I replied, "but what would you do during the remodel? It will be messy here for a long time."

"I would like to stay here through the renovation," Pete replied. "My preference would be for you not to make any changes in my studio. You're going to have plenty of other things to do. I'm gone during the day when most of the work will be going on. You might find it helpful to have someone on the site in the evening—especially when it's difficult to secure the premises."

Pat nodded, so I shook his hand and said, "I hope you don't change your mind. This is going to be a big project."

With a slight grin, Pete winked and said, "This old Spanish lady deserves a makeover. I'll be glad to see you git 'er done."

Chapter 11

The Traumas of Transformation

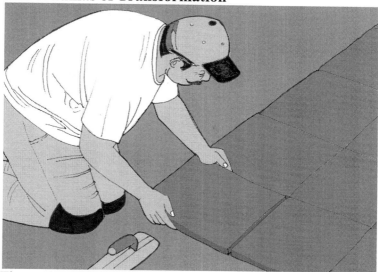

Those 'lazy, hazy, crazy days of last summer' were gone. Without deliberate design, I had become a bicoastal professor who sometimes felt bimodal. In the manic phase, I couldn't believe how lucky we were, but sometimes I got depressed thinking about balancing classes in Northern California and Virginia, taking on leadership roles in Newcomers, and navigating the maze of home ownership and renovation—all while building relationships with fascinating new friends. Starting with a blank calendar and knowing no one, we had managed, in just nine months, to find ourselves in a familiar pattern with too much to do and not enough time to get it done. It was a wonderful, self-inflicted problem!

With new roles in Newcomers, we learned that the fun required hard work and discovered the secret that enabled this transient organization with constant turnover of members and officers to operate with greater efficiency than most corporations.

> *Orientation for Board Members and Activity Committees Here's a chance to have a (free) dinner in a beautiful setting and learn about your new responsibilities. After dinner, you will receive your activity notebooks and have an opportunity to meet with your committee members and do some brainstorming and planning.*

We enjoyed the (free) dinner and seeing new friends, but the highlight of the evening was getting a look at those "activity notebooks." They were the magic elixir, like Coca-Cola's secret formula, for the organization's long-term success.

For years, committee chairs had articulated what made their activity successful. Each new chair was expected to follow the recommended protocol and suggest improvements to assist successors. Out-going committee chairs were available to answer questions and provide insight into the challenges the new group might expect.

Pat had her Visual Arts committee lined up with Julie Lopp, our Unitarian fashion critic; Estelle Meadoff, Pat's eighty-something-year old friend from Memphis with whom we had first talked at the Art Museum; and Dee Kruger, a sexy seventy-year old who had run a building and design firm with her ex-husband, a former professional football player for the Detroit Lions. The committee met efficiently for an hour and outlined half of their programs for the next six months.

I ran back and forth between the Money Talks group and the new Book Writing Committee. Unlike Pat, I accomplished little and was late getting to the Board meeting. I began to suspect that book writing couldn't be done by committee.

A Journey Begins

The next morning, I started on my "to do" list for the house. First, I called Michael Arth to ask if he would do the architectural drawings for the project. He was definitely interested, provided we considered his exciting idea to improve the view from the proposed great room. "You have a great opportunity," he enthused, "to turn that unattractive hillside into something beautiful and dramatic. I specialize in the design of 'water features,' and your back yard topography is perfect for a six-foot waterfall."

"That sounds great," I replied, "just don't create a shark tank in our back yard. How soon can you do the drawings?"

"As soon as Anita and Imo clear out some of the junk," he promised, "I will take lots of photographs, do measurements and run some elevations. After everyone moves out, I should have the drawings ready in a week."

Next, I called the number for handyman extraordinaire, Hector Torres. He agreed to meet us on Mission Ridge when he got off from his city job. We got permission from Imogene, and looked forward to meeting someone Barbara had described as "a part-time Superman."

Hector *was* impressive. Almost movie-star handsome and in his late 30s, he radiated a sense of calm, cheerful self-confidence. He immediately spotted the items that the city would require us to address. "As soon as you know the date of your closing, let me know and I will schedule the demolition that afternoon. I know you want to move quickly and get things started."

His quick grasp of the situation, pragmatic advice and engaging manner made both of us want to know more about him. "I'm one of five siblings," he told us. "My parents emigrated from Mexico when we were young. Some of us went to college, and one brother is in medical school. Three of us are in construction. I've been working for the city for twenty years."

"In a few more years, you could probably retire. Do you plan to do that or stay with the city's housing authority?" I asked.

"Right now, I'm trying to learn as much as I can about the construction business. With the City, I'm getting exposure to every aspect of housing and working with some of the area's best contractors. Also, I like having health insurance. At some point, I'll probably get my general contractor's license and go in business for myself," Hector explained.

We knew instinctively that we could trust Hector and would enjoy working with him. Pat asked, "Would you be willing to take on our renovation? That experience could be helpful in moving you toward your goal of becoming a general contractor. If things go well," she added, "we would be very supportive and do anything in our power to help you achieve that goal."

"To be honest" Hector replied, "I've never undertaken a project this large. I don't want to promise something I can't deliver,

137

but I will be glad to advise you as you work on the plans. Perhaps we can sit down with your architect and figure out what needs to be done. Then, I can let you know if I can handle the project or just do parts of it. If it's too big for me, I can recommend a couple of contractors for you to consider."

When we were back at East Beach, I called Barbara Sanchez to report on our conversation with Hector and to thank her for the gift of his telephone number. "I am pleased, but not surprised, that you like Hector so much," she said. "Your renovation would be the biggest project he's ever undertaken, but I think he could do it and it would be good for his personal development. Will you be home for a little while?" She wanted to come by and drop off a couple of other gifts for us.

After protesting, feebly, that she had already done enough, I invited her over. We greeted her with champagne and camembert when she arrived a few minutes later. "We are really grateful," Pat said, "for all of your assistance in making this work out. You have listened, responded appropriately, and nudged us and Imogene in just the right directions." We raised our glasses to toast "the best realtor we know!"

An Enchanted Evening

We waited for Barbara to reveal her additional gifts. "I admire your ability to see possibilities rather than problems," she said. "The path you have chosen won't be easy, so I'm giving you two things to be helpful. First is a gift certificate for dinner at your soon-to-be new neighbor, the El Encanto Hotel. I hope you go soon and make it a romantic celebration you look back on and remember when you're in the middle of problems with the project." Her second gift was two hours of consulting with a former city employee who now advised people on navigating the challenging maze of planning and permits.

We were overwhelmed, hugged Barbara enthusiastically, and repeated our proclamations of pleasure in working with her. As soon as she left, we called the El Encanto, made reservations for dinner and looked forward to exploring one of America's unique, small hotels located a block from our new house.

Tucked in the center of the Mission Ridge neighborhood and almost hidden by vegetation, we found a cottage-style hotel, a frequent weekend destination for Hollywood celebrities who wanted a quiet getaway. Before going to the restaurant, we explored their extensive grounds which featured flowering terraces and vine-covered arbors, a magnificent lily pond, and a trickling waterfall. The setting was breathtakingly romantic.

We were arm in arm as we walked into the hotel lobby and found the dining room. With twinkling lights all around the coastline, the view from the terrace restaurant at sunset was stunning. We listened to crickets enjoying amorous adventures in the gardens, sat back in wrought iron armchairs, examined the menu and realized just how generous Barbara had been. We probably wouldn't be popping in for dinner on a weekly basis.

We began by resisting the temptation to order some 1993 Dom Perignon for $194 and selected a local Foxen pinot noir instead. The champagne we had shared with Barbara wasn't Dom's, but was celebratory enough for one evening. Pat ordered a salad of organic baby field greens that included Stilton cheese, sliced pear, toasted pine nuts and balsamic vinaigrette, and I chose sautéed calamari with Fuji apple. As usual, we sampled each other's dishes and decided to share an entrée of herb roasted rack of lamb with garlic. This was filling, but we were in a sharing mood and split a large 'floating island' dessert while talking about how much we were going to enjoy living in the best part of Santa Barbara. This was a 'happy meal' that McDonald's would never match.

X Marks the Spot

After my next teaching weekend in Santa Clara, Michael Arth called to report that he was ready for us to review his drawings and a couple of suggestions. We coordinated a time that would also work for Hector and suggested that Michael come a few minutes early to discuss the proposals.

His external perspectives and internal layouts were crisp, clean, accurate and artistic. The sketches of the proposed water feature were imaginative and dramatic. After accepting our compliments, he continued, "I have one other sketch for you. Your comment about not wanting a shark tank got me thinking.

Remember Pat's idea of having eight-foot windows above an eight-foot retaining wall on the northern side of your great room? Just imagine how impressive it would be to go down six more feet and install heavy, pressure-resistant glass instead of a concrete retaining wall. Then, you could sit on your sofa and see large tropical fish swimming at the foot of the waterfall."

With a flourish, Michael presented a magnificent drawing that Sea World would love, if only they could afford it. I chose my words carefully, trying not to dampen his enthusiasm. "It's a brilliant concept, but we don't have the financial resources to build it or the energy to maintain it. I love your first drawing with a five-foot waterfall. That is even grander than the water feature at El Encanto."

Michael was partially mollified by the time Hector arrived, and we sat down to work on our proposed changes. Pat's earlier suggestions were accepted unanimously. They were good ideas, and she was the client. Michael tried to sell a reduced version of his aquarium wall, but Hector earned points by reminding us that he would probably need to dig down ten feet to create a drain that would divert the hillside runoff when Santa Barbara experienced an occasional heavy rain.

The best new idea of the day came when Hector pointed to the drawing of the small porches outside Pat's studio and Pete's efficiency. "Between these two porches, Michael shows the wooden stairway going down to the utility room. If we take out the stairs and utility room door, extend the two porches and connect them, you would have better aesthetics and create over 200 square feet of additional living space below."

It was an excellent idea. More importantly, it signaled that Hector was seeing himself as a major part of the renovation. He explained what we should expect at the planning department. "Each time you request a permit, you'll submit a drawing of the current situation and another that shows what you propose. You'll want to break the project up into segments," he explained, "Obviously, the certificate of occupancy issues will be first. That will be a piece of cake. Just use two copies of Michael's drawing. On the second, we'll put an 'X' indicating the removal of the carport, trellis and the unauthorized sinks."

Permits Please

"What permit should we request next?" I asked tentatively.

"You can do improvements like painting, resurfacing floors or upgrading bathroom fixtures without permits," Hector explained, "but I would start with a proposal to create a kitchen in what you call 'the dirt room' and moving the master bathroom. Both projects are pretty straightforward and will give you a sense of how the system works. We can tackle the great room and water feature later. Does that make sense to you, Michael?"

"It does," Michael answered, "I'll need a more time to do the cross sections and detailed drawings for the water feature and great room. We'll need a structural engineer do some calculations then. Can you recommend anyone?"

"Norm is a former city engineer who retired several years ago. I'll use him to review the work in the new kitchen. By the way," Hector added, "you should request permits as an 'owner-builder.' They will probably give you a little more leeway than they would a regular contractor."

"We'll try that as long as they don't ask too many technical questions," Pat replied.

As Hector and Michael started to leave, Hector wanted to make sure we understood the task ahead. "Building a basic ranch house involves 40,000 decisions. This kind of renovation will require many more," he said. "Most general contractors will recommend that you tear everything down and start over. That would be much easier, and I recommend that you talk to a couple and get estimates."

If he decided to work with us, Hector's goal would be to do the job for half of what a contractor would charge, but "I will only work on a time and materials basis." He explained, "That way, you can change your minds as much as you want to, and we will be less likely to have major misunderstandings."

"Actually, we prefer that," Pat said. "Contractors need to bid in an extra forty percent just in case they overlook something.

We like old houses and don't want to consider demolishing it for economic and ecological reasons. We like the flexibility you propose and hope we'll be working together."

Our lives seemed hectic before the closing, but the pace quickly moved to double-time. The closing went smoothly. Hector did the demolitions efficiently, and Michael prepared drawing for our new kitchen and master bathroom. We were ready to meet the fabled consultant who would show us how to breeze through the city's planning obstacle course.

Unfortunately, she wasn't in the same league with Barbara, Michael, and Hector. As with many professionals who are paid by the hour, she was an excellent conversationalist, interested in us and our backgrounds, and happy to tell us about her experiences. Before our two-hour gift had expired, she managed to make a few modest suggestions and to mention that she would be willing to continue working for us. We were anxious to test the waters and blithely set off to the Planning Department's Garden Street offices. Pat is generally more charming than I, especially to men, so she volunteered to submit our proposal while I graded papers in the car.

"That was simple!" she informed me cheerfully upon her rapid return. "They'll review our plan and let us know in four days."

"I didn't think that handing the proposal in would be hard," I quipped, "but let's see what they say next week."

Money Mumbles

We didn't just sit and wait for their response. Pat was coordinating a studio visit for the visual arts group. I had another trip to Virginia and a "Money Talks" program to manage. Dwight, a senior VP for a local brokerage firm, volunteered to help put together a description of the session.

> *Starting with ceoexpress.com (a website designed by and for busy CEOs), we'll take a quick look at some of the free resources on the Internet that can provide efficient ways to track finances, do research on stocks or mutual funds, manage your portfolio, pay bills online or screen investment alternatives according to your criteria.*

Dwight assured me, "I've been a consultant to several Internet companies and have decades of experience with the medium."

That should have been a red flag. At this point, even Al Gore didn't have decades of Internet experience! Dwight offered to host us at his office and promised to provide everything we needed. Just to be safe, I came directly from the airport and arrived two hours early to check on the setup.

"I must be missing something," I commented diplomatically, "this conference room is large enough, but I don't see a computer or Internet connection."

"Oh, I thought you would bring a laptop. We can probably run an extension cord from the computer in our reception area," Dwight replied with a breath that reminded me of the Scotch-tasting session a few months earlier.

"Do you have an LCD projector so the participants can actually see what we're talking about?" I asked.

"Oops," he grinned, "I must have forgotten that. Maybe we can just huddle together so we can all see your laptop screen."

None of our attendees were going to enjoy 'huddling' within range of Dwight's alcoholic aroma. Fortunately, I did have a laptop in my car and knew an attorney with offices in the same building. Even though it was almost seven o'clock, she was still drafting pleadings for a client and agreed to let us use her conference room, LCD projector and Internet connection. Pat volunteered to redirect any registrants to our new location while I hustled off to find my laptop and get the computer and projector in operation.

Everyone nibbled on refreshments while I played with cables and encouraged Dwight to have another cup of coffee. We were only a few minutes behind schedule when I demonstrated ceoexpress.com and some of the analytics provided by Schwab and Fidelity. Today, everyone has access to these resources, but most of the audience seemed to be learning about tools they had not used before.

After exhausting my limited repertoire, I crossed my fingers and asked Dwight if he was ready to elaborate on some more advanced concepts. He never made a single slurred reference to using the Internet. Instead, he rambled for ten minutes about important people he knew and companies that might be great investments before I thanked him and dismissed the session. The City Planning Department had to be easier than this.

You Can Fight City Hall

We were disappointed to learn that our initial proposal had generated twelve issues that had to be resolved. Reluctantly, we went back to the former city employee and asked her to translate some of these 'requests.' She was helpful in explaining the terminology and showing us how to mark the documents to indicate our projected compliance. Now, I thought we are starting to get the hang of this. We resubmitted and waited confidently for the full approval of our proposal.

Pat almost never cries, so I knew something serious had happened when she came home in tears, clutching our crumpled project submission. "You won't believe this," she sobbed. "We addressed their twelve issues, and they've come back with *fifty-eight* other requests. I don't think we'll ever get through this process. The department is run by Nazis! I wanted to tell the woman commandant that I've never had to deal with such stupid bureaucracy anywhere we've lived. I'm never going there again!"

"Perhaps it would be better for me to go next time," I suggested, "in case you really did tell them off. Let's look at the kind of requests they're making."

We spread out the plans on our kitchen table. I might be missing something, but they seemed to have moved from twelve broad directives to fifty-eight specifics with several iterations of the same requirement. For example, there were six notations indicating that we should provide information about the type of electrical outlet to be spaced throughout the kitchen.

Days later, we sat down with Michael's new set of plans and tried to address each of their fifty-eight concerns.

I went back to the planning office, with detailed notations on a fresh set of drawings to address each item. Keeping Pat's vivid description of the 'commandant' in mind, I waited a few feet away from the planning review counter until I sensed an opportunity to talk with someone who didn't sport a swastika and looked pleasant or understanding. Allison was an attractive blonde with a nice smile. I showed her our drawings and said, "Hopefully, we've addressed all the issues. We've never had to provide this kind of detail before, and my wife was traumatized when we moved from twelve to fifty-eight problems."

Allison checked the address of our project and replied, "I remember your wife. I really felt sorry for her and apologize for the way she was treated. Marina could have been much more diplomatic."

"Thanks for saying that," I responded. "We may not understand the Santa Barbara process, but we want the same thing as the Planning Department. We want to make a run-down house safer and more attractive. If we understand what you want, we will work hard to get it done. I know you can't give us a decision now, but could you take a quick look at our response to see if we are going about this in an acceptable way?"

About this time, Allison was joined by David, a tall, slender man, who looked like a former basketball player. He added, "I did the last plan check and tried to provide enough detail for you to see exactly what needed to be done. I'm sorry that no one explained to your wife why the number of issues seemed to increase so dramatically."

They were pleasant people who indicated that we were on the right track. I felt better about our prospects for approval. In just a couple of days, we received the official 'go-ahead.' Actually, we were already going ahead with the work that didn't require permitting. With the house empty and relatively clean, it was much less depressing. Hector had agreed to supervise the entire project except for the construction of the great room which would require a licensed general contractor, and introduced us to 'Uncle Beto' and his helper, Juan. They began laying tile in what Pat had claimed as her studio.

The Traumatized Tile Man

I didn't grouse very much about beginning the project in Pat's area. She was going to be spending lots of time in the house, and the studio area needed relatively little work.

She became increasingly frustrated as Uncle Beto, who was probably our age, carefully examined each piece of tile as if it might reveal the mysteries of the universe to him before adding the cement and slowly, very slowly, putting it in place. This relatively simple task took twice as long to complete as we had estimated. Pat checked on his progress regularly, and when she asked if Beto could work a little faster, I feared that Hector might complain about her interference. Instead, he calmly related the message, in Spanish, to his uncle.

The usually taciturn Beto responded with a dramatic torrent of *español.* I managed to catch, "¡*Mi dios! No puedo tomarlo más"* before my limited powers of translation lost track, but the message was clear. The traumatized tile man "couldn't take it anymore." In fact, Hector solemnly informed us that his uncle had decided to retire and would not be working with us on the other rooms that required substantial amounts of tile.

Pat refused to admit that this was a problem. "It's probably a good thing that we found out early," she reasoned. "We would have spent our entire renovation budget on tile. I'll bet we can find someone better and less expensive."

We quickly learned that Beto's helper, Juan, had many talents, including a facility with stonework and tile. Hector asked if we could provide lodging for Juan. "He's lost the place he was living and is sleeping on someone's porch. Would you let him stay in Bob's office area? There is a bathroom nearby, and we won't be doing work there for several months."

Juan was a cheerful guy, and we were happy to make this modest contribution to solving Santa Barbara's 'homeless problem.' We liked all of Hector's team. I don't know where the stereotype of 'lazy Mexicans' originated. Several workers lived in Ventura. They left home each morning at six o'clock and worked on other jobs until mid-afternoon, when they started on our project. They stayed until it was too dark for further work. On Saturdays, they arrived before eight o'clock and worked ten hours or more. Juan was full-time with us, and so was a pleasant, industrious young man, Alberto, who saw Hector as a role model.

They clearly enjoyed working together and kidded each other extensively. Several times, someone called Hector 'Kaliman' in a jocular manner. Occasionally, they would refer to Alberto as 'Solín.' Most of their communication was in Spanish, so I asked Hector, "Are they giving you a hard time or just kidding?"

"I like to think it's a sign of affection," he explained. "Kaliman was a famous Mexican comic-book hero when we were growing up. The comic books described the adventures of Kaliman and his young companion Solín, an Egyptian kid who descended from the Pharaohs. Kaliman had extensive mental powers like levitation, telepathy, remote viewing, telekinesis, and astral projection. I haven't gotten there yet, but it would be nice to levitate and not have to move these ladders around."

Pat also had a creative idea to expand our tile-laying options. Her son, Brad, was struggling in the movie business and agreed to supplement his Ivy League degree with a postgraduate class at Home Depot. Brad's wife Keiko joined him, and soon they had more than tripled our tile capability. Both were artistic, and our flooring moved from Beto's basic to a variety of intricate designs with inset diamonds of tumbled marble or a different-colored tile intermingled with the principal choice. Eventually, they graduated to applying the same creativity to shower enclosures, kitchen counter backsplashes and fireplace facings.

Architectural Flaws

Somewhere in the midst of dealing with the traumas of city bureaucracy and our first experience with labor unrest, Michael gave us his detailed drawings for the great room and water feature. Before submitting for City review, I checked them one more time. "Wait a minute, Michael, we didn't agree to a swimming pool and hot tub. That would push our costs way beyond what we can handle. Plus, we've found that a pool is more trouble than joy...and we're getting to an age when we don't enjoy lying around outside with most of our clothes off."

147

"The waterfall, pool and hot tub are part of an integrated design," Michael explained, somewhat defensively. "You're already doing most of the excavation so the incremental cost would be minor. This plan would greatly increase the value of your property and be the focal point in the house or yard."

"Give me some specific estimates," I suggested, "and we'll make a decision. Now, what happened to the new closet that was to replace Ruth's balcony?"

"That's not going to work," Michael replied. "If you enclose the balcony area, you won't be able to see the waterfall from your master bedroom. The overall effect will be much more dramatic if we open up your bedroom so you can see the water feature from your bed or the sitting area beside it."

My efforts to reason with Michael were proving unsuccessful when Pat entered and ended the debate. "Michael, let me be very clear about this. A walk-in closet is more important to me than the damn water feature!"

Michael put both hands on his head in a childlike gesture of disbelief and frustration and exclaimed, "It's a tragedy! It's a travesty! The Philistines win again! No one appreciates a true artist!" as he stormed out of the house.

Later that evening, I explained to Michael that there were only two ways to argue with Pat, but unfortunately, neither of them worked. Eventually, I managed to console him, complemented the original concept of the waterfall and persuaded him to re-draw the specifications according to his client's instructions.

In the second quarter of the year (and century), we celebrated the sale of our Virginia property and the completion of the upgrades for our East Beach townhouse. We went back to Virginia for my last classes and to supervise the packing for our move. Traveling between Santa Barbra and Williamsburg was the longest commute in my career, and the long-distance professorship was not very satisfactory for me or the college. I became *Professor Emeritus* at William & Mary and agreed to teach an extra course at Pepperdine.

United Van Lines delivered our furniture and other household goods to Mission Ridge. We put boxes and furniture in the master bedroom and throughout the downstairs. We bought a huge quantity of inexpensive blankets and tried to cover everything to protect against dust and grime. The house was looking, depressingly, very much as it had when we first saw it.

Fortunately, we made time for a few Newcomer activities to distract us, if briefly, from the bedlam on Mission Ridge. We enjoyed an ice cream social at the home of Tom and Judy Nelson, who had joined Newcomers with us. I asked Tom if they had 39 flavors, and he replied that Baskin-Robbins wasn't the apex of his aspirations. "I just heard a PBS story about an ice cream shop in Venezuela that sells 567 flavors, including onion, chili, beer, eggplant, smoked trout, chicken with rice, and spinach." Unfortunately (or, perhaps, fortunately), the Nelsons only offered vanilla, chocolate, and peach.

We assured Tom that we preferred homemade peach to eggplant ice cream, and began to mingle with friends we were starting to neglect. After working the room for a few minutes, I sat down with other members of the Nominating Committee and discussed potential leaders for the next six months. Darlene Amundson would succeed Ellen Lilley as president and Pat's friend, Dee Kruger, would become Activities Vice President. Dee was becoming an increasingly vital part of the renovation effort because of her extensive experience as a decorator and builder. Pat referred to Dee as my "editor" because she was a wise, dependable sounding board and source for ideas.

Summer was approaching with a new flurry of activities, but not the non-stop fun we had experienced the previous year. We missed the Big Dog Parade and only watched half of the Solstice celebration because we had to pick up supplies. The renovation was proving to be more of a wrestling match than a waltz. We'd been traumatized by bureaucracy and inflicted trauma on our architect and tile man. We were learning daily lessons in humility and hoping that our plans for transformation wouldn't include divorce, bankruptcy or a padded cell.

Chapter 12
Casa de Alégria or *Hoya de Diñero?*

Why did we agree to have a Newcomers' "Life Styles" party just as our renovation was getting started? Certainly, we had more than enough to do without agreeing to host an event for our favorite organization. But six weeks before the actual event, we were confident that everything was under control. We had gotten approval to move the kitchen and master bathroom. Our work crew was energized and efficient. Within a month, I would turn in grades at William & Mary and Pepperdine.

The work was just getting started, of course, but the possibility of sharing our project with friends seemed like a good idea at the time. Dee Krueger, Pat's 'editor' and Newcomer VP of Activities convinced us, "Hosting a Newcomers party is like having a party in a box," she said. "You really don't have to do anything except welcome people and explain your plans. The committee will arrange for the food with each couple providing *hors d'oeuvres* for ten, bring the wine, set up the event and clean up afterwards. What could be easier than that? I'll even write the announcement for the event."

We reluctantly agreed. After all, it was six weeks away. Then the newsletter came out, and the three remaining weeks felt very near as we read:

Life Styles: A California-Spanish Hacienda in the Remaking

Pat and Bob Fulmer have purchased a California-Spanish Hacienda built in 1920 and owned from 1964 until early 2000 by 'two women with great musical talent, but less architectural and aesthetic perspective.' The original owner christened the residence Casa de Alegría (house of happiness) but the Fulmers, in the midst of a major renovation, have renamed it La Hoyo de Diñero (the pit of money). Currently the Fulmers are trying to personally manage the labyrinth of securing permits and general contracting much of the construction work. That way, they can control the project to re-create the original excellence of Alegria with their own modern touches. Join us to hear the stories, hopes, plans, and frustration of these courageous Newcomers.

We were apprehensive, but there wasn't much we could do at the moment, so we took time to attend a picnic dinner and concert at the Music Academy of the West. For more than fifty years, scores of gifted young classical singers and instrumentalists, competitively selected for their talent, had gathered for eight weeks in Santa Barbara to study and make music with illustrious guest artists, conductors, and faculty. The public gets to enjoy over a hundred of these events each year, almost half of them free. We enjoyed cold fried chicken, potato salad and chardonnay on the luxurious grounds of *Miraflores*, ("look at the flowers"), the palatial former winter residence of John Jefferson. After eating too much, we headed to Abravanel (now Hahn) Hall to hear some of the best young musicians demonstrate their virtuosity in a variety of vocals and instrumental favorites. Afterwards, we mingled, chatted with a couple of the performers and got home past our usual bedtime, which we liked to describe as "1:30am, Eastern time."

A little too early the next morning, Hector gave us a wake-up call. "I've got some bad news for you!" he reported.

"Aren't you supposed to preface that with 'I've got some good news and...?" I asked.

"I'm afraid this is just bad news," Hector replied. "We've run into serious problems with the sewer lines in the house and

151

with the outside drainage. We're going to have to do a lot more digging and excavation than anticipated."

"That does sound a little frightening," I responded. "Just what does that mean? Could you talk me down a bit?"

"It just means that Juan and Alberto will be spending the next three or four weeks digging trenches inside your dining room and trying to get rid of the 'pour in place' concrete that is blocking our work on the French drain in the back yard."

"Slow down a minute," I asked. "I'm sure the French can make drainage sexy, but can't we just go with a plain American drain? You know we're on a tight budget."

Hector spoke slowly as he tried to explain. (I had been getting lots of patient explanations with an almost pitying concern about my lack of comprehension.) "There's nothing sexy about a French drain. It's just a ditch covered with gravel or rock that redirects surface and ground water away from an area like the back of your house. It looks like we're going to have to go down about twelve feet to accommodate the waterfall and keep water away from the great room. When the previous owner was trying to divert runoff, they just dug down and poured concrete in some key places without a form. That makes it difficult for us to dig it out and do it right."

"Okay," I said, "But what's the problem with the sewer?"

"Basically, the issue is age." Hector continued in his role as special ed tutor. "You've had a lot of ugly stuff coming through those pipes for eighty years and they are starting to crumble. We'll have to dig trenches to get at them in the old kitchen area and continue all the way to the exterior wall. Hopefully, we can use 'trenchless piping' once we get outside."

"That sounds expensive," I moaned, "but there doesn't appear to be a good alternative. We don't want to finish everything and find out that the sewage is leaking out under the house."

"No, I don't think you do," Hector agreed," We're probably lucky to have discovered it at this point. So, as we say in the sewer business, 'here's mud in your eye'."

Down Market Life Styles

Two weeks later, it was clear that we were in trouble when a battered old van wheezed up our drive and a shabbily dressed couple unloaded and started checking out the rubble and disarray. Cautiously, I walked out and asked if I could help them. "Oh," said the woman, "we thought the house might have been abandoned. I guess it isn't, huh?"

We had hopes for better days, for the house as well as our uninvited guests, and stopped complaining, at least for a little while, about our problems.

Three days later, a maze of open trenches welcomed seventy guests to a unique event for the Life Styles Committee. They had hosted reviews of "A Montecito Makeover," "A Transformation on Campanili Hill," and "Of House and Horse in Hope Ranch"—all impressively elegant (and completed) projects. They had never, and would never again, I suspect, have an event where participants walked across planks that covered open trenches to move from room to room. Furniture and boxes were draped with bedding. Two-claw footed bathtubs had been moved to the backyard for sanding and refinishing. The excavation for the plain French drain was only half completed, but still resembled a miniature Grand Canyon.

We doubled our umbrella policy's liability insurance coverage and still hovered around, constantly warning people about potential dangers. For most events, the committee only would serve Chardonnay because of staining carpets and rugs if red wines were spilled. For our event, Zinfandel and Merlot were cheerfully provided and no one worried about spillage. The guests were politely appreciative of the challenge, our audacity in undertaking the project and for allowing them to realize how much worse their own projects could have been.

The 'program' consisted of our standing on the stairway in the now totally open great room and attempting to explain our vision. I could have used Ruth's balcony, but it was already framed and partially enclosed for Pat's closet. I tried to convince our guests:

"You may find it hard to believe, but the house actually looked worse when we bought it. The open courtyard where you are standing is original. When we first saw it, it was covered by fiberglass sheets partially supported by flimsy panels from a demolished hothouse. We have restored the original clutter and added the trenches, excavation and outdoor bathtubs. I hope you appreciate our taste and decor."

We earned a bit of sympathy, but not much envy. As the committee members were packing up (there wasn't much cleaning to do), Dee shocked us with the suggestion. "You know, it would be fun to have another event in about a year when the project is finished. Several people suggested that they enjoyed the 'before' and would like to see the 'after'."

Pat and I shook our heads in disbelief and decided to bite our tongues rather than shouting, "No way, José!" We didn't want to upset Dee or offend any of our workers. Instead, we replied, "Let's wait and see how we feel in a few months."

Grandma's Enterprises

Julie Lopp was a serial entrepreneur who had started businesses in Nevada, Los Angeles and the Bay Area who was moving slowly in redecorating the house she and Don had purchased. Julie recognized Pat's artistic judgment and suggested that they join forces in one of her ventures. "Why don't you become a senior buyer for Grandma's Enterprises?" She asked, then added, "We can get into the LA Merchandise Mart, order items at wholesale or decorator prices, and maybe even make a buying trip or two to Mexico."

Pat was a veteran of the Atlanta Mart and always ready for a road trip or a chance to save money. She and daughter-in-law Keiko had made one exploratory Tijuana visit to purchase tumbled marble tile, along with some handmade Mexican tile. I tried to warn about potential dangers for two women traveling together, but Pat, who is typically fearless, responded, "Oh, there's nothing to worry about. Hector says we just go across the border and take the first exit past the airport and we should see lots of places selling tile."

They did return safely, but exasperated with the time spent trying to find their destination. Pat complained, "Hector, your directions were terrible! We kept stopping and asking, '¿Dónde es aeropuerto?' but no one would help. They just shrugged and said, 'No entiendo.' Do you think they didn't know where the airport was or didn't understand our pronunciation?"

"It's hard to say," Hector replied. "Many of the people would never have been to an airport. They could also have been confused by hearing an approximation of Spanish spoken in Tennessee or Japanese accents. You probably didn't gesture or talk loudly enough to compensate for that. Now, you've picked out some excellent tile, but did you save enough to justify driving six hours each way?"

We didn't get a satisfactory answer for a while. I recognized that Pat enjoyed a sense of adventure and having stories to tell her more cautious (or less foolhardy) friends. Julie spoke fluent Spanish, so I would worry less about the buying trip on behalf of Grandma's Enterprises they began to plan.

The next expedition included Julie and Dee. This trip to Rosarito was focused on ironwork and, hopefully, granite for countertops. They left Santa Barbara a little after noon, later than planned, with the same level of precision in directions as before, this time for "un maravilloso hotel" recommended by one of our workers. Rosarito is only twenty miles south of the border on a "modern scenic coastal toll road," but Julie's Spanish proficiency wasn't enough for them to find their 'wonderful hotel' without much confusion and wasted time.

Finally, in the dark and cold, they located the 'resort hotel' that charged twenty-four dollars for a room with two double beds and cot. They were too tired to look further, splurged an extra dollar for firewood, built a fire, enjoyed a light dinner in the hotel coffee shop and went to sleep quickly.

That's their official story. Neither of them will admit to having enjoyed or even known about the notorious nightlife of Rosarito. The next day they parked at the Rosarito Beach Hotel because they had to walk under the hotel's legendary sign, "Through these doors pass the most beautiful women in the world!"

A Deal Too Good to Good to be True

Eventually, they started shopping and discovered an excellent, but somewhat hidden, artisan *mercado*. They bought some wrought-iron outdoor furniture, a couple of wood carvings and a few artistic mirrors with hammered tin and tile—enough to fill the van to capacity and make the seating for the return trip cramped and potentially dangerous. The real find, however, was the discovery of Raymondo Franco's shop.

As we unloaded their bounty, much of it going to Julie's place, Pat was almost rhapsodic. "You won't believe what a great deal I found on granite countertops for the kitchen!" she said. "The best estimate I got here was almost four thousand dollars. Franco has a tremendous selection and gave me four samples. He showed us pictures of some impressive installations he's done in California. We'll choose the color and send the kitchen dimensions and a check for $650. Four weeks later, he'll come and install everything for us. When he finishes, we will owe him another $650. Isn't this is almost too good to be true? Hector can't say that this trip didn't save us money!"

I tend to be skeptical of anything that is 'too good to be true.' Nevertheless, the samples were attractive and the price was right. We made our selection for a color called 'golden oak' and sent off a check the next morning.

Hector didn't comment, but we thought he was impressed. As we became friends, Hector was beginning to feel free to tease us just as he did his work crew. We had talked a little about his family, his work for the City and the summer Olympics in Sydney when he asked, Do either of you know why Mexico didn't send any competitors to Australia?"

"I have no idea," I answered, "but I suspect you'll tell us."

"Because every Mexican who could run, jump or swim is already in California!" he informed us with a grin.

"That's a great line for you, Hector, but I probably won't be repeating it," I said. "On the other hand, I may get by with telling 'redneck' jokes better than you."

He turned to Pat and asked, "*¿Cuál es el próximo viaje de los tres mosqueteros?*" Seeing our blank looks, he explained, "I assumed that you were fluent in Spanish since you have now spent almost as much time in Mexico as I have. I'm just asking what the next road trip is for the three musketeers."

Pat explained that on my next drive to Pepperdine, she and Julie were going to check out a tile place she had heard about, explore the Merchandise Mart and, hopefully, find some decorative cabinets to use in the bathrooms.

Before that trip, I had to deal with a problem in our plans for the great room and water feature. Michael had convinced me to include a hot tub and swimming pool heated with solar panels in our application for permits. Our request had come back indicating that the solar panels would require approval from the ABR (Architectural Board of Review). Conversations with pool companies generated estimates running twice as much as Michael's 'rough guess.' "Look, Michael," I finally said, "We know you love the idea of the integrated design for the pool and spa area, and I agree with every aspect of the plan except the cost, but we *are* cutting back and need some drawings to reflect our reality rather than your aesthetic sense."

This was the firmest I had been, and Michael finally accepted that his dramatic design wasn't going to be constructed, at least not now and definitely not by us. He was a bit grumpy, and perhaps a little passive-aggressive, when he provided the revised drawings. There was a significantly more detail about the enclosed area where we wanted to eliminate a stairway to the utility room. Pat pointed this out and suggested, "Let's erase most of this detail. They haven't asked for it, and I'd rather not reduce our flexibility more than necessary."

The Devious Duo

"If you insist," Michael said, "I can see you want to be devious.

Hector thought this was a hilarious accusation. "Pat and Dee are the 'devious duo.' That sounds like fun." He added, "Perhaps I can learn to be devious too."

157

Some of my Pepperdine classes were at the beautiful Malibu campus. More often, they were in West LA near the airport. The commute was through two of the ten worst interchanges in the country. The trip could take less than ninety minutes (at midnight) or up to four hours during rain or after an accident.

One day, we made the trip; Pat dropped me at my office and went to check out the 22,000-square-foot warehouse of OTW Ceramic Tile in downtown Los Angeles. She came back that evening more excited than after the first trip to Mexico. "They have the best selection I've ever seen," she exclaimed. "I bought some porcelain tile, honed charcoal marble, limestone tile and Spanish pavers. We'll get the rest of our tile here. It's better than what we bought in Mexico, there's greater selection, and it's less expensive!" We agreed that we would go by to pick up her purchases the next day after I finished work and after she and Julie were through at the Mart.

We finally had an answer to the question about the value added by the additional twelve hours of driving time to Mexico.

Early next morning, the top executives of Grandma's Enterprises met at the overwhelmingly spacious LA Mart. With over three hundred permanent exhibitors, the choices were almost infinite. Julie and Pat had enough experience to focus on manufacturers they knew and trusted. Pat placed orders for several artistic cabinets to use as lavatory bases in our bathrooms from Decorative Crafts, a third-generation Italian importer. She also ordered plate racks and cabinetry from British Traditions, whose market niche was making affordable, new furniture that looked antique. Pat had bought from them before and appreciated their artistic design, attention to detail and the European country reproduction cabinetry she wanted for the newly christened "butlers' pantry." Regrettably, they didn't offer wholesale prices for butlers.

When we went by OTW to pick up our purchases, I got to meet the owner, Andre Obalek, and asked how they were able to sell at lower prices than we got in Mexico. "There's no great mystery," he explained in that patient, now familiar tone, "I buy a lot more than you do, speak the language better and have more experience negotiating. We purchase closeouts or huge quantities direct from factories all over the world, and probably sell more tile than all Tijuana merchants combined."

Thinking Global, Acting Local

Our station wagon was sitting low on the road and every spare inch was filled as we navigated up the 405, through those two insane interchanges I mentioned earlier, then on to the 101 and north to Santa Barbara. At home, Pat showed me pictures of some monkeywood columns she had ordered to help define the dining room we were attempting to create in what had been a kitchen. Technically, the wood was from the *Enterolobium* tree, but who could pronounce that?

This L-shaped area presented one of our major challenges. We wanted space to seat ten people, but had to deal with the kitchen door and the space on either side of the table. Pat had decided to partially address this with cabinetry from British Traditions: one unit for china, serving dishes and silverware on one end; a bar area with additional storage; and a small, under-counter refrigerator and dishwasher at the other. She was rerouting some of the furnace's ductwork to form soffits over the table. The columns would further delineate the dining area.

"Do you realize," I asked, "two transplanted Southerners are asking a largely Mexican crew to install ornate Corinthian columns made from Asian *Enterolobium* wood to provide space for our country French dining table in a Spanish Mediterranean house?" Globalism was sweeping the world, even at *Casa de Alégria*.

Globalism may be a positive for commerce, but not everyone agreed with our "small world" attitudes. Two potential contractors for the great room wouldn't' submit bids as long as we had "wetbacks" on the premises. Our workers were here legally, and we resented this obvious prejudice.

Apparently half of the property owners in Santa Barbara were engaged in a building or remodeling effort. Several contractors didn't bother to return our calls. Finally, we found a pleasant young general contractor who was starting his construction business and was willing to work on our great room.

Minor tensions were developing on jurisdictional or ethnic grounds. Dan, our licensed electrician, knew his business, but looked down on everyone else, especially the Hispanics.

Sometimes we thought he was trying to stir up the workers on the great room project who were not a part of our core team as he yelled across a couple of rooms, "I smell tacos!" We didn't have a ready replacement for Dan, but insisted this had to stop. Even if it wasn't meant to be insulting—he claimed to be asking other workers to share their lunch—we found the approach offensive. While Dan grudgingly complied, he continued to complain about a lack of professionalism among our workers and how, as a *gringo*, he was part of "an oppressed minority." He was the most expensive, arrogant, and generally unpleasant person we employed. No one regretted saying *adios* to Dan when the wiring was completed and the city inspector signed off on this part of the project.

Alberto, nicknamed Solín, was also taking abuse from Juan who appeared to resent anyone who wanted to better himself. Juan thought Alberto might be gay because he sometimes read a book during lunch. Juan was a great worker with many gifts, but enlightenment and ambition were not among them.

Stocky and muscular, Juan wanted to be a machismo, hard-working, hard-drinking Latin lover. He succeeded on all counts. One Saturday, we were checking the week's progress when Juan came out of his living area dressed for the evening. He wore a large white sombrero, a dressy white shirt with black cowboy piping, a broad leather belt with a huge silver buckle, and lizard skin boots.

Wishing again for more Spanish fluency, I tried to compliment his appearance and ask about plans for the evening. *"Usted es muy guapo esta noche ¿Vas a bailar?"*

His smile didn't reveal if he was amused by my grammar or pleased by the effort *"Sí, me gusta bailar mucho. La semana pasada, he ganado un trofeo en el concurso de baile,"* he replied and went back into his area. I understood that he liked to dance, but missed the rest of the reply until he returned to show us the trophy he had won in last week's dance contest.

Fall Features

By late autumn, we were beginning to sense a shift in the atmosphere of unmitigated chaos that had characterized our efforts to provide a makeover for our Dulcinea.

Despite their differences, Juan and Alberto had finished the excavation for the drainage and waterfall. Hector had brought in gravel and completed a very unsexy French drain. The sewer pipes had been replaced and the trenches filled in. The tubs had been refinished and relocated from our backyard to the bathrooms. Sal Pereura, who also worked for the City, was proving to be a genuine artist who enjoyed Pat's sense of color and appreciation for faux painting. Brad and Keiko had earned substantial increases in their hourly rate because of their artistry in blending the various types of tile in creative, designs. The framing for the great room was moving along and you could almost see how it would eventually look.

Hector and Jamie, another city employee, had framed in the space for new windows and French doors to replace the old Bavarian bay windows, and we had placed orders for windows and doors that would be available in eight weeks A truckload of red Mission roofing tile had been delivered and was stacked on the roof area that Imo hadn't completed, as well as on the new great room roof. The tile needed to sit there for a few weeks, we were told, for the roofing support to 'cure' or adjust to the additional weight.

We hadn't started the water feature and pond, and had a couple of more months work to do on the great room. The cabinetry had arrived but wasn't installed. We had yet to choose a variety of plumbing and electrical fixtures. The tile work was going well but was less than half completed. We hadn't heard from the Mexican granite guru, had not chosen the appliances for the kitchen, and weren't even thinking about landscaping.

We were also trying to make a final decision about locating the kitchen door. Actually, we had made that decision a couple of times, but afterwards, Pat or Dee would conclude it wasn't exactly right. As Hector framed the doorway for the third time, he commented, "You are paying by the hour, so I'm not complaining, but if there is an earthquake, this is where you want to go. This will be the safest place in the house. The door frame will be standing when the rest of the house is rubble."

A Fair Hearing

The third time they tried was charmed. From the kitchen door, Pat could see through the dining room, the bar area, and great room to the huge crimson bougainvillea in the courtyard. She could also see through the other butler's pantry and the living room to the entryway. The door swung open and aligned perfectly with the cabinets from British Traditions. There is an old saying, "If at first you don't succeed, lower your standards." Pat would never agree to that. Hector had learned, as had I, "If at first you don't succeed, just do it Pat's way."

By late autumn, we began to see some signs of progress; I became concerned that the stress and noise of renovation was affecting Pat's hearing. She was making hundreds of important decisions, and I was regularly impressed with her judgment, but I mentioned my concern to Bob Rottenberg, a retired physician from Connecticut, who asked for a little more insight as to why I thought she had a hearing problem.

"I repeat the same question over and over before she responds. She just doesn't seem to hear as well as she used to," I said.

"Most people lose some hearing acuity as they age," he said. "Before you go to Sansum Clinic, why not test to see how severe the hearing loss is? Perhaps you could ask a question from twenty feet away, then ten feet, and if she still hasn't responded, keep your voice at the same level and move to a distance of five feet. Just remember when she first hears you."

Of course, I knew how to test a hypothesis, so a couple of days later when I came home from Pepperdine, I walked toward the kitchen as she was preparing dinner. About twenty feet from the stove, I paused and asked, "What's for dinner?"

When there was no response, I moved halfway to where she was standing and repeated the question. There was still no response. Finally, I took two more steps and asked again, "What's for dinner?"

This time, I got a response, but her answer destroyed my hypothesis. "For the third time," she replied with a touch of exasperation, "we're having shrimp and pasta!"

Chapter 13
Two Weddings, a Funeral and a *Bandito*

The approach of winter brought significant signs of progress. Our work crew was growing in numbers and everyone was rushing to beat the brief, but sometimes intense, rainy season. Our window and door order arrived from Sierra Pacific. Burke, a journeyman carpenter from New Zealand, was responsible for adjusting the framing to be sure that they enjoyed a snug fit; he also oversaw others who were doing carpentry work.

Paul was a graduate of New York's Institute of Culinary Education who had tired of the pressure of being a chef and discovered that he could make more as a carpenter—and have time to catch some waves. If the surf was up, he sometimes failed to show up for our job, but promised to demonstrate his pre-burnout skills when the "Dynamic Cooking System," a commercial range and griddle Pat had ordered at the LA Mart, was installed. Nicolas and Jamie had a variety of handy skills and were part of the contingent of City employees who joined us, after hours, on a regular basis.

Sal Peryra continued to develop his artistry as a painter. He had graduated from simple 'sponging' of the peach paint on the rough stucco in our upstairs guest room to blending misty green over an azure blue base in our bedroom. He moved on to the more sophisticated layering of magnolia yellow over ochre in the living room and a darker ochre over the pale yellow in the living room annex. This area where Gus' cot had been now sported wraparound window seats in front of the large arched windows that replaced the discolored sliding glass doors. By adding multiple layers of color in what looked like random patterns, Sal had given our rooms what I thought of as the Old World charm of an aged fresco. He was the only person I knew who could really communicate with Pat about the blending and shading of colors, and she was the only person I knew who, as part of an M.F.A. program, had taken a graduate-level course in color. Some of us completed our study of color in the third grade with an eight-crayon set of Crayolas.

Belles at the Bank

On weekends, I arranged my schedule to pick up cash to pay the workers. Only the contractor for the great room, Hector, and Sal accepted checks as payment for their labor. I was getting to be on a first name basis with the tellers at Montecito Bank and Trust. We chose that bank partially because it looked like a bank is supposed to look. Each time I went in to cash a check, I expected to see George Bailey making loans to help Santa Barbara become an even better place to live. Come to think about it, despite the challenges of renovation, we were experiencing "A Wonderful Life."

We even attended a couple of parties hosted by the bank. The ornate lobby made a striking party venue for receptions after performances by the Ensemble Theater or CAMA (Community Arts Music Association). Greenbacks would have made nice party favors, but the cash drawers were always tightly locked.

At one of these events, Pat met a couple of women from the South who were members of a discreet 'by invitation' organization that modestly called itself "The Belles." The members were beautiful women of a certain age who had grown up in the South, had impeccable social skills and knew the difference between grits and polenta (none). Most were married to or involved with very successful, wealthy men. Fortunately, a wealthy consort wasn't a requirement, so Pat was invited to join and enjoyed regular, lengthy luncheons with "the girls," white gloves optional, and managed to keep her Scarlett O'Hara persona undiluted.

After one of the bank parties, I remembered to review our bank statement and realized that our check to Raymondo Franco had cleared almost two months earlier. "Pat," I called, "when is Raymondo going to deliver our granite countertops?"

"I need to call him again," she replied. "The number on his card doesn't work from Santa Barbara, and I'm not sure how to call Mexico. I can't seem to figure out the right combination of numbers to reach him. Would you call him for me?"

Usually, you would simply use the international access code, 011, then the country code of 52, followed by the city code which I thought was 615 for that part of Mexico, and then the seven-digit telephone number. Unfortunately, I kept doing something wrong, and got a variety of strange sounds or recorded messages in Spanish that exceeded my ability to translate. Finally, we asked Hector for his assistance. Even 'Kaliman's' magic couldn't make connection with the elusive Raymondo. "I'm getting a bad feeling about this," I finally admitted. "Do you think he might be a con man?"

"That's certainly a possibility," Hector said. "Most Mexicans are very honest, but there are a few 'rotten apples' who make people suspicious of the rest of us. It looks like you may have to make another Rosarito trip to know for sure."

I did an Internet search and the only significant hit was for a 'Raymond Franco' who had been charged with taking 34 drums of toxic waste across the Mexican border and dumping them in Tijuana eight years earlier; doubtless, a totally different person, but it wasn't reassuring. Pat and Dee, the 'devious duo,' started planning to cross the Rio Grande in pursuit of an alleged Bandito, but finding time would be a challenge.

When I was home on the weekend, I would usually made my bank run to pick up cash for pay day just before it closed at noon on Saturday's. Then I'd stop by Bennie's on Milpas to buy burritos for the crew. Pat had prepared lunch a time or two, but the workers seemed to prefer big beefy burritos with lots of beans to chicken salad sandwiches with the crusts trimmed off. On a gorgeous October Saturday, Hector told me to skip the stop at Bennie's. "Nicolas is going to fix lunch for everyone, but a supply of Dos Equis would be appreciated."

I picked up *dinero*, then *cerveza,* and a little after noon, and we were invited into the front yard, where Nicolas had rigged up a spit with what looked like a medium-sized dog roasting over coals. Fortunately, it was *"un pequeña cabra,"* the same dish I had enjoyed during our first Cinco de Mayo in Santa Barbara. The small goat made tasty tacos, and we enjoyed the food and camaraderie. After the feast, Nicolas invited us to his daughter Gabriela's First Communion party in eight days. We were pleased to be included in this celebration.

A Wedding Party for an Eight-Year-Old

Growing up in the Protestant South, I had learned how dangerous Catholic rituals could be. I remembered that the Inquisition had ended right after the Civil War, but was nervous about the practice of forcibly circumcising adult heretics. First Communion should be relatively safe, I reasoned, since it was one of the holiest and most important occasions in the life of a Roman Catholic child. Just to be sure, I checked the always reliable internet and discovered:

> *...every little girl becomes a bride of Christ in her first spiritual union with Him Who is fully present... (The celebration) means that person has received the Sacrament of the Eucharist, the body and blood of Jesus Christ...Catholic children receive their First Communion when they're seven or eight years of age, because this is considered the age of reason, and then get to make their first confession.*

Even by southern standards, eight seemed a little young to become a bride. I wondered what eight-year-olds might have to confess. "Forgive me, Father, for I overslept this morning. I watched MTV without permission and looked at the magazines that popi hides in his truck." We decided to skip the ceremony itself, but headed to Alameda Park for the *fiesta*.

We discovered Nicolas roasting another goat with extended family and friends. There were several cute, chubby little girls dressed in white dresses, veils, and gloves. I could almost get my mind around the "Bride of Christ" idea but, eight year old girls must have been terrified at consuming the transubstantiated body and blood of Jesus.

I remembered Frank McCourt's account of his first communion in Limerick when he was so frightened by the cannibalistic aspects of the ritual and the dire warnings, "You'll roast in hell for eternity...if ye chew the Lord's body," that he threw up as soon as the mass ended. His family wasn't prepared for the theological implications of a boy who had "thrun up the body and blood of Jesus in me own backyard," so Frankie makes multiple visits to the confessional and finally says, "Bless me, Father, it's a minute since my last confession," before a kindly priest assures him that ordinary water will wash away this sin.

Gabriela was handling the pressure better than Frankie, but was appropriately solemn at having become a member of the One True Church, an official sinner, and wearing, for a few hours, the most expensive dress she had ever owned. We enjoyed another *cabra taco con cerveza*, congratulated Nicolas, handed him a gift envelope, met Gabriela's mother, and did a lot of nodding and smiling at the other guests. Once again, I regretted my Spanish deficiency, but we lacked the ability to discuss Catholic theology or even the weather. After a few painful minutes, we offered our best wishes again and retreated back to East Beach.

A Questionable Election

A presidential campaign was in progress during this time. We didn't have time to be as obsessive as we often are. Since my father was a die-hard Democrat, my youthful rebellion included embracing the Republican virtues of individual responsibility and balanced budgets. Dad had doubts about the 'Holy Ghost' as a full member of the Trinity. The whole concept sounded vaguely Romanesque. FDR had brought TVA to North Alabama and provided jobs for young men coming to maturity during the depths of the Depression. Surely, Roosevelt was a more appropriate partner for the Father and the Son.

My uncle liked to tell the story of assuming that Dad would vote for Eisenhower, since they both had served under Ike (way under him) during World War II. "Nope," Dad declared, "I can't vote for a Republican."

Uncle Carter challenged him, "Robert, I don't think you would vote for Jesus Christ if he ran on the Republican ticket!"

167

"I wouldn't," Dad responded. "He would have no business changing parties after all this time."

For me to vote Democratic would mean admitting that my father might have been right about a few things. But by the 1990s, I had more respect and appreciation for my father and had to admit that Bill Clinton demonstrated greater mastery of complex issues than any recent president. The economy was proving that a balanced budget could create a rising tide that helped everyone. Early in 2000, when George W. Bush said, "Rarely is the question asked, 'Is our children learning'?" I knew I couldn't vote to deprive some village in Texas of its favorite son.

My younger son was completing the third week of a thirty-day Amtrak excursion before heading to a Guatemalan teaching assignment. Had my eyes not been opened about politics, it would have been a difficult visit when he arrived in Santa Barbara for Election Day. While we watched Burke and Paul complete the installation of the last windows just ahead of a forecasted rain, Burt informed us, "If Bush wins this election, I'm not sure I'll come back to this country." While at Georgetown, he had dated a Central American coed who was very negative about the Bush family's policies in the region. We were too committed to Santa Barbara to share Burt's resolve, but were on the edge of our seats all evening as the votes were being tabulated, analyzed and discussed.

We finally went to bed without knowing who would be our next president, and said goodbye to Burt the next day without knowing who had won the election. We still didn't know the outcome when we attended a pre-departure party for a trip to Cuba's 7th Biennial of La Habana with the UCSB Art Museum. At the orientation dinner, we met a new group of interesting Santa Barbara residents. They included a novelist, a sculptor, an architectural historian, the museum curator, the founder of one of Santa Barbara's leading law firms, and a former District Attorney along with a variety of philanthropists, art lovers, five people we knew from Newcomers, and a couple of ordinary folks. After mingling and enjoying *mojitos* and *tapas,* we moved to a dinner of slow-roasted chicken smothered in onions and garlic-citrus sauce, served with the requisite black beans, rice and plantains.

A Bridges Too Far

I sat by an attractive blonde woman who was rather quiet. In trying to find a topic for conversation, I asked what type of business was keeping her husband from going on the trip. "He's in the movie business," she responded.

After learning he was an actor, I tried to think of a way to inquire whether he had ever had a significant part. Finally, I asked, "What roles did he enjoy most?"

Almost shyly, she answered, "I think he enjoyed *The Great Lebowski* and *The Fabulous Baker Boys* more than most."

The name Bridges should have been a clue, but she had spoken softly and the mojitos had elevated the noise level in the room so I had missed that little detail. Completely embarrassed, I considered skipping dinner and hiding out in the men's room until the group departed in three days, but we had already paid for the trip, so I tried to act as if I had known that all along. I wondered what penance was appropriate for being slow and hoped that celebrities and their families get accustomed to ordinary folks trying to figure out how to show appreciation for their achievements without fawning or obsequiousness.

Our friends Kirby and Ingrid Warren came to visit for a couple of days before the trip. Ingrid was going with us to Cuba, but Kirby had to get back to New York for a board meeting. He had been the best teacher I had ever known, a great dean during my time at Columbia, and a master of dialects. Sadly, he was starting to show signs of Alzheimer's. He kept asking, "Now, who was just elected President?"—a question none of us could answer yet.

Despite his memory lapses, Kirby entertained everyone on our charter bus ride to LAX by doing a routine of one-liners with a Cuban, not just a generic Spanish, accent. As we rode down the PCH by the Pepperdine campus, he informed the group, "Señors and Señoritas, you know that Castro, he is the most important socialist in the world who does not live in Malibu. He *tiene setenta años.* Soon he retire and move to Miami so he can get good *picadillo.*"

169

At the airport, the bus dropped Kirby at the American terminal and took us to the international terminal for our Lasca Airlines flight. Despite the restrictions on travel to Cuba, this was a 'cultural tour,' so we didn't have to change planes in Mexico.

The flight was smooth and uneventful. The tour group was pleasant and intrigued by Havana's crumbling elegance. It reminded us of Dulcinea but, of course, almost everything made us think of the work that was going on without our oversight. The art lovers enjoyed the artist studio tours, the Musec de Habana and the Biennial projects. We all appreciated the mostly well-maintained American cars from the 1950's, the Tropicana Night Club where Julie Lopp did her Carmen Miranda imitation, the famous 'Blue Beach,' the obligatory cigar factories and meals at the traditional cafés as well as at the *paladars* or entrepreneurial home restaurants.

Poverty was rampant, but people were pleasant and appeared happy. We saw several families huddling around a single television set in the evenings. During the day, children played with homemade toys. Attendants at the museums appreciated tips in the form of toothpaste or shampoo that had been embargoed. There were probably more communists in Havana than the McCarthy-era State Department, but they didn't look particularly evil or threatening.

Although we would have enjoyed staying longer than a week, we were glad to board our return flight, bid our new friends *adios*, and rush to check on what, if anything had been accomplished during our absence.

We were pleasantly surprised to see that, even with shorter days, the work was proceeding apace. Hector introduced us to Bruce Garcia, whom he described *as un artista de piedras*—an artist who specialized in making stones. As a child, I assumed that God was the consummate rock artist. That was before I watched Bruce fashion latex forms or 'skins' to use as molds for concrete boulders that replicated nature but were exactly the sizes needed to fashion the backyard waterfall and ponds. In total, he created thirty-two boulders, which blended with six or eight huge stones from our back yard. Even today, I can't tell which stones are Bruce's and which are of an earlier vintage.

Hector recommended that Bruce include some steel rebar in the construction of the larger boulders, but the *artista de peidras* didn't think this was necessary. Bruce took more than six days to complete his creation and was installing pumps for the waterfall as we prepared for Thanksgiving. We still didn't know who had won the election, but we were pretty sure Gore had received more votes and had high hopes that this might be a factor in the ultimate decision.

Thanks for the New Memories

That Thanksgiving, we participated in a new tradition. Ron and Jane Freund, Newcomers from Kansas City, were organizing the second annual Thanksgiving on the Beach. I crumbled cornbread, then chopped onions and celery while Pat blended these and a few other secret ingredients into her famous stuffing, which we brought along with our own beverages to Goleta Beach. Jane coordinated favorite recipes from sixty newcomers, brought ceramic turkeys to go by each place setting, and pulled off a celebration unlike anything we had known. We set up an imposing buffet, commandeered a dozen picnic tables, took a leisurely walk along the beach in seventy-degree weather and talked about the twelve degree temperatures in Buffalo before sitting down with friends to share wonderful food and gratitude for all that we were enjoying in America's Riviera.

We continued trying to reach the mysterious Raymondo Franco. Finally Hector was reasonably confident that he reached Raymondo's answering machine where he left word, in English and Spanish: "In January, Señora Pat will be in Mexico and would like to hear from you as soon as possible. Just in case you've lost her telephone number, here it is again. She is very anxious about her order for granite countertops and the check that cleared almost three months ago." Hector paused and asked me, "Would you like for me to add, '*Su marido es un gran, hijo de puta?*' He might be more responsive if he thinks she is married to a big mean mother."

"You may just want to say 'big, mean *abogado,*" I suggested. "An attorney might be more intimidating than a *hijo de puta.*"

171

Pat interrupted our dialogue. "Just stop with the machismo and let me handle Raymondo. Dee and I are going to Mexico in a few weeks. We'll take care of everything without your having to prove that your anything is bigger or badder than his."

Early in December, my parents came for their first and only visit to California. They were in their mid-eighties and inexperienced travelers, so my younger brother, Joe, a professor at Western Kentucky University, traveled with them to be sure that they made all the connecting flights. Dad was not a happy traveler—in fact, he was never a truly happy person. Growing up with a stern, widowed mother, he worried about the judgments of a harsh, condemning "heavenly Father." Joe was exhausted from trying to allay his fears, complaints and concerns. For the first time, I sensed Dad's imminent decline. He had little energy, evidenced considerable confusion, and wandered into our bathroom several times without realizing where he was.

As expected, Mom was excited about exploring a new part of the world, and was particularly impressed by the Mission Rose Garden and the huge Moreton Bay fig tree near the railroad station—supposedly, the country's largest. She couldn't wait to dip her toes into the Pacific, and was ecstatic about what we were attempting to do with Dulcinea. "When I come back next time, the house will be beautiful, and I'll help you get your rose bushes in better shape," she promised. We had not started thinking about landscaping issues, but there were six or eight rose bushes in our front yard, and mother loved nothing more than nurturing roses and sharing her flowers with friends, shut-ins and "old folks."

Bicoastal Again

We treasured our brief time with them and correctly suspected that they would not make it back to see the completed restoration of *Casa de Alegría*. Pat said goodbye and headed to Mission Ridge to meet Dee and see if the great room project was ready for the city's inspection. It wasn't, but they were comfortable that we were ready for any rain that might come in the next few weeks. I loaded a mountain of luggage into my car and headed for the airport. About forty minutes after Joe and my parents boarded, I had a flight to Raleigh-Durham, where

Blair Sheppard, a friend from the Fuqua Business School, was leading a new venture called Duke Corporate Education, which would focus on custom executive-level programs for national and international companies. Their business plan called for employing a variety of talent from academia and the corporate world to become the global leader in helping firms "execute strategy through education." It was a bold, ambitious plan, and I wanted to learn more about it.

With three connecting flights and travel through three time zones, it took all day to reach Durham's Marriott Hotel. The next morning, I walked two blocks to find an energetic team of forty impressive people who radiated energy as they went about their work in new, off-campus offices in a recently renovated tobacco warehouse. Several key academics and friends from Duke, Emory, Dartmouth and McGill had taken leave from their universities in order to be part of this venture. I wanted to participate in this exciting activity but wasn't interested in leaving Santa Barbara, so we worked out an arrangement where I would be an Academic Director and work on demand as appropriate projects developed. This gave both of us greater flexibility and reduced their fixed costs. It was another bi-coastal arrangement, but I didn't see a downside as I returned to Santa Barbara in another almost manic state of excitement.

Pat was pleased by the prospect for increased income, as we were running substantially over our estimated budget for renovations. So far, I had resisted the temptation to scream, "We are hemorrhaging money!" But she knew me well enough to understand that I, like Oscar Wilde, could "resist anything but temptation," and would eventually revert to my Manhattan mantra.

We missed Santa Barbara's 48th Annual Holiday Parade, but watched the 15th annual Parade of Lights from the back yard of Mark and Barb Palmer's new house. They were still struggling with obstreperous neighbors, as well as with the city for permits to demolish the house and construct their two-story dream home.

According to Mark, "The neighbors are objecting because we would be able to see their pool from our upstairs bedroom, and they worry about our watching them swim or sunbathe in the nude. Since they are ten years older and thirty pounds heavier than we are, I don't think we will spend lots of time with binoculars checking out that view when we can see the ocean from the other windows."

Mark had rigged some portable, outdoor gasoline heaters to mitigate the fifty-degree winter temperatures, and Barb provided *hors d'oeuvres* for more than ten. We sipped local wines, sampled finger foods, caught up with the housing challenges of other newcomers, and watched about forty decorated boats parade around the harbor and compete for prizes in five judging categories. None of us could spot our friend Elden's entry so we relaxed, enjoyed more conversation, and the fireworks following the parade.

Justice for the Bandito

After a quiet Christmas and New Year's, Pat and Dee began to devise a strategy for bringing justice to Raymondo, whom they were now calling El Bandito. Pat followed Hector's call with a friendly letter:

> *I will be back in Rosarito in two weeks and hope to meet with you. If you still want to install our granite countertops, please try to contact us and schedule the installation before our trip. If you have decided not to proceed with this project, please return our deposit of $650 (check 879) before we visit on Thursday, the 18th of January.*

No one waited by the telephone in anticipation of an apologetic call from Raymondo and, early on Wednesday, the devious duo climbed into our ancient Voyager van, dropped me at the airport for another flight to Raleigh-Durham, and headed for the border. I kept thinking about the shooting scene in the parking lot outside The Silver Bullet cowboy bar from *Thelma and Louise*. Truthfully, I felt a little sorry for El Bandito.

They had anticipated that Ramondo would "be away on business" if they arrived on Thursday, so they managed to arrive twenty-four hours earlier. Pat was almost sure she saw Raymondo duck out the back of his store when they entered. She asked Miguel, the shop assistant, if they could speak with the owner and were told, *"Lo sentimos, tuvo que ir a San Diego, pero estará de regreso mañana por la mañana."*

Pat recognized three or four words and with the help of Dee's Spanish dictionary, they concluded that Raymondo had found it necessary to visit San Diego, but would be back the next morning. "Well, we will just have to come back tomorrow morning," Pat replied, "but while we're here, let's look at some of your other merchandise."

Miguel was delighted to show them the store's excellent collection of wrought iron fireplace screens and outdoor furniture. Pat negotiated reasonable prices on several items, took extensive notes, and finally said, *"Adiós, hasta mañana."* She had almost become bilingual.

After visiting a couple of other shops early in the morning, Dee and Pat arrived at Raymondo's just before noon. They were shocked to find that the owner had not returned. "While we are waiting," Pat suggested, "Let's pick out some other items we need for *mi casa*." They quickly identified four exquisite fireplace screens, three large candelabras and an attractive set of outdoor furniture from Wednesday's negotiations. Miguel added the prices of each item and announced that the grand total was $694. Always an effective negotiator, Pat inquired, "If I buy it all, could you sell it to me for $650?"

Miguel quickly agreed and started helping them load the merchandise into the van. Pat opened her purse and started writing a check. Miguel was a little hesitant about this until Pat reminded him that Raymondo had taken a check just a few weeks before. Reluctantly, he wrote "paid in full" on the receipt. Pat indicated that they would visit a couple of other stores and stop by again in an hour or two to see if Raymondo had returned. Instead, she and Dee began a mad dash for the border, checking the rearview mirror regularly to see if a Mexican posse was in hot pursuit.

As soon as they crossed the border, she called Montecito Bank and issued a "stop payment" on the check.

175

Hector was proud of the devious duo. I was relieved that they were home safely, and Juan observed, *"Él se siente muy mao porque una mujer le ha superado."* Even Pat didn't understand, until Hector explained, "Juan thinks the man will feel very bad because a woman bested him." Juan still hasn't been nominated as NOW's "Man of the Year."

Goodbye to a Groom

We were happy to hear that Alberto was engaged to be married; disappointed he was leaving our work team; and gratified to be invited to his wedding celebration. This wedding was age-appropriate, and his fiancée was the attractive daughter of the foreman for a large Carpinteria ranch that specialized in exotic fruit. We were two of the dozen *gringos* who attended, and sat with the ranch owners, Ralph and Betty Brown, who were charming hosts and *padrinos* (sponsors) of the event. We enjoyed traditional wedding foods including spicy rice, chicken and beef tortilla dishes and beans. Sangria, made from wine, brandy, fruit juice, and soda helped wash down the tasty but *muy picante* feast.

The meal was followed by what our hostess described as "the only thing that is more Mexican than tequila." She went on to explain, "This group of musicians dressed in *charro* suits is the essence of the country and its people. Mariachi music is cultural, traditional, spiritual and unique to Mexico itself."

We enjoyed the band until the *padrino* stood and asked the bride to dance and Betty began to dance with Alberto. Soon the dance floor was crowded as the mariachi band played a variety of *cumbias, rancheras, corridas,* and *merengues.* We didn't recognize any of the musical offerings, but appreciated being told what was happening. We dreaded the dollar dance when guests were expected to pin money on the bride or groom's clothing while dancing with one of them for a minute or two. Concerned about the pinning process, I handed Albert an envelope, shook his hand and we excused ourselves after only three or four hours. The celebration was just getting started, but we were finished for the evening.

The winter rains caused some erosion in Bruce's boulders and base. Hector had been right about the need for rebar, and Bruce agreed to repair the damage in May. He was an artist who wanted to be proud of his work—and to have this dramatic water feature as a reference for future prospective clients.

We took time to attend a Newcomers' event scheduled an at the area's oldest restaurant, the Cold Springs Tavern. Only twenty minutes out San Marcos Pass, it is like stepping back in time. In the late 19th century, stagecoaches (actually, mud wagons outfitted for rough terrain) made the dusty, grueling eight-hour trip to connect passengers from the rail line in Los Olivos to one in Santa Barbara. The stage would stop at the Tavern for new horses, food, drink and rest. The restaurant is located in the original ivy-covered wooden building, and its menu includes traditional fare as well as game meats and even a couple of vegetarian dishes. I enjoyed a half-pound Buffalo Burger while Pat tried the Wild Game Chili with venison, rabbit, and buffalo simmered with black beans and fresh chiles.

Paper Chase

We enjoyed making some new acquaintances and sitting with the Beurets and Rings. As further confirmation of the "small world" hypothesis, Peter Beuret and I had been hired at the same time, by the same Procter & Gamble recruiter. We both fully expected to retire from P&G. Peter had done that after returning from London and heading up an international marketing team. I explained to our table, "During my first winter in Ohio, when the temperature stayed below zero for a week and I reviewed a market research study where the two major variables were 'number of sheets per pull' and 'number of pulls per visit,' I decided to leave P&G. I didn't want to spend the rest of my life advertising bathroom tissue, so I applied to Ph.D. programs in Florida and California."

Richard Ring had been listening quietly, but retorted, "That's a good story, but I had a damn good career selling paper products." He had been a very successful sales and marketing executive for James River Paper and Georgia Pacific and would become a good friend despite my initial malapropos.

"Darn," I thought, "it's getting to where I won't be allowed out in public. I need to do penance and say ten 'Hail Emily Posts'."

A Death in the Family

As spring approached, we thought we were making good progress on the house, so agreed to let Dee, who was to be the next president of Newcomers, schedule an up-dated version of the Life Styles event that had so embarrassed us a year earlier. In truth, we were making *great* progress, planning to put our townhouse up for rent in April and move into our Mission Ridge home while the finishing touches were applied. We were overly optimistic again—a trait that had become part of a pattern in our Santa Barbara adventures.

There were still major decisions to be made, and the incredibly dependable Hector was a bit distracted. We knew he was expecting a second child during the summer and were saddened to learn that his mother was seriously ill. We never met her, but knew she was a great mom because her children were all hard-working, pleasant and successful. Hector may not have been up to his usual peak performance, but he was still amazingly proficient. Our workers had almost become extended family, and Hector was like a younger brother. When his mother died, we tried to share his grief and asked if we could attend her memorial service. He was pleased and provided the details of the service.

The tiny Church of God of Prophecy was filled to overflowing. We learned that this Pentecostal-type denomination, but learned that it had over a million members and 10,000 churches in over 120 nations. The service was long and energetic. I recognized four words, *Dios, Christos, Aleluya* and, finally, *Amen.* After the service, the family went to the front of the sanctuary where the oldest thanked the attendees, in Spanish, for their support, and Hector conveyed the family's appreciation in English.

Our early months in Santa Barbara had been filled with exciting "hellos." Now, we were starting to experience some sad "goodbyes" that we feared would become more numerous as we, our parents and friends grew older.

Chapter 14

Lifestyles of the Nervous and Stressed

What George Bush meant to say was, "Fool me once, shame on you. Fool me twice, shame on me." It didn't come out quite that way, but we couldn't blame anyone but ourselves for agreeing to host a second Life Styles event to "celebrate the completion of our renovation." For the four months after agreeing to this event, our lives centered on the existential question, "Are we going to be ready?"

Brad and Keiko were nearing the completion of the tile work for our bathrooms and kitchen. Some contractors charge for each "cut" they make. Our team worked by the hour and, as artists, insisted that each tiled surface have something to break the monotony of consistency in color and material. They often used a simple diamond of a contrasting color to connect four of the primary tiles. Four cuts were needed to create a diamond and four more provided space for the contrasting diamond. Fortunately, Brad had a good eye and steady hand so no one lost a finger in the pursuit of variety and creativity.

Their ingenuity was tested as we moved to the final flooring project. Pat had purchased some excellent cement tile for ten percent of the usual price from a contractor who had ordered too much for a big Beverly Hills project.

She thought there would be just enough for the dining room and two butler's pantries. Unfortunately, her math was a little off and we were about twenty tiles short. There were no concrete tiles to be found in Santa Barbara, and we were frustrated until Keiko suggested that they cut three- and six-inch segments of Saltillo and intermingle that with cream-colored diamonds from the tumbled marble for a creative design. I wasn't sure it was possible to make all of our constraints work, but Brad sat down and wrote a computer program that utilized our remaining tiles in a pattern that was unique, attractive and economical. That worked so well, he adapted the program and created configurations that used our remaining tile to cover two outdoor tables Pat had brought at Raymondo's shop in Rosarito. Every tile man should have at least one year of engineering and computer science.

Not to be outdone, Keiko sketched out some Moorish modifications to the plain, brick fireplace in the downstairs guest bedroom. She asked Juan to build nine-inch curved concrete pillars on either side of the fireplace mouth. These were covered with plaster and faux painted by Sal to match the layered peach over dark ochre that we were using for the walls and ceiling of this room. Next, she created a Moorish arch over the opening by doing some difficult curved cuts on charcoal marble tile and adding a downward pointed triangle of dark marble a few inches above the arch as a feminist statement.

The plain bedroom Anita had shown us a few months earlier was now an attractive, distinctive space. Dee designed and built a Moorish canopy daybed with matching pillows. We still hadn't addressed the issue of the wonderful office area Pat had promised to create in the narrow space behind this room. I couldn't imagine how we were going to squeeze book cases, filing cabinets, a desk and computer stand while still having access and a place to sit, but I was starting to have supreme confidence in the creativity of our team.

The Matchmaker and the Cross-Country Trucker

We were worried about our friend, Berkeley, who had been President of Newcomers during the first six months of our membership. She was smart, sexy, intelligent and had a beautiful estate in Hope Ranch that overlooked the Pacific, but she wasn't doing well with men. She didn't have trouble attracting them, but we didn't feel that the guys in her orbit were good enough for her. She was breaking up with John when we first met. He was a good dancer but didn't match her intelligence or energy. After they officially split, she allowed him to housesit while she traveled to Australia and he looked for another place to live.

Shortly after her flight departed, he apparently transferred her portfolio to the brokerage firm where he occasionally worked. Management was pressuring him to generate business, so to satisfy them; he transferred the funds without her knowledge.

Berkeley was shocked when she stopped at an internet café in Sydney to check her e-mail messages and financial holdings. What had happened to her net worth? She wasn't much happier when she figured out what had actually occurred. I didn't hear her yelling from Sydney, but only because of the construction noise on Mission Ridge. Gene, another newcomer friend, offered to take care of things until she returned. He was a big, burly extrovert who had one of those stomachs with its own zip code. He strode into the brokerage office and demanded that everything be transferred back. The threats of legal action, physical retribution and jail time were quite motivating.

Berkeley was grateful for this assistance and began dating Gene. He matched her energy, but was like the proverbial bull in the china shop. Our prejudice was confirmed when he barreled through a stop sign in her Lexus and crashed into an oncoming Mercedes. His seatbelt was unfastened so the impact hurled him into Berkeley and contributed to her three-day coma and seven broken bones. He was appropriately apologetic and solicitous, but we sensed that their relationship would not be made into a romantic Broadway musical.

A few weeks after leaving the hospital, she started to venture out (alone). We invited her to join us and a few other newcomers at the James Joyce pub for Dixieland jazz. After socializing with our group for a while, Pat introduced Berkeley to Mike, a city engineer and regular at the Joyce. He asked her to dance, and they have been dancing ever since. They may have had an argument or two along the way, but so far, she and her assets remain reasonably safe.

181

Back on Mission Ridge, most of the rooms were now painted and the tile floors were done. As spring approached, we started thinking about actually living there. We needed to get the wood floors refinished and then could start enjoying this house that had consumed our lives for fifteen months. The upstairs bedroom floors were heart of pine, the living room floors were white oak, and all of them needed to be sanded and refinished.

We checked with a couple of flooring contractors and decided to use Brent, who was just restarting his business after serving hard time for an undisclosed felony. He might have been a relative of "Stan the Moving Man," but wasn't quite as elegant. Still, he understood what needed to be done, wanted the job, and gave us a competitive price to refinish the floors, add oak to the living room annex, and then finish it to match the rest of the room.

Brent was ready to start immediately, and we began working through a checklist of things to do before moving in. Pat remembered some antiques we had stored in the Atlanta house that we absolutely had to have in Santa Barbara, and we both wanted to visit parents, other relatives, and friends in the Southeast. After watching Brent for a couple of days, we were satisfied that the flooring was in good hands, especially with Hector's oversight. Then, we flew to Atlanta to prepare for another transcontinental drive.

Driving Concerns

The house in Atlanta was a mile from Emory. Keeping it had been a long-term point of contention between Pat and me. We had added a room and bath in the basement and the house had come with a garage apartment, so Pat argued, "The house isn't costing us anything since the rental income pays for the taxes and utilities."

My counter-argument was, "There's a fair amount of capital tied up in the house since we've owned it long enough to pay off the mortgage. If we sold the house, we could reduce our other mortgages or generate additional income."

Despite my greater experience in finance and college forensics, she had, for over a decade, consistently won this debate, but I thought there were signs of détente.

We researched cross-country truck rentals and reserved a medium-sized vehicle for the trip. Pat suddenly decided we should stay an extra day to visit with long-time friends. I tried to explain, "That would be fun, but my classes in Los Angeles on Friday and Saturday aren't flexible. If we spend an extra day, I won't be able to make it back."

"That's not a problem," Pat responded, "We can go to Tennessee together, and I'll drive from there. I enjoyed my first cross-country drive last April. Let's just load up on Wednesday, visit with your parents in Alabama and spend the night there. I'll drop you at the Nashville airport on Thursday for your flight. Then, I can spend a day with Mother in Dyersburg and not feel rushed. "

I wasn't happy about the arrangement, but this debate didn't look winnable, so I conceded and enjoyed seeing friends. We went to pick up our rental late on a Tuesday, and discovered Budget didn't have a medium-sized truck available. "Don't worry," they assured us, "We'll give you a larger one at no extra cost."

That was a generous offer if we had enough furniture to fill a larger truck, but the behemoth they offered us would have lots of potentially dangerous empty space and be much more difficult to drive. Budget provided dozens of straps to secure our load, and we nervously made our way back to start loading.

After we found a place for everything, the truck was only half full. Pat had another idea. "Let's go by Atlanta House Parts in the morning," she suggested. "They have all kinds of materials for architectural restoration. We can certainly use some of their pottery, and we'll probably find some other outdoor items that will help fill up the truck."

I groused about the added time, but it was a reasonable idea so we drove slowly to a warehouse filled with a fascinating variety of remnants from old houses including lots of columns and moldings they made from a variety of materials. We quickly identified a few Grecian urns that could be stained to look Spanish, as well as concrete garden benches and a couple of molded statuettes.

It was noon when we loaded our purchases, so we stopped at Harold's for real Southern barbeque and Brunswick stew before heading west on Interstate 20.

Almost six hours later, we arrived at my parents' house, where Mom had prepared dinner with six vegetable dishes, fried chicken and three desserts. She was definitely slowing down now that she was 85.

We said good-bye the next morning after Mom insisted on serving us eggs, bacon and biscuits, and drove to Franklin where we visited briefly with my son, Jeff, before Pat dropped me at the Nashville airport and went on to see her mother in Dyersburg. I arrived back in Los Angeles in the evening, checked into the Sheraton and was ready for another sixteen-hour teaching marathon. When Pat called me after class on Friday evening, she reported, "I decided to bring Mother's fountain, since she isn't using it any longer. I couldn't get away until after lunch because it took a while to find two guys to load the fountain and base. The truck still isn't crowded, and I am almost to Oklahoma City." She described the truck as slow, cumbersome and hard to drive, but she was in relatively good spirits.

A Crack in the Belle

During my Saturday lunch break, however, I received a less positive call. Immediately upon picking up the phone, I heard. "As soon as class is over, get your ass on a plane and meet me in Albuquerque!"

"Excuse me, but you have a wrong number," I said, "My wife is a sweet southern belle who doesn't use profanity. Who is this, and how would you expect me to get a flight in the next few hours?"

"I don't give a damn how you get a flight , but if you aren't in Albuquerque by tomorrow morning, I will leave this fucking truck in the airport parking lot and fly back to Santa Barbara. It is totally up to you!"

Well, what could I do? After a few moments of silence, I timidly suggested, "Why don't you have some warm milk, no more coffee please, and call me back in thirty minutes? By then, I'll know the options."

When she called back, I had reserved a Wyndham hotel right at the entrance to the Albuquerque airport, and booked a Southwest flight that would allow me to finish my class and get to New Mexico by 9:45. Pat had calmed down a little and offered to meet me at baggage claim. "I don't think so," I replied. "You go to the Wyndham just off the intersection of Interstate 40 and 25, have a few glasses of wine with dinner and get some rest. I'll take the shuttle to the hotel."

I didn't suggest taking a couple of tranquilizers or offer to bring flowers, but I did get my ass on the plane, caught the shuttle and got to the hotel by 10:30. We didn't snuggle very much that night, but after a silent but filling breakfast the next morning, we were on the road again. After a few hours of driving the tank-like truck, I understood why Pat needed help.

We drove eleven hours before stopping for the night in Barstow. Only six hours from Santa Barbara, it was in a different world. The temperature was 110 degrees at nine o'clock in the evening, and El Pollo Loco was the classiest restaurant in town. We shared a very forgettable hotel with other long distance truckers, and were happy to leave early the next day.

Pat enjoys apologizing about as much as I do. But around ten o'clock on Sunday morning, she admitted, "I was surprised by how well you handled my asking you to meet me."

"Well," I said, "your *demand* was overly dramatic, but I was worried about you and thought you needed company. I remembered the agreement that Barbara asked us to sign before starting the project and that lame joke about how many divorced men it takes to change a light bulb."

Reluctantly Pat asked, "And how many divorced men does it take?"

"None," I answered, "men never get the frigging house! Moreover, I really like what you're doing to Dulcinea and would hate for us to wind up with joint custody or like Michael Douglas and Kathleen Turner in *The War of the Roses*."

Saint Hector and the Acolytes

When we arrived at Mission Ridge, we were pleasantly surprised at how much better things looked. Hector and his men had removed the dust coverings and placed our furniture where Pat had sketched it after first seeing the house. The floors were finished perfectly, and the best surprise was that the city had signed off on the great room and water feature. We had a renter for our townhouse and were ready to become residents of the Riviera.

The next day, we thanked Hector profusely. "You are an absolute saint!" Pat exclaimed.

"I don't know about sainthood," Hector responded, "but there is some new evidence that the founder of Christianity may have been a Mexican. His first name was Jesus. He was bilingual and was always being harassed by the authorities."

"Well, I've always wondered if Jesus could have lived in California," I countered. "According to the pictures, he had long hair, wore sandals and started a brand new religion. It sounds like he must have been a California Mexican."

Now that we had settled the theological issue of the day and could see where the project stood, Hector outlined the remaining priorities. "We're going to install the gas stove, hood and convection oven this week. You have to decide how you're going to deal with the kitchen counter tops, and then we'll connect the sink, dishwasher and faucets. We are also starting to stretch chicken wire over the stair banisters and outdoor walls so we can start the stucco process next week."

Pat agreed and added, "I've got to decide what color of stucco to use before we get to the third coat. That will be at least two weeks. By then, I will have chosen the color and find someone to handle the kitchen counters."

"Let's don't forget about the landscaping," I suggested, happy to have something to contribute. "Berkeley has been through the Botanic Garden's 'master gardener' program. I'll ask if she has any suggestions."

Devine Insights

"Why don't you wait until I check out a lead that Pete provided," Pat said. "One of the best landscape architects in town used to live next door. Her work on Rob Lowe's estate was featured in *Architectural Digest*. Let me see if I can get Sandy Devine to spend a couple of hours with us. And, yes, I know that we don't have Rob Lowe's budget."

Sandy came over a couple of days later and shared her impressions of Ruth and Imogene. "They were truly an odd couple, but they enjoyed life and loved living here," she recalled, then focused on what could be done in the front yard. "The jacaranda and pepper tree should come down. I would take out everything in the front yard except the roses and palms, put in the tubing for your sprinkler system, bring in good topsoil and tamp it down to make it stable, and then put in your ground cover and other plants."

She and Pat talked for a few more minutes. Sandy took out a felt tipped pen and sketched a simple design that showed the two large palms as they were, a new, smaller palm where the badly pruned jacaranda tree now stood, a circular garden with slices of different herbs. Roses would continue along the front wall and low succulents along the entrance path. On the left side of the walkway to the house, she drew a birdbath and small shrubs along the wall. It was a basic but elegant concept.

I spent hours with the *Sunset Western Garden Book* and concluded that we wanted to emphasize plants that were low maintenance and required little water. We already had a small cactus garden, and wanted to learn more about how succulents could save money and reduce fire risks. Berkeley agreed to meet me at San Marcos Growers, a wholesale nursery specializing in "plants for California's Mediterranean climate."

She whipped an electric golf cart up and down rows of an almost infinite variety of plants in their twenty acres of nursery production. We purchased a few more white rose bushes and lots of lavender and Mexican sage to create a purple and white color scheme for the yard.

Berkeley recommended that we use *Dymondia margaretae*, a low-growing South African perennial succulent, as a ground cover. I bought enough to sprig our small front yard and to use between the flagstones Juan was to use in our pond area. Dymondia spreads slowly, but I hoped that it would almost cover our front lawn in three months before the Life Styles event.

Barbara Sanchez stopped by as I was unloading plants from our van and was impressed by our progress. We asked if she knew a good roofer or stucco person. She consulted her little black book and said, "Francisco Vasquez is a very good roofer, reasonable in price...and he's a real hunk. I enjoy watching him work. He has a cousin with a stucco crew. I don't remember his name, but Francisco will know."

Needless to say, Pat called Francisco immediately. He came out, gave us a good price for the job, and, while good looking, wasn't as handsome as Hector. He wanted to start in ten days, but Pat was planning to accompany me to a Pepperdine class in Orange County. "Will I need to leave a door open so your crew can come in to use the bathroom?" I asked, after we agreed on the price and schedule.

"Oh, no," he said. "My workers, they're like camels."

We decided not to pursue the topic any further. Juan would be working outside and could provide access if needed. We could see the progress when we returned, and for another few days, we lived with camel-like roofers clattering over our heads and the pungent smell of the sealant they used before applying the two-piece mission clay roofing tile that Francisco said had been utilized since the Bronze Age. They were a happy group who enjoyed harmonizing on songs whose melodies we appreciated even if we couldn't follow the words. One phrase, "*El propietario, es un idiota*," seemed to be a frequent refrain in their musical collaborations.

Hector explained that this was a Mexican folk song about the many good ideas of the boss-man, but I wasn't convinced this was an accurate translation.

Juan was working outdoors, using rocks unearthed during the excavation for the French drain and water feature to extend a retaining wall with stone amphitheater steps. He found stones that fit perfectly, or would use a saw to trim them as needed. After finishing the retaining walls, he used smaller rocks to fashion cobblestone pathways around the back doors. We brought in a load of thin flagstone that Juan used to create patio areas on both sides of the waterfall.

Juan was a good worker, but had three problems. Even using the Spanish version, he had failed the California driver's license exam three times. I suspected that he might be dyslexic, although he always spelled my nickname correctly. Juan had tremendous native intelligence about how things worked. I was intimidated by his ability to figure out practical concepts, but, unfortunately, he didn't possess the skills that are appreciated in modern economies. Our second worry was that he might be drinking too much. Now that we were living in the house, we couldn't miss the growing number of beer cans that filled the garbage cans. We expressed some concern to Hector who relayed the message to Juan whose response was, "*Si yo puedo trabajar todo el día, no estoy bebiendo demasiado.*"

Hector shrugged and translated, "Juan says that as long as he can work all day, he's not drinking too much." Dr. Weil might not agree, but Juan had another explanation for his drinking. As he told our housekeeper, Teresa, her 17-year old daughter, Laura, and every female he encountered, "*Estoy tan solo. No tengo a nadie.*" He seemed to believe that talking about how lonely he was might generate some feminine sympathy, even though he had a wife and two daughters in Mexico. We also noticed that he frequently had company on Sunday mornings after his Saturday excursions to the Copa Nightclub.

Pat finally found an alternate source for the granite countertops. Walker Zanger's price was double the quote from Raymondo, but they carried the 'golden oak' we wanted, made their own measurements, actually delivered and were on time.

Now we understood the secret of Raymondo's bargain prices. If he didn't deliver the countertops, any price was profitable.

Hector recommended two brothers, Silvestre and Armando Vega, who were excellent cabinet makers and worked on contract assignments for P.J. Milligan & Co. Pat provided detailed sketches for my work area and a large entertainment center/book case for the living room that would enable us to hide a stereo system and television. She didn't want people to know we actually had a television set—this might undermine our reputation as closet intellectuals.

Now that we had chicken wire covering almost every exterior surface on and around the house, we were ready for Antonio's crew to start the stucco process. We soon learned that stucco is plaster with a cement base that is applied in three layers over a base of wire mesh and wooden-slat spacers. Antonio went on to explain, "We need to let each layer or 'hand' dry for a day or two after applying it. By late next week, you will need to let us know if you want to add color to the last application. It's almost as difficult to do a fast, aesthetic stucco job as it is to get quick six-pack abs, so we don't want to rush."

We already knew that color pigment could be mixed in or the stucco could be painted and agreed that we wanted to avoid the need for regular painting. We had a slight disagreement about what color to use. I liked the popular pale peach tint that some houses in the neighborhood employed; Pat preferred clay-colored La Habre 20/30 pigment mix, which she described as a pale beigey brown. I recognized that the pale peach designation lacked specificity and wished that I had pursued the study of colors at least through the fourth grade.

A Blast for the Future

"One other thing," Antonio added, we'll need to sand blast the house's exterior before we start applying the stucco. Our crew will come out with compressors and literally blast the old stucco off. This will give us a clean, fresh surface for the next layers to grab hold of."

Oops! We hadn't thought about that when we moved in. "What about cleanup afterwards?" Pat asked weakly.

"Sand blasting is a messy job that can fill your gutters with sand," Antonio explained. "It will even blow dust inside the house. You'll need to put painters' tape around all of your windows and doors." We didn't need to worry about the sand filling up our gutters since we didn't have gutters yet. This was another detail I had forgotten about.

"All right, folks," I said, "We have a month until 'curtain time,' when more than a hundred people show up and want to see a finished project. Let's walk around the property and see if there is anything else that we've forgotten about or let slide."

The sand blasting was to begin immediately, followed by the first or 'scratch' coat of stucco. That process should be completed in a little more than two weeks, including our unanticipated interior clean up. The tile roofing was almost done so we probably wouldn't be seeing Barbara as often. The irrigation system and plants were in place and our dymondia was spreading nicely. The water feature was functioning perfectly and the hardscape was nearly ready. Brad and Keiko were laying tile for the 'Woman with Urn' fountain in the courtyard—Pat insisted that no one refer to it as 'woman with jug.'

She and Dee were concerned about the color of some floor tile and were mixing stains to get it just right. They would spend several days wearing knee pads and applying their concoctions in the pursuit of perfection. Silvestre and Armando would deliver and install my office furniture in five days and the entertainment center a week later. Dee had purchased some fabric and ordered curtains and cushions to be delivered in two weeks. There was no slack in the schedule, but it just might be possible to finish on time. Then I remember one important project that we hadn't considered.

"Wait a minute," I gasped, "What about the driveway? The asphalt was in bad shape when we started. We've had trucks and earth moving equipment in so often that there's no pavement left. Hector, what can we do?"

"It's going to be tight," Hector replied, "But I can rent a Bobcat this weekend, scrape up the residue and get my brother to haul it away on Monday. We'll work through the weekend, and your neighbors won't like the noise, but it's our only choice. We'll pour the concrete on three weekends, starting with 13 yards for the upper drive next Saturday. Juan can build in the frames ahead of the pour, smooth the concrete, let it cure for a few days and then build separators with wood or brick for the next portion so we'll be ready for the next stage. If it doesn't rain or my wife doesn't deliver our daughter on a Saturday, we should finish the third segment about four days before your party."

"Thanks, Hector," I said, "My first job is to get the gutters scheduled. There's lots to do, so it's time to get started. Remember, let's be careful out there…and *git'er done!*"

Fortunately, I couldn't think of any other motivational clichés, so I called California Rain Gutters, specialists in popular residential applications of extruded, seamless aluminum gutters and downspouts. These were available in a 'desert sand' color that would match our exterior walls.

The core team, subcontractors, suppliers, the weather and even Hector's wife performed perfectly. Jimena was born on a Sunday in late July. Hector didn't miss a day of work. Just a few days later, he showed up with a pink bow in his hair. "Is this a tribute to Jimena?" I asked.

"Nope, but I've seen how too many children creates financial hardship, so I had a vasectomy. The guys will give me a hard time. I'll just help them start and they'll get over it quicker."

"If you had told us, Hector, I could have saved you some money." I launched into a tale I'd heard about an Alabama couple. "They couldn't afford more children, so Bubba went to his veterinarian and explained their situation. The vet told him that there was a procedure called a vasectomy that would fix the problem but that it was expensive. A cheaper alternative would be to go home, get a cherry bomb, light it, put it in a beer can, then hold the can up to his ear and count to ten. Bubba wasn't sure. 'Ah don' see how puttin' a cherry bomb in a beer can next to my ear will help,' he said, but the vet assured him that the advice was trustworthy.

"So Bubba went home, lit a cherry bomb and put it in a beer can. He held the can to his ear and began to count:'1, 2, 3, 4, 5.' At this point he paused, placed the beer can between his legs and kept on counting with his other hand."

Hector winced and replied, "Thanks for sharing that. I was already very grateful to the city for health insurance, and now I'm happy to live in Santa Barbara rather than Alabama."

An Affair to Remember

For the last fortnight, everyone worked long hours, seven days a week. On the big day, we still had lots to do. We cleaned, scrubbed and mopped. We re-arranged furniture. We barely had time to take a shower before it was time for "The Blessing of the House." Gail Saunders came early, burned some sage, dabbed lavender oil on the doors, and wished us and the house much happiness. A few minutes later, Rev. Jim Grant arrived and delivered a simple Unitarian-Universalist homily on home, hospitality and the union between head, heart and hands.

The Life Styles event was oversubscribed, with more than seventy people attending at four o'clock, with the same number scheduled for the next day. Were they really interested, or were they there to gloat because they had made decisions that involved less stress and hassle? The first order of business for attendees was to sample the finger foods, get a glass of wine and catch up with their friends. We nervously watched their reactions. At least, everyone was enjoying the wine and food.

Then it was time for Dee to introduced us to say a few words to the group before leading tours through the house. My primary objective was to express our appreciation:

> *"Gracias. Hoy, nuestra casa es su casa."We welcome you to a house that has been called Dulcinea , the money pit, and much, much worse. Today she reclaims her original name from 1920, Casa de Alegría—house of happiness. We hope you notice that a few modest changes have been made since some of you were here over a year ago.*

"About one-third of you have mentioned that you looked at this house, considered purchasing it before we did and said, 'No way!' You are probably smarter than we in other ways too.

"This transformation wouldn't have happened without help from many people. Juan has lived here for the past 18 months and has worked on too many projects to mention. He is a hard-working, hombre, muy intelligente. Bruce designed the water feature and created rocks that God would be proud to claim as her own.

"Lots of other people made contributions but couldn't be here today, but el hombre más importante is here—the person who guided us through every crisis with calm, caring expertise. He is both 'superman and saint.' Muchos, mas y grande gracias to Hector Torres!"

Hector bowed and graciously accepted applause from the crowd.

"Newcomer president and Pat's editor was a gentle, wise counselor at every step of the journey. We would christen the downstairs bedroom where she made the drapes and designed the décor as the Dee Kruger Memorial Room if that didn't have a negative connotation, but we will think of her every time we are in that room. Dee, Hector and Pat probably made 60,000 decisions in this renovation, and, for my money, they made great choices in full recognition that my money was quite finite.

"Finally, I hope you appreciate my wife's talent as an artist. I am the proud owner of the world's largest collection of Pat Fulmer's work. Throughout the house, you will notice several of her four by six foot paintings. But to me, her biggest and best canvas is Casa de Alegria.

"Thanks, sweetie, for taking a tattered, frayed Old Master and making it an even greater work of art—and for letting me share it with you. Al salud y felicidad !Con mucho amor!"

Chapter 15
Different Paths to Paradise

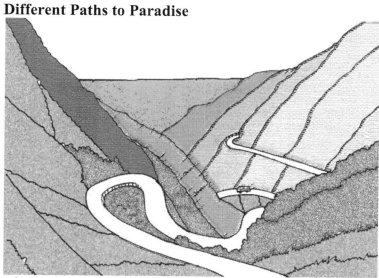

After surviving the Newcomers' event, we wanted to celebrate with a couple of other constituencies; most importantly, the artists who contributed to Pat's biggest canvas. Almost every day during the past eighteen months, we had spent time with these folks. Since they regularly worked until late every evening and on Saturdays, we invited them to come on Sunday afternoon to share tacos, tamales, chips, salsa, sangria and beer with us—no chicken salad tea sandwiches this time. Pat insisted we should ask the men to bring their wives, girlfriends and children. As she pointed out, "The families will like to see the finished work and appreciate what their men folk have helped us accomplish." Hector nodded, but made no comment.

We printed invitations in English and Spanish and gave them to almost 30 people whom we considered to be a vital part of the project. Only about half of the men came by, and many of them were by themselves. Bruce, the rock artist, brought his wife and children and Hector brought his family. Juan was still living with us but was about to move in with Kathy and her two sons. We liked Kathy and had given her boys a computer and Internet connection, so we were anxious to hear if they were making progress. Only Bruce and Hector appeared comfortable at the party, and the children were quite shy.

In an effort to establish rapport, Pat took Sal's daughter by the hand and showed her the faux painting that her father had done. "Look at this," she said, "Your father is an artist. You should be *muy orgullos*, very proud." She didn't respond, and after a few minutes of awkward politeness and one beer each, the men started saying goodbye.

Hector stayed behind to explain. "This was a nice gesture that everyone appreciates, just as they liked the respect you showed and the little things that made working on this job pleasant, but they have already moved on to other projects. When they get off work, they want to be with their families."

This explanation made a lot of sense. We didn't want the workers to think that we were too good to socialize with them, but they didn't live in a house as nice as the one they helped create for us. We might respect each other, but despite our best efforts and good intentions, we weren't going to be best friends.

Since our reclamation efforts had disturbed the tranquility of Mission Ridge for more than eighteen months, we also planned a neighborhood party to get acquainted and express appreciation for everyone's patience. We also wanted to know the neighbors better because we weren't planning to move for a few years—or maybe decades. We hoped that they would be as likeable as the circle of Newcomer friends, and planned our traditional ecumenical Sunday brunch, blending Southern roots and New York experience by serving garlic cheese grits, bagels and lox.

As we were coming to expect of any collection of people in Santa Barbara, the neighbors were a diverse assortment of interesting individuals. We had already met Mercedes Eichholtz in her role as Board Chair for the Santa Barbara Museum of Art. She had welcomed us to the neighborhood shortly after we purchased the house next to hers, and told us bluntly, as is her style, that she looked forward to our getting the house in shape and helping make the neighborhood more respectable. We breathed a sigh of relief when she gave our renovation her seal of approval.

Greg and Lisa Young were the other next door neighbors. Probably in their late thirties, they were the 'kids' of the neighborhood. We thought they were unduly reclusive until we learned, a couple of years later, that Greg's grandfather was the founder of Gibraltar Savings and Loan, and while growing up in Beverly Hills, his brother had been kidnapped and held for the largest ransom ever paid in California. At the party, Greg sipped a glass of Sauvignon Blanc, and we talked about the utility wires that interfered with our ocean views, agreeing that they had to come down. (It only took eight years for us to accomplish that objective.)

The folks directly across the street had moved away during our modernization efforts. We didn't feel responsible for their departure since they had just sold a successful business and were moving to a historic property in one of the toniest areas of Montecito, where they could keep horses. Chris, an entrepreneurial dentist, had purchased their house and was doing his own renovation. We got along with Chris better than we did with his Jack Russells, who were the culprits of the "Curious Case of the Dogs in the Day." Every morning, when Chris left for work, the dogs would begin to bark. They refused to take a break, even for lunch, until he returned in the evening.

Bob Pohl and Susan Strong, who lived next to Chris, became two of our all-time favorite neighbors. Bob was a hunky former banker and inner-city principal who was working with the UCSB School of Education and planning a race for California's General Assembly. Susan was putting the finishing touches on her book, *The Greatness of Girls,* and was finding it hard to concentrate with the constant doggie concert next door. We loved the way that Bob and Susan would sometimes knock on our front door and ask if we could spare a glass of wine. Often, they brought their own, but we always enjoyed their company.

Neighbors a couple of houses away had lived on Mission Ridge for thirty or forty years. Because of California's infamous Proposition 13, some still paid less than $100 per month in real estate taxes. Everyone was welcoming, seemed to appreciate our improvements, enjoyed the garlic cheese grits and added to our repertoire of Imogene and Ruth stories. We liked everyone we met, and were starting to agree with Pete: the Riviera *is* the best part of Santa Barbara.

From Bombay to Santa Barbara

After the Newcomer celebration, I started thinking about some about the different paths that had brought our guests to Santa Barbara. I wondered why so many of us felt that we had discovered a paradise that was perfect for us and decided to see if there were common themes to the stories.

Bob Nourse, who helped register us at our first meeting of Santa Barbara Newcomers, had agreed to make a presentation at Pepperdine's next Executive Learning Forum and was willing to talk about how they decided to settle here rather than any of the other options he and Alex could have chosen. We met for lunch at the appropriately named Paradise Café, a local favorite located in a vintage brick and stucco building that has housed an Italian bakery and Mexican restaurant before becoming "The Paradise" in 1981. Their specialties are fish and beef, grilled with Santa Maria live oak wood. I had fish tacos and Bob ordered a hamburger that many fans believe is the best in town. As we waited for iced tea, he made some positive comments about our reclamation of *Casa de Algria*.

"That's very kind," I said, uncertain about how to respond to a compliment from someone accustomed to much more and wanting him to know that I recognized the differences in our situations. "We are very happy with our house, but I've seen the plans for your place, and we're not in the same neighborhood—literally or figuratively!"

Bob was the founding CEO of Bombay Company and had been named Entrepreneur of the Year by *Inc. Magazine*. He and Alex were building a magnificent showplace that would be featured in *Architectural Digest*, but he responded modestly with an apt phrase that captured the essence of our experience in America's Riviera. "Well, the point is that we both made it to Santa Barbara."

Thinking back to the scores of people whom we had met at various local functions, I realized that Santa Barbara's former CEOs, professors, engineers, nurses and divorcées may live in differing degrees of luxury, but anyone who manages to buy, rent or visit gets to enjoy the same glorious climate, culture and scenery in a very democratic community.

Bob began to tell me about his path to paradise. "We had a good run with Bombay and grew to about 450 stores at the peak. Perhaps we stayed a bit too long. Some of the excitement was gone, and Alex had been telling me for a year that it was time for us to do something else. By the time we actually left the company, I was in my late fifties. We decided to spend a few months looking at places we might want to live next. Neither of us had ever made a move that wasn't because of school or work."

At first they focused on Florida, and made a couple of trips to Naples to explore the Gulf Coast. That didn't click. Then, they spent six weeks in Biot, in the South of France. They brought their family over and had a wonderful time, but it didn't feel like a potential home.

Since Bob had been born in British Columbia, they considered moving to Vancouver Island. After visiting his only cousin for a week that included seven days of rain, Bob said, "Suddenly, I remembered why I left." About that time, he received a call from a private equity firm that almost took them to the East Coast. The firm was negotiating the purchase of a retail chain and was interested in having him run it with Alex as its chief merchant.

Ultimately, the acquisition fell through, so they explored the San Francisco area, especially Belvedere Island. They heard about an interesting company in Carlsbad, California that was for sale, and even checked out real estate in the San Diego area, but were bothered by the traffic. Fortunately, friends in Ventura, whom they had come to know as vendors, insisted that they consider Santa Barbara.

"We knew, almost immediately, that this was it," Nourse recalls. "We started looking at real estate quickly and found three lots together in Montecito with great ocean and mountain views that we loved. The property wasn't actually on the market, but we started negotiations and wound up buying it."

They had never lived on the ocean, so they rented a beach house for three years and fought with City Planning, watched over the building of their spectacular house, got active in

Newcomers and were co-chairs of the Welcoming Committee when we attended our first meeting.

We talked a bit about the amazing differences in people who had made it to Santa Barbara, and agreed that our adopted home was unusually accepting and welcoming.

Bob suggested that I should talk with Linda and Peter Beuret, who had been featured in a recent *Wall Street Journal* article about the wave of retired managers, executives, attorneys, physicians and other professionals who were settling in Santa Barbara and the surrounding area.

Two Paths Diverged

Pat and I had met the Beurets at the Cold Springs Tavern a few weeks earlier. Although Peter and I had started our business careers together in Procter & Gamble's brand management program, our paths had quickly diverged. I wasn't sure which of us had taken "the road less traveled," but we had each arrived in Santa Barbara at about the same time.

Peter had retired from Procter & Gamble in his late fifties. He and Linda spent three years doing extensive research about where they wanted to spend the rest of their lives. Their research had been more concentrated, and perhaps more organized, than ours. They developed six critical criteria. First and foremost, they wanted a temperate climate. As Peter explained, "We're bird-watchers and snorkelers, and we need to have warm weather all year long to enjoy those activities." That certainly made sense to me. That first stretch of below-zero temperatures in Cincinnati had convinced me to look for a warmer climate years earlier.

As music buffs, Peter and Linda also wanted a location with "a healthy dose of classical music and culture." He went on to explain their other criteria. "We also wanted proximity to hiking trails and other outdoor activities to enjoy in that temperate climate. Ideally, we wanted to live somewhere with low humidity, a nearby college or two that could provide continuing education and culture, and an international airport to make trips overseas more convenient."

With this checklist in hand, the Beurets made extended visits to Charleston and Savannah. "They were nice, but much too hot and humid in summer. Next we spent some time in Miami and Coral Gables, Florida. They were exciting, but seemed somewhat dangerous and also suffered from excessive summer heat and humidity. Finally, we turned to California. Palo Alto and San Francisco were very, very exciting culturally, but with too much traffic and unreasonable home prices. San Diego had great weather, but the symphony was foundering and there was a little too much military influence for our tastes."

When they visited Santa Barbara, the search was over. "It met five of our six criteria," Peter said. "The only thing it lacked was an international airport. We decided we could take a commuter plane to Los Angeles or one of the other hubs served by the Santa Barbara airport when we wanted to fly overseas."

In house-hunting, the Beurets were decisive or lucky. Peter saw a great place on their first visit, but it wasn't for sale until they returned for a second trip. They bought the octagonal-shaped residence on a lot high in the Mesa area of town with a panoramic view of the ocean, the city and the mountains. It was easy to understand their pride as they showed us around their house on one of Santa Barbara's brilliant blue-sky days, and Peter pointed out key locations from the living-room windows.

"Everything is five minutes away," he bragged. "The historic Mission Santa Barbara, the beach, hiking trails, downtown and Santa Barbara City College—they're all nearby. The icing on the cake is the quality of health care. Cottage Hospital has one of the few graduate medical education programs between Los Angeles and San Francisco. The area is attractive to doctors who enjoy the same qualities that appealed to us."

The Mesa includes Santa Barbara City College, one of the best community colleges in the country, and Shoreline Park, a beautiful 15-acre bluff-top strip that the Beurets and many others think of as the finest park in Santa Barbara. The Beurets also claim that the Mesa's winter temperatures are ten to twelve degrees warmer than downtown and ten to twelve degrees cooler in the summer. Peter and Linda are convinced that "the Mesa is the best place to live in Santa Barbara," but we had heard that phrase before—applied equally as enthusiastically to other neighborhoods in this special place. And, of course, we know that the Riviera is *really* the best part of town.

Peter's career at P&G sounded exciting and rewarding; however, I never regretted my decision to pursue another path. I was pleased that we had both arrived in the same place after making other different life choices.

A Japanese Assignment Leads to Santa Barbara

Bob and Ellen Lilley were the engine and drive train of Newcomers. They were involved in almost every one of the group's myriad activities. I couldn't help but wonder how all that energy and organization had been utilized before Santa Barbara, so we scheduled a luncheon conversation with them at our house.

The Lilleys had it made in Ohio. They had met on the campus of Ohio University in Athens, fell in love, married, and were well on their way to "living happily ever after." Bob was a popular professor of electrical engineering and Director of the Avionics Center. Ellen was a leading distributor for Shaklee vitamins and natural health products and served as executive director of the International Loran Association (ILA), a trade group involved with global navigation satellite systems. A few years earlier, they had built their dream home by a one-acre lake in the middle of a wooded area. Their life was almost perfect. Sure, some people complained about the Ohio climate, saying that "we only have two seasons here: May, and bad weather," but they didn't expect perfection.

They had been so successful in Ohio, other opportunities never seemed worth upsetting a very nice apple cart. The turning point came when Bob was asked to represent the university at their sister institution, Chubu University in Kasugai, Japan. It was only a three-month assignment, but it stimulated them to start thinking about other opportunities for adventure.

Just before agreeing to accept the Japanese assignment, they attended an ILA conference in San Diego. John Illgen, an entrepreneur and longtime friend, encouraged them to visit him in Santa Barbara and asked Bob to consider joining his startup as a senior engineer and limited partner. Ellen described her thought process. "The Chubu opportunity helped us realize that we were capable of change. Old dogs *can* learn new tricks. That's probably how they get to be old dogs.

"Fortunately, a friend offered to housesit, handle my Shaklee orders, and keep us informed via e-mail. We no longer had an excuse to turn down the Chubu opportunity, and that gave us some time to think about the Santa Barbara option."

Bob elaborated. "The chance to live in Santa Barbara and take on a new non-university challenge was exciting. Deep down, all academics probably harbor a secret desire to prove that they could have survived and prospered in 'the real world.' We had visited Santa Barbara a couple of times and knew it was a wonderful place. John's offer was an opportunity to apply some of my engineering skills in a very applied setting. We really enjoyed Japan and decided to settle our affairs in Ohio when we returned and grab this once-in-a lifetime opportunity."

Back in Ohio, they were surprised when their house sold in just two weeks. That meant consolidating accumulations from a 30 year marriage, saying goodbye to long-term friends, and providing a destination address for the moving van. They didn't find anything suitable on the first house-hunting visit. "We were absolutely blown away by the prices," Ellen recalls. "Some of the houses cost more money than I knew was in circulation. Then, our realtor called and told us about a new development that was opening and encouraged us to come out immediately. Bob was in the middle of a big project, so I flew out alone. Although it meant moving from 38 acres to a lot that was only slightly larger than 38 feet, I thought Cathedral Pointe would be ideal for us. I called Bob and told him that we needed to make a decision immediately. Fortunately, he trusts my judgment, and we've been very happy here."

The Lilleys found Santa Barbara to be everything they had hoped it would be. Bob described their first party, "We invited about forty people and everyone came. In less than a year, we had just as many friendships as we had enjoyed back in Athens.

People weren't as competitive and weren't constantly trying to impress you." Bob went on to become senior engineer and vice president for Illgen Simulation and Technologies and played a major role in their sale to Northrop-Grumman. Ellen, of course, was president of Newcomers and the major force in a follow-up organization called The Graduates which was based on the principles that made Newcomers so successful.

A Youthful Dream Fulfilled

Tom and Lee Walsh figured it out early. It just took a while to work out the details. When they were in their early 20s, they drove their Volkswagen bug from Chicago to visit Tom's brother in San Diego. They headed west on Interstate 80 and, in California, traveled down that dangerous PCH, stopping when they saw something interesting. Lee reports, "Tom had read about the famous Biltmore Hotel and wanted to check it out. I didn't think we were dressed appropriately, but Tom insisted that we roll up our cutoffs and act like we were rich kids out for a lark."

After visiting the Biltmore bar, they walked across the road to the beach and watched the sunset over the Mesa. Tom made a resolution and told Lee, "One day, we're going to live here."

Lee recalled thinking, "There's no way a son of Irish immigrants and one of twelve kids raised in the inner city of Chicago, would ever live in Santa Barbara. I should have more faith, because thirty years later, we bought a Bonnymede condo almost adjacent to the Biltmore."

They made this purchase in 1998 and planned to use it use for vacations, thinking that perhaps, sometime in the distant future, they could retire there. They had the *Santa Barbara News-Press* sent to their home in Wisconsin, where Tom was a financial executive for a division of Nortek, a NYSE company. He checked out every employment opportunity in Santa Barbara, but didn't find a situation that matched what they had in Wisconsin—better weather, perhaps, but not opportunity.

They were starting to experience an addiction similar to the one that we had known. In 2001, they came out for a fundraiser at John Cleese's ranch. Tom managed to schedule an interview with a small start-up company. He thought the interview went well, but they didn't make an immediate offer, so the Walshes continued their vacation trip and negotiated, via Internet, from towns in Peru and Ecuador, terms that might bring them to Santa Barbara.

Upon returning to Milwaukee, they decided to accept the offer and sell their primary residence, lake house, and much of their furniture in order to move from a five-bedroom home to the Bonnymede condo. Tuesday, September 11, 2001, was the official day for the movers to come and pack everything. Tom was already in Santa Barbara, but Lee was stunned by the news and amazed that the packers continued working as she stared at the coverage of the tragedy.

They saw an article in the *News-Press* about a Newcomers meeting at the Doubletree Hotel. They had joined groups with similar names in other states, but these had focused on babysitting co-ops and play groups. The Walshes were pleasantly surprised by the Santa Barbara group and made lots of new friends, including people from Milwaukee—even one woman who had had worked in the same school district as Lee.

Is Everyone Rich?

In the middle of exploring the various paths to paradise, my son, Jeff, came out for a visit. He had seen the house at the beginning of the project, was impressed by the improvement, and captured some of it with his digital video camera. We talked about my interest in how people got to Santa Barbara. He immediately cut to the chase and asked, "Isn't everyone who lives here rich?"

After thinking for a moment I responded, "Probably a few think of themselves as wealthy, but most of us believe we are rich. We live in a beautiful city, enjoy a wonderful climate, and have great friends. That makes us rich whether we have money or not."

Jeff wasn't sure he could accept what he thought was an overly glib response. "Do you know anyone who has moved here without having more money than the average person?"

205

Pat jumped in with a couple of good illustrations, "You've met my friend Dee who moved here to take care of her sister. Although she had a successful career, Dee invested in a son's business venture that failed, so she lives in a nice mobile home park, but was a popular president of Newcomers and is just as appreciated as the big-time professionals and executives."

So Jeff wouldn't focus on Dee's support for her son's business venture, I quickly added, "Remember how Dorothy moved here even though she couldn't find an affordable rental? She's managed to arrange house-sitting assignments for almost two years, and probably has as many Santa Barbara friends as Oprah."

Before returning to Tennessee, Jeff finally conceded the point, but added an insight I had missed. "I was just talking with your renter," he said, "and realized Pete is living in the same house as you do, and it costs him a hell of a lot less money."

After Jeff's departure, I started focusing on people who were very successful, but not corporate executives. Tom and Judy Nelson were high school teachers in the Los Angeles School District. I was curious how teachers could afford to live in Santa Barbara. Public school educators are typically paid even less than professors. Tom and Judy were native Californians and chose the teaching profession, not because of the big bucks but because they believed in the importance of education.

In psychological terms, Tom was maze-bright. He could figure out how systems operated and how to make them work for him. For example, with every fifteen units of academic credit, teachers move to a higher salary grade. For every week of an "educational trip," one credit was earned. Tom and Judy planned their family visits and vacations to include museums and historical sites, wrote up the key insights garnered from these experiences, and moved steadily up the hierarchy. And, of course, those educational trips were clearly tax-deductible. When they were audited, the IRS agent checked their records and concluded, "I don't see how you made those trips for as little as you've claimed in deductions."

Tom became a principal, and then part of central administration for LA County's Department of Education. He commuted from the San Fernando Valley to downtown Los Angeles, and fortunately enjoyed a flexible schedule. As we walked on the beach one day, Tom explained, "When our children were young, we all enjoyed coming to Santa Barbara for day trips. I couldn't figure out how to get academic credit for these visits, but they were educational and fun."

In the mid-1990s, they rented an El Escorial apartment in East Beach as a weekend getaway and would sometimes sublease it for a few weeks during the summer. Tom admits, "We became addicted to Santa Barbara. Eventually, we retired, sold our place in the Valley, bought a house on the East Side and moved where we plan to stay for the rest of our lives. We were lucky that our house in the Valley appreciated more than if it had been in Lake Woebegon. We don't have a mansion on the beach, but we enjoy the beach as much as anyone."

Estelle Meadoff and her physician husband had planned to retire in their fifties so they could move to Paris and enjoy the expatriate experience. "I never liked Baskerville," she confessed. "In many ways, it was a hellhole."

Just as they were planning to make their dream a reality, Dr. Meadoff died from a heart attack. Though devastated by the loss, she carried on with their plan, just as she thought he would have wanted. After thirty years abroad, most at the Mayfair Hotel in London, she concluded that it was time for her to come back to the United States. She had lived simply, invested wisely and was in excellent health. After spending a little time in Mill Valley with her son, she set out on a four-week expedition to find the perfect place for the rest of her life.

"I spent a week in each of four possibilities: Carmel, San Luis Obispo, Santa Barbara and Ventura," she explained. "I took a Greyhound bus to Carmel, which I remembered as a charming little village. I found a taxi driver who drove me around for a couple of hours each morning and afternoon. At my age, I wanted to keep things simple, so I checked with hotels about monthly rentals, but they weren't very interested. Also, Carmel was colder than I remembered."

"Did you have a checklist or set of criteria?" I asked.

"Not really," she answered. "But I was confident that I would know the best option after a short visit. At each location, I checked out the hotels, restaurants and things I might enjoy doing. I took the train to San Luis Obispo and quickly knew it wasn't for me. Of course, I fell in love with Santa Barbara and wanted to live here, but I kept being told that hotels couldn't rent on a monthly basis without having to pay a punitive tax. I went to every hotel in town and they all said the same thing."

As we spoke, Estelle was living at the Encino Lodge, directly across from Sansum Clinic (just in case she is ever old enough to worry about health issues), so I inquired, "What's the rest of the story?"

"Eventually, I went to the county tax collector's office and asked for an explanation. They assured me that there would be no transient occupancy tax if I had an agreement, written in advance, specifying that the rental was for a period greater than one month. Naturally, I asked if someone would put that in writing, and they did. Living in a hotel is a perfect arrangement for me since they provide housekeeping and all utilities. I sold or gave away most of my silver, china and furniture. One monthly check covers most of my expenses. After a couple of years, I had enough friends and didn't need to make more. As you get older, simplicity is the key to successful living."

It's the Destination, Not the Path

As I reflected on these and other Santa Barbara stories, I remembered Pastor Marshall Keble, the only African-American minister who could draw a "separate but almost equal" assortment of blacks and whites to a revival meeting when I was growing up in North Alabama. He told a story that contributed significantly to my doubts that Dad's congregation was the only 'true church.'

"The judgment day," Keble would explain to an audience of people who were accustomed to a four-week suspension of school in September for cotton picking, "it be like taking yo' cotton to the gin. When you git there, the gin man, he don't say, 'what road you come on?' he say, 'how good is yo' cotton'?"

My father quickly explained the error of this logic. "Of course, if the gin owner had said that he was only buying the cotton from people who came to his gin by driving on the Savannah Highway, then everyone else would be disappointed. The Scripture says, 'straight is the way and narrow is the road that leads to life eternal, and few there be that find it'."

Even at ten, I found Keble's argument to be more convincing. As a future business professor, I couldn't help but think that a gin that only accepted cotton that arrived from just one of several possible routes wasn't likely to be very successful.

Bob Nourse had captured the heart of the matter when he reminded me, "It doesn't matter what we did before. We both made it to Santa Barbara."

As I thought back to the direct-mail piece that had started our dreams about parachuting to paradise, I realized that Santa Barbara met all the requirements except for that minor detail about finding perfection *and* a low cost of living. I pulled the ad from a file and made just a couple of minor changes to describe life in our chosen destination.

> *You look out your window, past your gardener, who is busily pruning the lemon, orange and pomegranate trees...admidst the splendor of bougainvillea that surrounds your fountain or the lavender and roses that adorn the entry to your hacienda.*
>
> *The sky is clear blue. The sea is a deeper blue, sparkling with sunlight. A gentle breeze comes drifting in from the ocean, clean and refreshing, as you sip your organic fruit smoothie.*
>
> *For a moment, you think you have died and gone to heaven. But this paradise is real, and almost affordable. In fact, it costs only twice as much to live this dream lifestyle...as it would to stay right where you were.*

Chapter 16
Walk By the Ocean...As We Slowly Grow Old

This book wasn't ready to be written when I first suggested it as a Newcomers project. Hopefully, the story is like a Santa Barbara County Cabernet that needs to age before being shared. After our failed efforts at creating a community writing experience, I put the idea aside but continued to ponder the themes that grew out of conversations about the different paths people had travelled to arrive with us in Santa Barbara.

Perhaps we are the advance guard for an important segment of the 78 million baby boomers just beginning to address issues of aging and finding the best place for their retirement years. Of course, a majority of retirees will stay where they've always been. They have deep roots and have learned to be happy where they are. Some will think of retirement as their 'reclining years.' My father's preparation for retirement consisted of buying a rocking chair and putting it on the front porch. "My plan," he declared, "is to sit in this chair. Maybe in a few months, I'll start rocking...slowly."

When back in North Alabama to visit family, I always spend time with some of my high school classmates. Most wanted their children and grandchildren to go to the same school we attended. I can't make Santa Barbara sound interesting enough for them to even consider leaving long-time friends and family.

On my last visit, James Ray Jones asked, without a trace of irony, "Now, Bob, when you finally retire, you will be moving back to Florence, won't you?"

As a seventeen-year-old high school graduate, I found happiness, like country singer Mac Davis, by seeing my home town in a rearview mirror. Three undergraduate colleges, two graduate schools, an early marriage and five states later, while discussing an exciting opportunity at Trinity University in San Antonio, my soon-to-be ex-wife wondered plaintively, "When will you ever be satisfied?"

For many years, I sincerely believed that contentment would be found at the top of the next mountain. Eventually, it became difficult to deny that I was part of a significant minority who find joy in the challenges of the climb rather than the destination. Neither total contentment nor a constant search for something better is inherently virtuous. Either can be carried to extremes, but a couple with different definitions of success is likely to have occasional disagreements.

Despite the virtues of contentment and the allure of inertia, many baby boomers will go through a process of looking for a better retirement venue. Most Newcomers looked for a more perfect place than where they were and exerted considerable effort to find that place that was just right for them.

To my knowledge, no one ever turned down a transfer to Santa Barbara because they couldn't stand the idea of living here. Being a destination of choice may mean that new residents are more adventurous and open to new experiences then their more easily satisfied compatriots. In other words, they probably had to *make* it happen. A few people in Santa Barbara inherited the resources to enjoy the lifestyle, but most had to be successful enough to afford some of the country's most expensive real estate or creative enough to "live well with less." The climate, culture, and aesthetics contribute to the decision to move here, but the availability of interesting friends is a major reason to stay. The rich aren't necessarily more interesting than the poor, but successful people who have led lives of great variety often have compelling stories that they have learned to tell in engaging ways.

The number of Santa Barbara couples who had actively explored alternative venues for their retirement was striking. In other words, the decision to come here involved considerable, thoughtful analysis. Few moved here without considering other options, and none were truly surprised at the cost of living because they checked out the positives and the negatives. Most had factored the cost factor into their analysis, decided they would get by in a smaller residence, and concluded that the price of admission, though high, represented good value.

For several friends, moving to California's central coast represented a creative response to a negative event. A board conflict or a corporate downsizing presented an opportunity for early retirement; an entrepreneurial venture sold earlier than expected; or a major consulting project fell through at the last minute. Rather than bemoaning life's unfairness or focusing on the negatives, they found ways of creating zestful lemonade. Like George Herbert, the seventeenth century British cleric, they decided "living well is the best revenge."

Speaking of which, I must confess to feeling a tiny twinge of pleasure when *Leading the Revolution* failed to become Harvard's greatest publishing success story. When Gary Hamel's opus finally came out, it lavished praise on one firm as having "achieved an almost magical mix of entrepreneurship with the ability...to get things done." When Enron collapsed shortly afterwards, HBS pulled the book and Gary did a major rewrite for another publisher. In this edition, Hamel didn't mention the innovativeness of his friend, Ken Lay. While Hamel was mistaken about Enron, he is, of course, still brilliant and successful. *Acceptance* did take a while, but today, I am pleased that Gary 'encouraged' us to move to Santa Barbara earlier than we planned.

The concept of an omnipotent power that crafts a master plan for each of the six billion or so people on this planet eludes me, but I am grateful for whatever cosmic forces kept me from staying in Cincinnati, moving to Palo Alto, or buying any one of those other 71 houses we looked at in Santa Barbara.

Walk by the Ocean

For Christmas, Jeff presented us with a DVD started during his recent visit to Santa Barbara. He was working for a video production corporation and carried a digital video camera everywhere. He began with scenes and music from the Farmers Market, added images along the beachfront and blended the "before" photographs utilized in the second Life Styles event with shots of us talking about the challenging changes in *Casa de Alégria*. In my totally objective view, it was superbly edited, and was made more memorable by a short musical finale featuring Glen Phillips, a local song writer, musician, and leaders of a group called "Toad, The Wet Sprocket."

The title of the song was "*Walk on the Ocean*." None of us has learned to do that (yet), but "walk *by* the ocean" has become a regular part of our social and fitness routine. After that first almost sleepless night in the East Beach townhouse, I had walked across the street for breakfast and met a retired pharmaceutical executive who was chair of a Newcomers committee called "Beach Walkers." It wasn't a very imposing committee, with only four people at the table, as he explained their routine of walking along the beach for three miles three times each week—an impressive workout for someone in his 80s, but I didn't think about the conversation again for years.

Ultimately, I became a bit jealous of Pat's increasingly close friendship with Estelle Meadoff—jealous because I recognized that someone, now in her nineties, still alert and active, had much wisdom and life experience to share. I didn't take out a personals ad, but did brazenly mention to a few associates that I was looking for a new friend who was in his nineties.

Ron Freund, who commutes from Kansas City to run an order fulfillment company, provided a potential lead. "I just went to the ninetieth birthday party," he explained, "for someone who invented Triaminic, was an executive for Bristol Myers, then bought a small pharmaceutical company and ran it until his mid-seventies. For this birthday, he invited ninety of his closest friends to a dinner party at the University Club. He still stays up with what's happening in science, regularly walks three miles on East Beach, and is a real babe magnet—at least a dozen or so women like to walk with him and drink coffee afterwards at East Beach Grill. You ought to check it out."

Initially, this information didn't ring any bells, but I did show up the next Monday, and met Tom Watson, who was the same person who had described a much smaller walking group during my first visit to the Grill. Anyone who wants to walk just shows up on Mondays, Wednesdays or Fridays around eight o'clock. At 8:05, according to Tom's cell phone, the walk begins, with everyone choosing a suitable pace and partner. An hour later, most of the group, frequently more than twenty, reassemble at the East Beach Grill for conversation and Peet's coffee. Pat and I try to make it twice a week, and yes, we still occasionally share a Santa Barbara omelet.

Walking with Tom is more intellectually stimulating than physically challenging. He doesn't walk quite as fast as he used to, but his mind hasn't slowed down at all. He reads *Scientific American* from cover to cover and points out articles I might understand. We swap books, usually agree on politics, and discuss his philanthropic interest in encouraging early reading opportunities for disadvantaged children. After discussing the news or the people who make it, Tom frequently observes, "We are an endlessly fascinating species."

Carl Sandberg once said, "The most hateful word in the English language is 'exclusive'." Carl would have liked the Beach Walkers—and would be welcome to join us—as are you. The Beach Walkers group is a community, but not exclusive. Muriel collected e-mail address for almost 50 some-time participants and circulates information about events like a potluck holiday party at Lynda and Pete's or breakfast at the clubhouse of the group's official hugger. Dottie greets everyone with a robust embrace and has just given her 30,000[th] Santa Barbara hug. At least once a month, Albie will bake cupcakes or brownies to celebrate recent birthdays after breakfast, or someone will send out an invitation to stop by for tea and crumpets or beer and pretzels.

Not long ago, Antonia invited everyone for "an evening of entertainment." She and Raul live on a spacious lot with ten chickens and a variety of exotic fruit trees. They had cooked a ham and turkey for the main course. The rest of us were encouraged to "bring your spouse (if you have one) and one other covered dish." Tonia had been mysterious about the evening's entertainment, but after filling our plates and glasses, we sat down to watch a 1947 black and white movie.

A few eyebrows were raised at this choice until we recognized that Anabel Shaw, star of *Killer at Large*, was the stage name for Marjorie Henshaw, one our walkers who had been on the cover of *Life Magazine* in 1940. Marjorie had turned down a couple of movie contracts until she graduated from college, and discovered that, at twenty-two, she didn't have the same choices as when she was younger.

By Marjorie's admission, her starring role was in a B movie that took a whole week to film and for which she was paid the grand sum of $1000. Although more than sixty years had passed, Marjorie still had the good bones and vivacious personality that had attracted Hollywood talent scouts. In my opinion, the film slowed down when she wasn't on screen, so I looked around the room and realized that most of these ordinary people had enjoyed extraordinary lives because they took responsibility for how those lives evolved.

Next to Marjorie was May, who is in her forties, the youngest member of the group and a retired Philadelphia lawyer who studies and gives lessons on the harp and organ.She lives simply, rents a small guest cottage, and keeps one vestige of her former demanding profession; a 2000 Porsche which alternates with a ten-speed bike for local transportation.

Mike now spends much of his time volunteering for the Red Cross and travels to problem spots around the country to help facilitate the organization's fabled disaster response efforts. He attended eleven colleges before completing an undergraduate degree in business and an MBA that qualified him for a good career in the aerospace industry. Once, as I was about to leave for Peoria to facilitate a Leadership Quest program with high-potential leaders at Caterpillar, Mike confided that he had worked for CAT when he was only fifteen years old.

"I'm not saying that you didn't work for CAT," I challenged, "but I am pretty sure that they observed child labor laws even back in the dark ages when you were a teenager."

"Oh, they wouldn't have hired me if they had known my age," he explained. "But my family needed a wage earner and I was the logical choice, so I took a bus to Peoria. When the hiring agent questioned that I was eighteen and told me to come back with proof, my uncle helped me modify my birth certificate, so I was suddenly three years older. I'm still grateful to Caterpillar because they paid me well, taught me good work habits and inspired me complete college no matter how long it took."

"Did they encourage you to take classes at Bradley College?" I asked.

"Actually, I wasn't even in high school, but during orientation, they introduced us to a man who had been at the same inspection station for thirty-five years. The thought of doing the same thing for more than twice the time I had been alive made me a believer in higher education."

Mike did complete high school, and found a job in the mail room of the CIA in Washington. After proving himself trustworthy, he became a secure mail courier, and picked up assignments in the Far East as a security assistant. I would have asked for more details about his adventures, but still worry that he would have to kill me if I knew the whole story.

Nan is the only person I know who is able to hear because of a cochlear transplant. She works for the deaf at the California Department of Rehabilitation, and coincidentally, before we joined the walkers, purchased our East Beach townhouse.

Before I finished circling the room with my rumination, the movie ended, so we talked about Marjorie's performance and what being a "star" was like in the 1940s. When the conversation lagged a bit, I shifted the topic, "Tonia, that's a very unusual statuette you have on the mantle. Can you tell us where you found it?"

"Oh, that," she replied, "It's one of my grandfather's Oscars."

"Don't tell us," I said, trying to gauge the correct timeframe. "Let me guess…your grandfather was Alfred Hitchcock."

"No, but Gramps did work with Hitch on a couple of pictures."

We learned that Tonia was the granddaughter of Frank Lloyd, one of the founders of the Academy of Motion Picture Arts and Sciences and the first Scottish Academy Award winner. Lloyd received three Oscar nominations in 1929 for his work on a silent film, a part-talkie and one of the early all-talkies. During a distinguished career, he worked with most of Hollywood's legends and is probably best remembered for *Mutiny on the Bounty* which he produced, scripted and directed.

As we started to leave, I looked again and realized that our little group included two Canadians, three folks from the British Isles, and one person each from Peru, Uruguay, Tennessee, and Alabama. There are a couple of former civil rights workers, three retired teachers, a nurse, an accountant a Peace Corps volunteer, and at least three Republicans. I suspect that each of us is a little surprised when we look in the mirror and wonder who that aged stranger can be. Sally kiddingly comments, "When I was young, I was always interested in the latest hip joints, and I still am. It's just that the definition of 'hip' has changed for me." Yes, hip replacements may account for the speed and mobility of some of the group. Tom may skew the average a bit, but the median age is well past sixty.

Everyone is ordinary, and everyone is special, with a unique story of how they came to be who and where they are.

The walking group doesn't impose many rules, but Tom and I have one inviolate requirement for our stroll. Each day, after we've reached the halfway point and turned around to start back toward the Grill, we look ahead and see friends with a faster pace heading toward coffee and conversation. To the left, we look over the red tile roofs of downtown and the Riviera to the purplish peaks of the Santa Ynez Mountains. To the right is the curving coastline of the Pacific, dotted with palm trees. The weather is almost always perfect. We alternate the responsibility of picking the point to turn to the other and say sincerely, "Aren't we lucky to live here?"

Circles within Circles of Community

In an era where an old-fashioned sense of community is often lacking, we feel especially lucky to enjoy overlapping circles of community that are common to the South Coast.

Two afternoons each week, we go to Lark's yoga class with a dozen other friends. Twice a month, I meet for dinner with eight guys from the Unitarian Society to talk about whatever 'issues' seem worthy of our collective consideration. We move from house to house for the meetings, with the host being responsible for drinks, dinner and dessert. For the most recent meeting at our house, the group learned about Brunswick stew and cornbread, neither of which I had made before. For dessert, I made a cake from persimmons grown in our backyard. The guys weren't quite ready for fried possum.

We've joined two movie groups that meet every few weeks where we rotate the hosting and movie selection. One was organized by some of our favorite former Newcomers and requires everyone to see the same first-run movie and come prepared to discuss it without prior conversations. We usually find lots to disagree about in the interpretations of the film's message and execution. Unencumbered by any real knowledge, we still have strong opinions and expect everyone else to listen to them, so we've recently had to impose a two-minute rule so no one pontificates too long.

For the past nine years, we've been the newest member of the other film group. Most are Unitarians, so "generally speaking, we are generally speaking." Rather than trying to impose a curfew on the conversation, we catch up over an appropriately themed dinner, turn down the lights and watch the hosts' selection for the evening. At our first hosting, we served fried chicken, lima beans, mashed potatoes and gravy, then added peaches and homemade ice cream for dessert as a prelude to watching *Driving Miss Daisy*—our favorite movie, only partially because it was filmed on our street in Atlanta.

We were living in New York during the filming and could have rented our Atlanta house to Dan Ackroyd, but foolishly declined because of his performance in *The Blues Brothers*.

Perhaps the most serious group uses the American Foreign Policy Association's materials for a consideration of "Great Decisions" facing the world. This distinguished group includes the founding partner of a leading Santa Barbara's law firm, the founder of the Self-Esteem Foundation, the former chairman of a global private bank, a George H.W. Bush political appointee, a former AIG Vice Chairman, the president or chair of three important non-profits, a community college president, three artists, an astrologer and a token business professor.

Earlier in his career, the discussion group's community college president, John Romo, was responsible for one of the most comprehensive adult education programs in the county. I just finished taking a course, "Hors d'oeuvres From Around the World" that has better equipped me for those requests to provide appetizers for ten. This is just one of 830 classes Santa Barbara Community College offers each year, and I am just one of more than 44,000 residents who enroll annually. From the Mind/Supermind lecture series and GED classes to landscape painting or an intro to the iPod, there's no limit to learning in Santa Barbara.

I usually miss the beach walk on Fridays because of an investment group that addresses the challenges of global finance over breakfast. About one-third of the group attends the Unitarian Society, at least on occasion. Another third is active in the Jewish Federation, and the remainder fall into the 'all other' or 'none of the above' categories. The conversations aren't usually religious, but since 2008, more and more deistic terms have become part of the conversations.

There are some heavy hitters in this investment group, but the name sounds more impressive than the meetings really are. Basically, it's just a bunch of old guys who like to get together to lie about how well their investments are doing. Because of a youthful interest in loud music, there are a few hearing aids around the table. Today, this group has more interest in acid reflux than acid rock. After the hearing concerns in Chapter 12, Pat and I both had auditory exams at Sansum Clinic and were told that our problems could probably be resolved by simply paying more attention to each other.

In this community, there is no reason for anyone to ever be bored. Ernie Marx recently complained, "I get up in the morning with nothing to do, and by night, I'm not half done."

Did You Used to be Important?

Changing planes at LAX, someone once actually asked me, "Did you used to be someone important?"

As you may recall, "In Santa Barbara, everyone is ordinary, and everyone is special, with a unique story of how they came to be who and where they are." Each person you encounter may or may not choose to tell that story. Santa Barbara is a great town for people who don't have much left to prove. That doesn't mean that they've conquered the world—just that they have accepted who they are and are willing to let you make the choice to accept them, too, without telling you how important they used to be.

Some people, like my former high school classmates and probably a majority of others, find an acceptable peak early and learn to grow where they are planted. Others aspire to an epitaph once placed on a tombstone for an anonymous Swiss guide that reads: "He died climbing." I'm happy to have finally reached a point in life where opportunities for growth still abound, but where there is little reason to keep climbing—or looking for a better place in which to grow.

Our impression is that Santa Barbara is a very welcoming community, but one that is difficult to impress. Unlike back home, the African-American woman at *Tre Luna*—the one who is wearing a baseball cap, sunglasses and looks like Oprah—may actually *be* Oprah.

If you have lots of money, you can go to two or three galas every week, be on dozens of boards and regularly get your picture in *Scene and Heard*, but you are still unlikely to be as famous as Oprah or as respected as Michael Towbes. On you can join Newcomers or the Graduates, become involved with a couple of non-profits, occasionally invite new acquaintances over for wine and cheese on the patio, and still get to complain about "so many social obligations…so little time."

As Glen Phillips sings:

> *…somebody told me that this is the place*
> *where everything's better, everything's safe.*

Of course, no place is completely safe in today's complex world. Since celebrating the reclamation *of Casa de Alégria,* our neighborhood has been evacuated twice because devastating fires were near—most recently, just days before almost a thousand people were scheduled to walk through as part of the Pearl Chase Society's tour of homes. When mud slides closed a major portion of Highway 101, I got to Ventura by boat and rented a car to meet my Pepperdine classes. Our house survived the 1925 earthquake, but there's no guarantee that it will withstand the next "big one," although Hector assures us that we should have no problems if we seek safety under the thrice-reinforced kitchen door.

This is the place where we've found everything is better and where we feel comfortably safe. We've found friends we expect to keep for life, even though that isn't as distant a horizon as it used to be. At a recent *Gatsby* parties, I stepped back to observe a hundred friends, all dressed in white, looking out over the horizon as the sun began to set. I couldn't help but comment, "You know, I really do like these people."

Tom Schleck, a hardnosed former banker, retorted, "Yes, and it's a good thing too, because we'll probably bury each other."

And he was undeniably correct. We've already seen a few of our Newcomer classmates die and have mourned their passing just as we treasure their memories. We've forsaken those places "where the air makes you choke....and trust is a joke."

We've made our choices and are determined to make these choices right. We enjoy the climate, the scenery and the friends we've selected. This is the life we choose.

We have more than …

> *…just memories to hold*
> *that grow sweeter each season*
> *as we slowly grow old.*

Acknowledgments

This book is non-fiction, but based on a sometimes faulty memory. My apologies if anyone recalls events differently.

Thanks to all the wonderful people who shared their stories, experiences and perspectives. I am particularly indebted to Santa Barbara Newcomers and The SB Graduates who provided many of the experiences described in this book. In addition to those mentioned by name in the text, but I am also grateful to people who provided context but not specific content. Former presidents of Newcomers and Graduates, especially Berkeley Meigs, Ellen Lilley, Dee Kruger and Julie Morrow were excellent leaders and helpful to this project in many ways. Lee Walsh provided historical details about property listings and the story of their path to paradise.

Melissa Block, Bill Fulmer, and Jeff Fulmer and read the entire manuscript at least once and made many helpful suggestions. They pointed out numerous typos and mistakes, but with every correction came other mistakes—all my responsibility. Christian Menard helped rescue my computer and software applications. I also appreciate the comments of other friends who read portions of the book and made encouraging or helpful comments. Obviously, I am grateful for the talented, insightful folks willing to risk ridicule by making positive comments for attribution on the back page or on the book's website, newcomersinparadise.com.

In Chapter one I quote Josh Sens about travel on the PCH (*Budget Travel* February 2006). In Chapter 6, the discussion of homelessness was enhanced by Rene Sanchez; *Washington Post* article, December 23, 2000. The overview of Santa Barbara philanthropy was influenced by William Overend, *Los Angeles Times*. September 21, 2003. Some information about first communion drew on Dr. M. T. Horvat's internet article *"The Secularization of First Communion:* Part of Chapter 15 was inspired by Earl Gottchalk, Jr's, "Santa Barbara's Charms Well Heeled Retirees," from the *Wall Street Journal Online*.

Of course, my greatest appreciation is to Pat, who read the manuscript a couple of times, did the chapter opening sketches, transformed *Dulcenia* into *Casa de Alegría*, and makes living here a source of great happiness.